The Great and Close Siege of York 1644

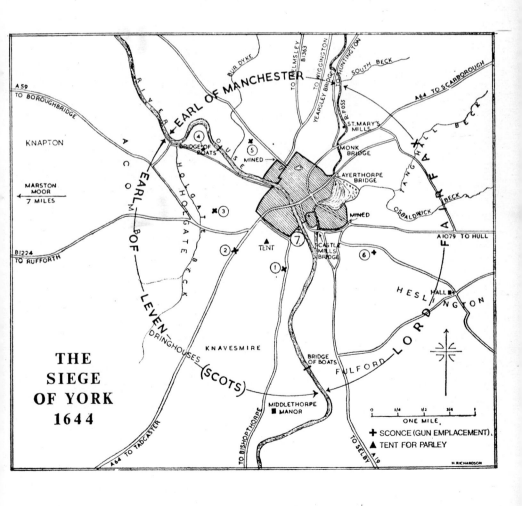

THE
SIEGE
OF YORK
1644

ONE MILE

+ SCONCE (GUN EMPLACEMENT)
▲ TENT FOR PARLEY

H. RICHARDSON

Ferdinando, second baron Fairfax.

Artist Edward Bower
(*floruit* 1629 – 1667/8)

The GREAT and CLOSE SIEGE of YORK, 1644

Peter Wenham
MA, M Litt, M Ed, FSA

SESSIONS BOOK TRUST
YORK, ENGLAND

First Published 1970

© 1994
Peter Wenham's Literary Executor

ISBN 1 85072 147 5

The production cost of this reprint has been financed by the
Sessions Book Trust, with greatly appreciated assistance from
the Sheldon Memorial Trust.

Facsimile Reprinted in 1994 by
William Sessions Limited
The Ebor Press, York, England

. . . the very best Harmonical-Musick that ever I heard . . . was in the year 1644 . . . in the stately Cathedral of the Loyal City York . . . The occasion of it was, the great and close Siege . . . strictly maintain'd for eleven weeks space, by three very notable and considerable great Armies.

THOMAS MACE, *Musick's Monument*, 1676

If York be lost, I shall esteem my crown little less.

KING CHARLES I to PRINCE RUPERT
in a letter dated 14 June, 1644

Acknowledgements

The publishers acknowledge with gratitude the assistance which they have received from the following bodies, institutions and individuals.

For the Frontispiece and Plate XXV : York Art Gallery.

For Plates I, II, III, IV, VI, X, XXIV and XXX : York Public Library.

For Plates V, VII, IX, XI, XII and XV : The Royal Commission on Historical Monuments.

For Plates XIII, XIX, XXI, XXII, XXIII : The Library of the Dean and Chapter, York.

For Plate XIV : The Scottish National Portrait Gallery.

For Plate XXVI : Robert Innes-Smith, Esq.

For Plate XX : His Grace the Archbishop of York.

For Plates XXVII, XXXI, XXXII and the Plan of the excavation on Holgate Hill on p. 154 : Yorkshire Architectural and York Archaeological Society.

For Plates XVI and XVII : The Star Inn, Harome, near Helmsley.

For Plate VIII : His Grace the Duke of Portland.

For Plate XVIII : The Governors of Kimbolton School, Huntingdonshire, and Edward Leigh, F.B.P., F.R.P.S., Cambridge, who took the photograph.

The Tailpieces were drawn by Stephen Beck and John Yale.

Contents

List of Illustrations

MAPS AND DIAGRAMS

The front End Paper shows the disposition of the
Parliamentarian armies around York,

and

The rear End Paper indicates the route of Prince Rupert's
march on York, June–July 1644.

Estimated numbers of troops taking part in the Siege of York 1644

ROYALIST

Marquis of Newcastle.

Garrison already in the city on 16 April	500	foot
Army brought in on 16 April by the Marquis	4,000	foot
(N.B. Most of Newcastle's cavalry, numbering some		
3,000 more left the city during the night 22 April;		
although a few were left behind — see pp. 14-15)	300	horse
Total	4,800*	

Prince Rupert

Relieving army arriving before York 1 July	8,000	foot
	6,500	horse
Total	14,500	

PARLIAMENT

Earl of Leven[1]

Army besieging York 22 April	14,000	foot
	2,000	horse
	600	dragoons
Total	16,600*	

Lord Fairfax

Army besieging York 22 April	3,000	foot
	2,000	horse
Total	5,000*	

Earl of Manchester

Army besieging York 3 June	6,000	foot
	3,000	horse
Total	9,000*	

*As the siege progressed these numbers decreased through casualties — killed, wounded, prisoners, illness and desertions. Newcastle probably took about 3,000 foot and 200 horse to join Rupert at Marston Moor on 2 July.

[1] He left Scotland with 18,000 foot, 2,000 horse, 1,000 dragoons and a train of artillery numbering 120 pieces (SHS. vol. XVI, p. xxiii).

Abbreviations[1]

BM	British Museum
CSP Dom	*Calendar of State Papers, Domestic.*
DNB	*Dictionary of National Biography.*
DAJ	*Journal of the Derbyshire Archaeological and Natural History Society.*
EHR	*English Historical Review.*
ER	East Riding of Yorkshire.
HMC	Historical Manuscripts Commission.
HMSO	His [Her] Majesty's Stationery Office.
l	line
LJ	*Journal of the House of Lords.*
NG	National Grid Reference.
NR	North Riding of Yorkshire.
NS	New Series.
TRHS	Transactions Royal Historical Society.
TT	*Thomason Tracts* in the British Museum.
Wing	Donald G. Wing, *Short-title catalogue* . . . 1641–1700, 3 vols., 1945–51. (This is the standard bibliography covering this period)
WR	West Riding of Yorkshire.
YAJ	*Yorkshire Archaeological Journal.*
YAS	Yorkshire Archaeological Society.
YAYAS	Yorkshire Architectural and York Archaeological Society.
YCHB	*York Corporation Housebooks.*
YPRS	Yorkshire Parish Register Society.
YPSR	Yorkshire Philosophical Society, *Annual Report.*

[1] See also Bibliography, pp 220-8

Introduction

All the general histories of York include accounts of the siege of 1644,[1] the earliest being that of Hildyard[2] published in 1664. Torre (1719) and Gent (1730) repeat his account almost verbatim. Hildyard also constituted Drake's chief authority in 1736 though other sources available to Drake included Mace (1676), Rushworth (1692) and Bernard (1697). Drake's version remained the most authoritative until the early 19th century, when the publication of Slingsby's *Diary* (abridged version 1806: complete version 1836) added to it materially. Cooper (1904) used some of the additional information available in the *Calendar of State Papers, Domestic* (1888), while Benson (1925) added to earlier accounts by using some selected entries from the unpublished 'Housebooks,' 'Chamberlains' Rolls' and 'Constables' Accounts' in the York City archives and elsewhere.

None of these writers tapped the richest collection of original material relating to the siege — the dozens of contemporary tracts (usually entitled *Relations* or *Intelligences*) written by eye-witnesses of the events they described. The most prolific of these was Simeon Ashe (or Ash), chaplain to the Earl of Manchester. Naturally his accounts look at events from the standpoint of Manchester's army. A few of the tracts were, however, written by Scotsmen and, consequently, refer more particularly to the activities of Leven's forces. The greatest collection of these documents is in the British Museum where they are known as the Thomason Tracts: many are duplicated in the Minster Library, York, where there are some not listed in the London Collection. Terry (1899) in his biography of the Earl of Leven made use of some of these and, up to the time of writing, his account of the siege has been the fullest published. Those tracts consulted in the present work are listed in the Bibliography under 'A' (pp. 220–2).

Other published contemporary or near-contemporary material used in this work is listed in the Bibliography under 'B' (pp. 222–5). Use has also been made of the information contained in the contemporary 'Housebooks,' 'Chamberlains' Rolls' and 'Constables' Accounts' in the archives of the city of York. All entries having any bearing on the siege have been extracted from these and are included in Appendix II. Another source has been the Parish Registers of those York churches which contain entries of this period, eleven of which have been published.[3] The titles of the published registers are listed in Bibliography 'D' while the appropriate entries themselves are reproduced on pp. 132–9.

Three new documents throwing light on the siege have come to notice in the Borthwick Institute of Historical Research, York (pp. 9–10, 138–9 and 187–9), two in the York Public Library (pp. 72 and 120), while in the City of Leeds Public Library, among the Temple Newsam papers, a reference to the Ingram Hospital in Bootham soon after the siege has also been discovered (pp. 110–11).

An original plan (see Plate X and p. 154) detailing the defences of York, drawn c. 1682 by a Captain James Archer, an officer in the Royal Engineers, and now in the York Public Library, has been useful in working out the topography of the siege. Archaeology, too, has made a minor contribution. This book, in fact, stemmed from an historical-*cum*-archaeological article which I wrote in 1953 on an aspect of the Romano-British cemetery on the Mount, York.[4] Philip Corder's excavation on Holgate Hill, published in 1952,[5] that of Dr. John Thurnam on Lamel Hill as long ago as 1849[6] and that of Peter V. Addyman on Baile Hill as recently as 1968–9 have also been significant.

I wish to thank the following who have helped me in this work :– Mr O. S. Tomlinson, Librarian of York Public Library and his staff, particularly Mr M. Smith, Head of the Reference Department; Mr Bernard Barr, Librarian of the Minster Library; the staff of the Borthwick Institute of Historical

Research, especially Mrs K. M. Gurney; Mr F. G. B. Hutchings, Librarian of Leeds City Library and Mr M. Collinson, Head of the Archives Department there; Mr H. Ramm and Dr. R. M. Butler of the staff of the Royal Commission on Historical Monuments (England); Mr N. Higson, Archivist of the East Riding of Yorkshire and Mr J. T. Brighton, an erstwhile colleague in the Department of History of St. John's College, York. Brigadier Peter Young, Lecturer in Military History at the Royal Military Academy, Sandhurst, has read this book in MS. and has made numerous valuable suggestions.

All the plans and line drawings in the text are the work of the late Mr H. Richardson of York. Photographs used as illustrations have been taken by Mr Robin A. Hill of the Huntley Museum, Edinburgh and Mr William Farnsworth of York.

Finally my warmest thanks are due to Miss C. J. Hatcher, Mrs Edna King, Miss M. Moore, Mrs J. Walker and Miss P. M. Widd who have typed and re-typed this work in manuscript, corrected numerous textual errors and given considerable help in compiling the index.

1   Widdrington might be considered the exception, though his *Analecta Eboracensia* (written *c.* 1660, published 1897) does refer to the after effects of the siege on the city's economic life (see p. 98).
2   For titles of the works referred to, see Bibliography (pp. 220-8).
3   Twelve, if the Minster be included.
4   Reproduced as Appendix VIII.
5   'The Excavation of the Earthwork on Holgate Hill, York, 1936' YAYAS Report for 1951-2, pp. 31-35.
6   *Arch. Journal* vi (1849), pp. 27–39 and 123–136. For a shorter version see YPSR i (1847–54), pp. 98–105.

Chronology of the Siege

1642[1]

15 January	Edmund Cooper elected Lord Mayor of York.[2]
17 „	King Charles I came to York.
20 „	The King knighted Cooper.
16 August	The King left York.
22 „	The King raised his standard at Nottingham. The Civil War began.
2 September	The Earl of Cumberland commissioned as Lieutenant-General of the Royalist forces in the North. The repair and fortification of the defences of York begun.
20 „	Ferdinando, Lord Fairfax appointed General of their forces in the North by Parliament. He began raising a Parliamentarian army in the West Riding.
30 November	Cumberland resigned his royal commission to the Earl (later Marquis) of Newcastle.

1643

15 January	Edmund Cooper re-elected Lord Mayor on the insistence of the Earl of Newcastle despite considerable opposition from the Common Council and the citizens generally.
22 February	Queen Henrietta Maria landed at Bridlington from Holland.
8 March	The Queen entered York with 500 waggons containing munitions of war.
4 June	The Queen left York for Oxford.
25 September	Solemn League and Covenant signed between the Scots and Parliament.
27 October	King Charles I created the Earl of Newcastle a Marquis.

1644

15 January	Edmund Cooper re-elected Lord Mayor for the third successive time on the insistence of Newcastle.
19 January	The Scots army, under the Earl of Leven, crossed the Border.
11 April	The storming of Selby. The defeat and capture of John Bellasis, the Governor of York, by Lord Fairfax.
16 April	Newcastle's army entered York.

21–23 April	Leven's and Fairfax's armies took up their siege positions around York.
3 June	Earl of Manchester's army arrived to take up its siege position.
5 ,,	Fairfax raised a battery on Lamel Hill.
7 ,,	Leven attacked the three Royalist gun emplacements to the S.W. of the city, capturing two of them.
8 ,,	The suburbs of the city fired. Fairfax started an abortive mine under Walmgate Bar.
8–15 June	Parley negotiations.
16 June	Mine fired under St. Mary's Tower. Abortive attack by some of Manchester's forces on King's Manor.
30 ,,	Prince Rupert's relieving army reached the Knaresborough area. Parliamentarian armies raised the siege and concentrated their forces near Marston Moor.
1 July	Rupert's army reached York and bivouacked over-night in the Skelton-Clifton area.
2 ,,	Battle of Marston Moor.
3 ,,	Royalist leaders fled from York, Newcastle to Scarborough, and Rupert to Richmond. Sir Thomas Glemham left in command of the city.
4 ,,	Parliamentarian armies resumed the siege.
16 ,,	York surrendered. The Royalist garrison marched out and the Parliamentarian armies marched in and held a Thanksgiving Service in the Minster.
18 ,,	Parliamentarian armies left York, leaving a garrison, a force of Yorkshiremen under the command of the new Governor, Lord Fairfax.
3 September	Edmund Cooper deposed as Lord Mayor and Thomas Hoyle elected in his stead.[3]

[1] The modern notation has been used.

[2] Elected Lord Mayor for the first time in 1630. For his biography see R. H. Scaife, *Civic Officials of York and Parliamentary Representatives* (MS. in York Public Library), pp. 183–5, no. 762. The circumstances of the election of Cooper as Lord Mayor in the Januarys of 1642, 1643 and 1644 are outlined in the paper by Robert Davies, 'An episode in the municipal history of the City of York,' YAJ v (1879), pp. 52–62.

[3] 'January the 30th [1649/50] much about the same houre of the day that our late Soveraigne was Murdered the year before, Thomas Hoyle . . . . became his own Executioner, by hanging of himself in his house at Westminster, and was there found dead by his Lady.' (Hildyard, p. 61).

Hoyle's first wife Elizabeth had died on 9 December 1639. Why her funeral sermon, printed by 'Tho[ma]s Broad, dwelling in Stonegate over against the Starre,' was not published until 1644 is a mystery. The front page is printed as Plate XIII.

Chapter One

THE STAGE IS SET

BY THE AUTUMN of 1643 the Royalist and Parliamentarian armies had virtually reached a position of stalemate in the Civil War. Neither had proved strong enough to gain a decisive advantage over the other. Each sought a way out of this impasse by seeking help outside England — the Royalists in Ireland and the Parliamentarians in Scotland. The former, about twelve regiments in all, while proving of some help to the King, were a political and religious embarrassment because of the Roman Catholic religion of many of them. The Scots on the other hand proved of immense value to Parliament. It was the entry into England in January 1644 of the Scottish army of some 21,000 men (18,000 foot: 2,000 cavalry and 1,000 dragoons) that set in motion the train of events that led to the siege of York later in the year. The Scottish army was commanded by Alexander Leslie, 1st Earl of Leven, (Plate XIV) with David Leslie (Plate XXVI) as his second-in-command. By the end of April when it besieged York its numbers were reduced by some 4,000.

The events of the first three months of 1644 in the north of England are best understood by a brief reference to the various combatant forces of the two sides which were ultimately to play a part in the siege. The Scots crossed the border on 19th January and progressed very slowly southwards, being delayed by bad weather, the obstinate resistance of the Royalist garrison of Newcastle and the harassing tactics of the army commanded by the Marquis of Newcastle. By late March they were still only threatening Durham. William Cavendish, Earl and later 1st Marquis of Newcastle (Plate VIII) commanded the Royalist army of the north, which in late April, numbered some 7,000 (4,000 foot : 3,000 horse).

In the south of Yorkshire, drawing its greatest strength from the West Riding, was the Yorkshire Parliamentarian army, some 5,000 strong, led by Ferdinando, 2nd Baron Fairfax, (Frontispiece) whose second-in-command was his son Sir Thomas (Plate XXV). In the early months of 1644 one of the objectives of this army was the containment and neutralisation of the Royalist garrison in York, numbering about 4,000 under the command of John (later Sir John) Bellasis.

In East Anglia was the Parliamentarian army of the Eastern Association under Edward Montagu, 2nd Earl of Manchester (Plate XVIII); while near Oxford, lay the Royalist army commanded by Lord Forth. Prince Rupert commanded those of Forth's forces which were in the Shrewsbury area, having his headquarters in that city. These two armies had no part in the first part of the siege but were to play important roles later.

The event which precipitated the Siege was the storming on 11 April of Selby where the Fairfax forces were to rendezvous. Bellasis intercepted a letter containing details of the plans of the Fairfaxes to unite their scattered forces and march north to assist the Scots near Durham.[1] To prevent this he marched out of York with three-quarters of the garrison, (some 3,000 men) to Selby. Bellasis was defeated and was himself captured. Two contemporary tracts[2] refer to this battle : they put his losses at about 100 officers and 2,000 other ranks. The news of this disaster reached the Marquis of Newcastle the following day at Durham. He realised immediately that this defeat had completely altered the balance of power in the north and that the initiative had now passed from the Royalists to the Parliamentarians and their Scots allies. Apart from a few small, isolated manor houses, the only remaining Royalist strongholds in Yorkshire now were the garrisoned castles of Pontefract, Sandal, Tickhill, Helmsley, Skipton, Knaresborough and Scarborough and, most important of all, the fortified city of York. York, left with a weakened garrison of doubtful morale, as the natural capital and military centre of northern England, had to be succoured. Newcastle had no alternative but to retreat. He left Durham on 12/13 April and

2

by a series of forced marches reached York on the 16th. The Scots followed him closely and on 20 April had joined up with the Fairfaxes at Tadcaster. During the next few days their combined armies, totalling some 20,000 men, marched on York. They took up their positions around the City: the siege had begun.

Three accounts — two from Scots sources[3] and the other by Lord Fairfax[4] — enable us to follow closely the itinerary taken by the Royalist and Scottish armies between Durham and York:—

April

Fri. 12/	Late at night/	
Sat. 13	Very early in the morning	Newcastle's army left Durham for Darlington via Ferryhill. The Scots were not aware of this until 3 p.m. on the Saturday; they then followed, and reached Ferryhill that night, by which time Newcastle had reached Darlington.
Sun. 14		The advance guard of the Scots reached Darlington by 7 a.m. before the whole of Newcastle's army had departed, they took 40 (killed and wounded); captured 2,000 marks worth of silver plate, together with cheese, pork and bread. The last of the Scots crossed the Tees late that night.
Mon. 15		The Scots reached Northallerton with Newcastle somewhere ahead of them.
Tues. 16		The Scots reached Thormanby; Newcastle reached York.
Wed. 17		The Scots reached Boroughbridge. The inference is that while the Royalists continued on the direct route to York via Thirsk and Easingwold, the Scots (presumably wishing to link up with the Fairfaxes whose army was in the Selby area) branched off westwards to Boroughbridge.
Thurs. 18		The Scots reached Wetherby. The Earl of Leven met Lord Fairfax.
Sat. 20		The Scots reached Tadcaster where some of Fairfax's troops joined them.
Sun. 21/Tue. 23		The Scots (from Tadcaster) and the rest of

Long before the siege began the Royalists had envisaged
such a possibility and the city had been put in a posture of
defence. In order to appreciate what had been done, a brief
description of the city and its walls and fortifications is necessary.
The site of the city was determined by the Romans who built
their legionary fortress on the tongue of land between the rivers
Ouse and Foss, and their civilian town on the south bank of the
Ouse in what is now the Micklegate area. In turn, the Angles,
Danes and Normans occupied all, or part, of this area, while the
latter threw up defensive mounds over some of the long-ruined
Roman walls, erecting on top of these mounds a wooden palisade.
This was replaced during the Middle Ages by the stone walls
which existed in 1644 and which substantially survive to the
present day.

These mediaeval walls are just over $3\frac{1}{2}$ miles in circumference and enclose an area of some 260 acres (Plate X and front
end paper). From Skeldergate Postern to North Street Postern
(via Micklegate Bar) and from Lendal Postern to Layerthorpe
(via Bootham and Monk Bars) the walls were built on the Norman
earth mound. From the Red Tower to Fishergate Postern the
walls were much less formidable, being built on a lower, post-
Norman mound. From Layerthorpe Postern to the Red Tower —
a distance of over a quarter of a mile — there was a gap in the
city walls, because the area was taken up by an expanse of nearly
stagnant water known as the King's Fishpond or Fishpool. This
had come into being at the time of the building of the York
Castles (1068) when the River Foss had been dammed just below
one of these, the wooden predecessor to Clifford's Tower, thus
flooding the low-lying land half a mile to the north. Seventeenth-
century documents suggest that by that time the Fishpond was
shrinking in size and gradually filling up:[5] it is clear, however,
that during the siege it presented a formidable obstacle to the
besiegers. It is now (1970) completely drained and the land
reclaimed, the area being known as Foss Islands.

Outside the city walls at the foot of the mound was the outer
moat, varying in width and depth, and in most parts containing

water. This was often choked with weeds and debris thrown over the wall and in hot weather was prone to dry up. However, between the Red Tower and Fishergate Postern the moat was generally filled with water at all times. Appendix III suggests that an attempt had been made to deepen this some months before the siege began. This moat compensated for the comparative weakness, noted above, of the wall in this sector. As well as this outer moat there was an inner one at the foot of the mound inside the wall. It was mostly dry, was in some places filled up, and was in others used as an open drain or as a convenient dumping ground for rubbish.

The walls were strengthened by the building at irregular intervals of small towers. Entry through the walls was by the four great gates or bars (Micklegate, Bootham, Monk and Walmgate: Plates I–IV) and by six smaller gateways or posterns (North Street, Lendal, Layerthorpe, Fishergate, Castlegate and Skeldergate). All the bars were similar in structure, consisting of a gateway, closed by a portcullis and heavy wooden doors, and flanked and surmounted by a massive tower. Outside each gateway was an additional defence work — the barbican. The one outside Walmgate Bar, heavily restored in 1648 owing to damage it received during the siege, is the only one still surviving, the other three having been pulled down in the 19th century. All four were standing in 1644. All the posterns (except Layerthorpe, which was large enough to allow wagons to pass — Plate VI) were nothing more than small doorways allowing egress and ingress to people on foot, cattle and pack animals.

The hub of York's defence system was the castle (Clifford's Tower — Plate XII) built near the confluence of the Ouse and Foss. This and another keep on the other side of the Ouse (Baile Hill — only the mound of which now remains), were built of wood soon after the Norman Conquest. In the 12th century Clifford's Tower was rebuilt in stone, by which time the Baile Hill keep had been abandoned. Alongside Clifford's Tower was the bailey. Castle and bailey were both surrounded by a deep moat fed from the Foss. Access to the castle and bailey was provided by two drawbridges. The castle, a royal stronghold and largely independent of the city, had been neglected in the 15th and 16th centuries and at the outbreak of the Civil War (1642) much of it (especially the tower itself) was in a ruinous condition.

Outside the city walls were the suburbs. These were not extensive; a few score houses clustered around each bar. The largest area was outside Walmgate where there were two churches — St. Lawrence's and St. Nicholas' — both of which were to play important roles in the siege.

Finally, in any military appraisal of York in 1644, reference must be made to St. Mary's Abbey. The Abbey Church had been ruined since its dissolution in 1539, but near to it, adapted from what had been the Abbot's Lodging, was the Manor House (now called the King's Manor) which since 1539 had been the official residence of the Presidents of the Council of the North. The Abbey grounds — 10 acres in extent — were enclosed by substantial walls on all but the river front; had corner towers (one of which, St. Mary's Tower, was to play an important part in the siege) and had a gateway adjoining St. Olave's church. These defences formed a salient on the north west of the City walls which would constitute an embarrassment to the defenders.

Although basically a strongly fortified city, the defences of York had been so neglected that in 1640, the year of the so-called Second Bishops' War against the Scots, urgent representations were made that they should be mended. Under the Treaty of Ripon (16 October) which ended that war King Charles I had to accept humiliating terms. The Scots were left in occupation of the six northern counties of England and the King had to pay them £840 a day until a final settlement was arranged. Many of the King's closest advisers were bitterly opposed to this treaty, fearing that the Scots would soon repudiate it and advance further into England. Edward, Lord Herbert was particularly outspoken and urged the necessity of fortifying York. Here are some extracts from his argument as reported by Rushworth :—[6]

> First, that Newcastle being taken, it was necessary to fortify York; there being no other considerable place betwixt the Scots and London, which might detain their army from advancing forwards.
>
> .... this agreeth with the custom of all other countries, there being no town any where he knew in Christendom, of the greatness of York, that hath not its bastions and bulwarks.

As for the charges, the citizens of York might undertake that by his majesty's permission; for since it is a maxim of war, that every town may fortify its circumference, within the space of two months, the expences cannot be great.

And for the manner of doing it, nothing else is needful, but that at the distance of every twenty five score paces round about the town, the walls should be thrown down, and certain bastions or bulwarks of earth be erected by the advice of some good engineer.

For the performing whereof every townsman might give his helping hand, digging and casting up earth, only where the said engineer should appoint. And for ordnance, ammunition and a magazine, the townsmen, likewise for their security, might be at the charge thereof in these dangerous times; it being better to employ some money so to prevent the taking of the town, than to run the hazard of being in that estate in which Newcastle-men now are . . . .

I shall conclude therefore, with your majesty's good favour, for the fortifying of York, as assuring myself that if for want of such fortification it fall into Scotchmen's hands, they will quickly fortify it as they have already done Newcastle.

It seems that little or nothing was done. This is not surprising when we realise that the cost and labour of the 'bastions or bulwarks' proposed under this scheme was to be borne entirely by the city. Further, the deliberate destruction of all houses within 'twenty-five score paces round about the wall' (about 200 yds.) was hardly likely to be acceptable to those citizens whose property was threatened.

However, before the 1644 siege began the deficiencies were, in part, rectified. In the Spring of 1642 King Charles I came to York as he distrusted the loyalty of London. On 16 August he left after a stay there of five months : six days later he raised his standard at Nottingham and the Civil War began. On 2 September, Henry, Earl of Cumberland, was commissioned by the King to put York into a 'Posture of Defence : And on the next day was Ordnance mounted on the Barrs.'[7] Now began a period of feverish activity during which the long neglected defences were repaired ; the City Trained Bands were put on a permanent war footing ; the city was amply provisioned with food, drink and fodder ; and the magazine was filled with powder, shot and match. Clifford's Tower 'being exceeding ruinous, was re-edified and strengthened with Fortifications . . . December the third [1642],

William Marquesse of Newcastle came to York with a great army, ten pieces of Ordnance, and ammunition for the King's service.'[8]

On 22 February 1643 Queen Henrietta Maria arrived at Bridlington, from Holland, with a convoy of ships loaded with munitions of war — 30 brass cannons, 2 iron cannons, and small arms for 10,000 men. With her was James King, Lord Eythin, who joined the Marquis of Newcastle's army as second-in-command. A fortnight later the armaments were transported to York in 500 carts, the ammunition being temporarily stored in the Common Hall on Ouse Bridge. Most of these supplies were taken in July to the main Royalist arsenal in Oxford.[9] It is not clear what exactly was left behind and was therefore available when the siege began in the following year.

In the autumn of 1643 the Marquis of Newcastle won a series of minor battles and skirmishes over the Fairfaxes in Yorkshire at Sheffield, Wakefield, Leeds, Halifax and Bradford and spent December and most of January in Derbyshire. However, when he heard of the invasion of England by the Scots and their occupation of Newcastle, he marched north to oppose them, revisiting York on 27 January 1644.[10] It was probably on this occasion that he left behind him in the city a considerable quantity of lead, doubtless from his Derbyshire mines. We know of this because on 8 August Parliament ordered[11]

> .... that all the lead found in the city [York] at its surrender, which had been brought thither by the E[arl] of Newcastle, should be sold, compensation being afterwards made to such owners thereof as were well affected and proved their title within six months.

Soon afterwards a Brian Dawson of York petitioned[12] the House of Commons for the value of 34 fothers of lead brought to the city by Newcastle 'which was sold [presumably after the siege] and the proceeds applied to the use of the Parliament's army.'

A wealth of material, largely unpublished, concerning these military activities exists in the 'Housebooks', 'Chamberlains' Rolls' and the one surviving 'Constables' Accounts' of the City. These give intimate glimpses of what was going on at this time. In Appendix II all relevant extracts from these documents are listed.

Drake[13] gives the most detailed account of the preparations. He says that, after the arrival of the Queen and the ammunition train from Bridlington

.... the city was every where strongly fortified, and above twenty cannon, great and small, were planted about it. Two cannon were planted upon old Bayle [Baile Hill], one at the Fryers, two sling pieces, and one small drake in three or four barks which cross'd the river in a breast near the Crane-house; two at Micklegate-bar, two at Monk-bar, two at Walmgate-bar; out of which last was a strong bulwark erected. At several lanes ends, within the city, were ditches and banks made and cast up, with hogsheads filled with earth for barricadoes. By the general's orders the magistrates were to find eight hundred men to work daily at the repairs of the walls, and securing the ditches of the city; and they had likewise eight hundred more out of the county to help them. This must be a vast expence and fall heavy upon every particular inhabitant; when besides, adds the writer of a manuscript,[14] each citizen paid two pounds a month, that maintained a man in arms, towards provision for the army. And if their own servants bore not their arms it cost five shillings a week for one to bear them. Add to this six shillings a month for firing at the several guards in the city, with two, three or four soldiers billeted upon free billet in a house, and it will make their case very deplorable.

Hildyard[15] adds further details :—

This year [1643] Clifford's Tower, being exceeding ruinous, was re-edified and strengthened with Fortifications. Sir Francis Cobb Collonell, was Governour thereof, who with his Lieutenant Collonell, Major, and Captains, had their Lodgings there during the Siege of the City.

During the same period, stores of food and drink were laid up in the city. This was done so well that the garrison and citizens suffered no real privation during the three months' siege. Stocks of provender for the horses and cattle were also arranged. The following document,[16] endorsed 'Sir Tho[mas] Glemham's protection for Uskele [Ulleskelf],' shows that this was done at places some distance from the city itself: Ulleskelf is 9 miles from York.

Whereas Thomas Squire Providore Generall for the Garrison at Yorke, hath layd upp Provision of hay and Corne att Ulliskelfe for the use of the said Garrison. Theise are therefore to will and I require yow and every of yow to forbeare to molest or trouble the said Mr. Squire or his servants in the quiet possession thereof and not presume to take or carry away any part of the same without his the said Mr. Squire's Privitie or Consent. And in case any shall doe contrary to these my Commands then I doe authorise the said Mr. Squire his deputie or deputies to take a competent number of Musqueteirs for his or their Assistance and bring all such before me or the Governor of the aforesaid Cittie for the time being, to the end they may receive condigne Punishment according to their demeritt.

Given at the said Cittie of York the xvi[th] day of October Anno Domini 1643.

Tho[mas] Glemham
To all Officers and soldiers under
the Command of his Excellence the
Marquesse of Newcastle, and to
every of them.

Finally, as early as the autumn of 1642, at least three gun emplacements had been constructed on the west side of the city — and there may have been more on the other sides as well as linking circumvallation trenches — as a series of outer defence works beyond the city walls. These are discussed in some detail in chapter IX, their positions being shown on the front end paper. They played an important part in the siege and many references to them occur in subsequent pages. One of their purposes was to screen the open fields which lay between them and the city walls, so that cattle might be pastured there. As late as 7 June — six weeks after the beginning of the siege — Henry Slingsby,[17] one of the besieged, could write 'we still send to ye feild to keep our cows and horses.'

---

[1] *CSP. Dom.*, p. 25 and Appendix I.

[2] *A Letter sent from the Right Honorable, the Lord Fairfax, To the Committee of both Kingdoms: concerning the great Victory lately obtained (by God's Blessing) at Selby in Yorkshire* .... Printed for Edw. Husbands, April 19 1644. (Not a T.T. Copy in Minster Library, York) Reproduced in Appendix I. *A Victorious Conquest near Selby in Yorkshire, certified by a letter from the Lord Fairfax his Quarters* .... London, printed by Andrew Coe, and Published by Order [April 1644]. (Not a T.T. Copy in Minster Library, York).

[3] Somervell, p. 53 and *Extract of Letters*.

[4] Fairfax, p. 60 b.

[5] Raine, p. 14.

[6] pp. 1293-4. Reproduced in Drake, p. 141.

[7] Hildyard, p. 54. Drake, p. 160.

[8] *Ibid.*

[9] Ian Roy, *The Royalist Ordnance Papers 1642–1646 Part I.* Oxfordshire Record Society 1964, pp. 107-8.

10 Newcastle, p. 31f.

11 HMC Portland MS., vol. i, p. 182.

12 *Ibid.*

13 p. 162.

14 This has not been traced. The Hildyard tract dated 1664 (of which Drake makes extensive use in various parts of his work) does not mention the details in the passage quoted.

15 p. 55.

16 Borthwick Institute of Historical Research, R. Asquith 11/25g.

17 p. 110.

Chapter Two

THE SIEGE BEGINS

ON 18 APRIL Lord Fairfax and his son Sir Thomas with some of their cavalry went ahead of their main force which remained around Selby, and met the Earl of Leven and the Scots' army at Wetherby; two days later they reached Tadcaster.[1] The time was spent by the two commanders and their staffs in 'several consultations how to proceed against the common enemy.'[2] It was evident that, in themselves, the two armies were insufficient to beleaguer the city completely and, in fact, unless their dispositions were made carefully, they might even put themselves at an actual disadvantage *vis à vis* the garrison. In a letter dated 20 April, probably addressed to the Committee of Both Kingdoms, Lord Fairfax summed up the situation thus :—

> . . . . the Marquis of Newcastle . . . . hath drawn all his force, both horse and foot, to York, where the bridge near Ouse [i.e. Ouse bridge, the only one then crossing that river in the city] gives him advantage at his pleasure to bring his whole army over the river either into the West Riding, where our armies are now quartered, or into the North and East Ridings, when opportunity presents itself, which we cannot suddenly prevent without apparent hazard of some part of our forces. So, for the present, my lord of Leven, with his army and part of my horse, are drawing to quarter nearer York upon the West side, until a way be contrived to put part of the army by a bridge or float over the river to straiten the enemy on the East side also.[3]

The same point is made in *Extract of Letters*. Another danger — one which hung over the besiegers like a nightmare during the whole time of the siege — was that a Royalist army might come upon them from the West or South. Later in the letter quoted above Fairfax expressed this fear thus :—

> I have had sundry intelligences that Prince Rupert is already upon his march towards Newark, intending Northwards.

Actually Rupert made no such move direct to York for another six weeks, but his eventual relief of Newark (21 March) was a swift and brilliant feat of arms, and caused widespread alarm in the ranks of the Parliamentarians that the Prince might continue his advance northwards to York.

On 22 April the joint forces reached Askham Richard and on the following day Acaster Malbis where a bridge of boats was made across the Ouse.[4]

Meanwhile Fairfax's foot moved up the east (left) bank of the Ouse from Selby, doubtless crossing the river at Cawood where there seems to have been another bridge of boats.[5] Within the next few days the allied armies took up the positions which they were to maintain during the entire siege. 'This year [1644] on 23 April, the Scots faced York at a distance, on the West bank of the River Owse,'[6] their line extending from the right bank of the Ouse, from somewhere below Poppleton to the river near Fulford: Leven had his headquarters at Middlethorpe, presumably in the Manor there. Fairfax took the sector from Fulford on the left bank of the Ouse, by Fishergate Postern and Walmgate Bar, to the Red Tower situated alongside the marshy region of the King's Pool, a backwater of the river Foss; his headquarters was presumably at Heslington Hall. Slingsby[7] is explicit in stating that until the army of the Eastern Association arrived five weeks later, the city remained open on the north side :—

> Thus we were blockt up upon two sides of ye town, and ye rest we had open for about 3 (*sic*) weeks, until such times as my L[or]d Manchester came with his Norfolk men.

It seems, however, that both Leven and Fairfax had squadrons of cavalry, and perhaps small bodies of foot as well, patrolling the open northern sector. A Parliamentarian tract — *Hulls Managing* — which probably gives an exaggerated account of the effectiveness of the blockade during these early days, describes the situation thus :—

> These two armies thus joyn'd amount neer to the number of 30000 horse and foot[8] which are quartered in all the Villages around about the City,

13

keeping their guards within lesse then [than] a mile on all sides; their Scouts are in continuall skirmishes on all sides with the enemy, and march up many times to the Walls of the City. Our guards are so many on all sides of the Citie, that not a man can goe in, or come forth without discovery, much lesse can the least provision be carried in to them.

Our guards being at such distance from the City, they cannot well sally forth in any parties to our prejudice, for first our men have more time to make ready, and then while they assault one quarter, the two next can more easily strike in betwixt them and home, to intercept their retreat, as very many times they have found to their cost. In particular, upon Munday the third of June instant a partee of horse sallyed out of our Quarters at Clifton,[9] intending to breake through and advance towards Scarborough, being discovered, our horse divided themselves into three Squadrons, the middle charged them, the other two wheeled about upon their right and left, and charged them in the reare, and so having encompassed them, cut most of them off; took 67 horse, very few escaped to carry the news to Yorke.

Concerning the Country, it is well affected towards the siege,[10] affording what provision they can for the Armies, according to the ability of the poore plundered people; it were well if such Counties as have lesse tasted of plunder, would give their speedy assistance in supplying them with provision, that so neither the Armies may want convenient food, nor the County be undone; the Scots desire nothing but meale, of which they boast they can make nine severall dishes.

Meanwhile, the Marquis of Newcastle within the city had his problems. He viewed the joining of the two hostile armies with alarm and on the very day that Leven and the Fairfaxes were meeting at Wetherby wrote to the King for assistance[11] :—

May it please your Majesty

The unfortunate defeat of Colonel Bellasis [at Selby, by Fairfax] wherein he lost himself, being taken prisoner, with all his officers; and the Scots and Fairfax having joined near Wetherby, are now too strong for us in matters of the field . . . . they have already p[ut] themselves in such a posture as will soon ruin us, being at York, unless there is some speedy course taken to give us relief, and that with a considerable force, for their army is very strong . . . . We shall be distressed here very shortly. This is my duty and shall be ready with my life to serve your Majesty, who am

Your Majesty's &c

W[illiam] Newcastle

York, 18th April, 1644

The advance of the allies on 22 April to within a mile or so of the city decided Newcastle, while the opportunity still remained, to send away most of his cavalry under Sir Charles

14

PLATE I

Micklegate Bar in 1806.   Artist Henry Cave.

PLATE II

Monk Bar in 1806.   Artist Henry Cave.

Lucas to join the King's forces in the Midlands where they could be of greater service :[12] at the same time he thus lightened the difficulties of his commissariat inside the city. As the Venetian ambassador put it[13] — 'As York did not contain enough forage for all the cavalry, the Marquis has sent out a part of it.' Somervell[14] — a Scot, and therefore possibly 'colouring' the episode — describes the departure of the Royalist cavalry thus :—

> .... in the nicht the haill trouppes that the Marquis of Newcastell had in York went out and fled; and our troupes with my Lord Fairfax and his troupes followed and tuik 60 prisoners and many horses; and they war so hard chasit that they war forcit to tak the culloris from the standaris and ryd away with them and live [leave] the staff behind them.[15]

Another problem to which Newcastle[16] turned his attention was the conservation of the food supplies within the city. Somervell[17] is again our informant :—

> The souldieres that we tak of thairis sayes they gatt a mutchkin[18] of bean an unnce of butar and a penny loaf evirrie ane of them per diem and thair is ane ordinance that evirrie ane within the citie of York sall have bot [but] ane maill [meal] per diem; for the Marquis of Newcastell and General King has causat search all the citie for provision and takin all into the stoir hous and gives out to the people that is within the citie efter the mainer foirsaid.

It may be that during the early part of the siege at least (when the northern sector remained wholly or partly open to the surrounding countryside, in the fields of which the garrison pastured cattle) only certain foodstuffs — bread, butter, etc. — were rationed.[19] In any case the usual 'black market' doubtless existed inside the city. Hildyard[20] has this to say :—

> .... a quarter of Veale and Mutton was sold for sixteene shillings a piece. Biefe [beef] at four shillings per stone; A Pigg at seven shillings; A Henn at foure shillings; Eggs at three pence a piece; And fresh Butter at two Shillings eight pence per Pound; yet the Souldiers and Citizens were well contented, and Couragious, having no want of salt Meat, nor of any sort of Graine, which was Sold at reasonable Rates; and of Wine, Beer, and Ale, there was plenty.

Slingsby[21] who was in the city, says that 'provisions we had in good store,'[22] but adds 'mon[e]y we had none ;[23] w[hi]ch bred us some trouble to help out & many complaints both from soulgiers and Townsmen.'

This introduces us to another of the problems facing Newcastle — the billeting, feeding and payment of the soldiers he brought with him into the city after his precipitate retreat from Durham. Two quite independent sources explain what was done. Slingsby wrote :—[24]

My L[or]d took a course to have ym [them] billet'd, & proportionably laid upon, both ye Gentlemen & Officer, either to find ym [them] meat, or mony after a groat a man pr. diem; w[hi]ch for my share came to 4*l.* 5*s.* a week, ye mony being rais'd out of ye corn w[hi]ch I brought into ye Town; this fell heavily upon some, yt [that] being Sojourners & in great want, yet was fourc'd to maintain a Soulgier, tho' they were put to ye shift to borrow; and their was no remedy, for ye soulgier, knew him yt [that] was appoint'd to pay him, & if he refus'd, ye soulgier lays hands on him or anything he had.

The second source is an entry in the 'York Corporation Housebook.'[25] This is also important in that it gives the figure of Newcastle's troops billeted in the city as 4,000. That these exactions were implemented in the city even on the richest and most influential Royalists is borne out by an entry in the 'letter books' of Sir Samuel Luke. During the period covered by the siege the latter was Scoutmaster-General to the Earl of Essex, the Parliamentarian Captain-General and, as such, was responsible for co-ordinating what we should now call the intelligence services on the Parliamentarian side. Under the date 6 December 1644 he notes[26] the capture of a Royalist, Sir Thomas Ashfield, variously described as a 'great recusant,' 'very rich' and a 'patentee of coals at Newcastle,' and goes on to say :—

He carried £800 into York with him which the Earl of Newcastle seized and during the siege, when every man was to allow so many groats a day for so many soldiers, he refused to pay and had two horses worth £60 distrained for actual sum of money, but afterwards underhand he got a man to redeem his horses and they were sent him home again.

To ensure loyalty inside the city walls Newcastle ordered everyone to take the following oath :—[27]

An Oath taken by the Gentrie and Inhabitants of the Citie and Countie of Yorke.

I A. B. doe hereby testifie, and declare, that our Soveraigne Lord King Charles is the true and lawfull King of England, and of all his other Dominions; and that neither the two Houses of Parliament, the people nor any part of them have any power, or authoritie over him, or the Crowne; neither ought they, or any of his Subjects of this Kingdome of England, or his other dominions, upon any pretence whatsoever, to take up Armes against his Sacred Majestie, His person, his Crown, his Generalls, or Souldiers authorized by him, nor may they by any authoritie or pretence whatsoever, make or levie War within this Kingdome, or his other dominions, or any way use his Royall authority, or name for that purpose, without his evidence, & pub-like [public] consent before obtained. And I do further sweare, that I will beare true faith, and Allegiance to His Sacred Majestie, and his Crowne; and to my might and power will assist him, his Generalls and all under their command, against all such as have taken or shall take up Armes against him, or that have or shall take up armes within this Kingdome, without His Majesties evident publike [public] or reall Authoritie, and especially against Robert Earle of Essex, Ferdinando Lord Fairfax, (pretended generalls for the Parliament), and all their associates & confederates, and all others whatsoever that derive not their authority by particular Commissions from His Majestie, and his Generalls.

And I doe further declare, from the bottom of my heart, that diverse of the Scottish nation, having presumed to enter into this Kingdome, in a warlike manner without his Majesties evident and publike [public] authority first obtained, and published; I will readily, and to the utmost of mine abilitie with the hazard of my life, and fortunes, assist his Majestie, his Generalls, and all under their Commands, in resisting, opposing and pursuing such Scots, in a hostile way, as rebells, and traytors against his Maiesty, and enemies to the Crowne of England. And I doe further sweare, that I will to my power assist, and defend all such as shall take this Oath, in pursuance of the same, and particularly defend this Citie, and Garrison of Yorke, and during my residence there, oppose all such, as shall make any attempt against it, and all such plots, and designes as shall come to my knowledge, that may bee preiudiciall to his Maiesties service or destructive to the Forces raised by His Maiesties Commissions. I will from time to time discover to His Maiesties Generall, or the Commander in Chiefe of this Country, and in their absence, to the Chiefe Officer for the time being of this Garrison, and all this I doe unfainedly sweare, without any equivocation or mental reservation, so help me God.

During the first phase of the siege the Parliamentarian troops were insufficient to invest the city closely. For most of the time they seem to have remained at some distance from the walls making a few attacks in strength to remind the Royalists of their presence and opposing the occasional sallies made by the garrison. They erected no batteries and, except for an attack on a 'little Strouse [sconce — gun emplacement] before Akhame [Acomb]' (see below, p. 23 under 14 May), made no determined effort to destroy the screen of outworks (numbering at least three and possibly more) erected by the Royalists before the siege began in the Clementhorpe/Mount/Bishopfields area to the west of the city (see further pp. 143–7). Parties of cavalry and foot — particularly the former — were detached from the main forces near the city and sent to capture other Royalist strongholds in the surrounding countryside;[28] these included Stamford Bridge, Buttercrambe, Waltham Hall, Crayke, Cawood, Airemouth, Bramham Hall (near Boston Spa), Sandal Castle (near Wakefield) Mulgrave Castle (near Whitby) and 'Mr. Elmer's house within a mile of Barnsley.'[29]

The fullest account of the happenings connected with the siege during the five weeks before the arrival of the army of the Eastern Association is contained in the diary of Robert Douglas, the Scottish chaplain of the Earl of Leven. Below are printed all the entries in it covering these weeks, together with annotations, and a few interpolations relating to other events, gleaned from other contemporary authorities, not mentioned by the diarist. All Douglas entries are prefaced by an asterisk (*).

> *24th April.   Our horses pass by the bridge, and joining Fairfax horse face York, take much provision from the wind milnes by the toun.
>
>   A Lieutenant, and 80 muscateers, yeeld Stamford bridge, upon condition to leave their armes, and march into the toun.

The bridge of boats at Acaster Malbis which Douglas had already mentioned in an earlier entry (see p. 13) is clearly intended. Stamford Bridge is the first of the seven 'strongholds' which Douglas (and other authorities) lists as captured around York during these weeks. One tract — *Hulls Managing* — comments on the leniency and understanding which Lord Fairfax showed towards the prisoners captured in these forays :—

> Parties have been sent abroad to many strong holds in the County, which after some assaults have been surrendered upon composition; for such is the Lord Fairfax his clemency towards their forced men, giving them leave upon taking the Covenant to take up arms under him, or to goe to their own homes, that he hath won all their hearts to him, in so much that when they see themselves but a little straitened, they lay downe their armes, and refer themselves to his mercy, but all their Officers he keeps prisoners.

> *25th April.   The Horses joyned, goe by Selby toward Ferribridge, to meet with most of the enemies horse, who were to march that way, as we understood from Knaresburgh, whither they had gon the night before from York.

This doubtless refers to the Royalist cavalry under the command of Sir Charles Lucas sent out from the city. Other authorities (see pp. 14-5) suggest that this incident took place two or three days earlier.

> *27th April.   To Midlethorp [Middlethorpe], within a mile to York.

The Earl of Leven had his headquarters at Middlethorpe; Douglas, as his chaplain, would accompany him. Nearby was the Scots ordnance depot from which artillery, shot, powder, etc. was issued (see Appendix VII).

> *28th April.   Psal. 83. 14, 15, 16.[30]

These entries, which occur on every Sunday and occasionally on other days (designated 'Fast Days'), doubtless represent the texts from which Douglas preached.

> *29th April.   Sixteen prisoners of the enemie.

> *30th April.   York blocked on all sydes. The bridge of Kavie brought up.

Hulls Managing in a passage quoted above (p. 14), makes the same assertion — 'Our guards are so many on all sides of the Citie, that not a man can goe in, or come forth without discovery.' Perhaps the northern sector, later taken over by Manchester, was lightly held, being no more than occasionally patrolled.

Reference has already been made to the bridge of boats mentioned (see p. 13): Cawood is presumably intended.

> *3rd May   Seven wind milnes burnt off on the other syde Ouse, near York.

Hildyard[31] has this to say of this incident :—

> May the second, the seven Winde-Mills on Heworth-Moore were burnt by the Enemy: And the next day the Water-Mills, called Abbey Mills, and the Winde-Mill, adjoyning with the Pepper Mill, were also Burnt.

Raine,[32] describes the position of these Abbey Mills thus — 'on the rising ground above the Foss where Park Grove is today, stood a windmill of the Abbey; below, on the Foss, were three Abbey water-mills.'

On the same day the two Houses of Parliament wrote a letter [33] of congratulation to Leven on his 'diligent Pursuit' of the Marquis of Newcastle :—

My Lord,

We are commanded, by both Houses of Parliament, to represent unto your Excellency their just Sense and hearty Acknowledgement of the Affection which you have so constantly and faithfully expressed, not only to themselves, but to the Cause and the Kingdom, in whose Assistance and Defence your Excellency hath so freely engaged yourself, notwithstanding the manifold Streights and Distractions they meet with, rendering them (at present) unable to give those Encouragements which they desire, to a Person of so great Merit, and the Forces under your Command; but as all the Hardships and Disadvantages which your Excellency conflicts with in this Cause are Additions to your Honour, so do they account them to be to their Obligation, which they shall be ready upon all Occasions to express. We are further commanded to take Notice of the great Advantage which may come to the affairs in the North, by your diligent Pursuit of the Lord of Newcastle's Forces, and joining now with the Lord Fairfax, for the more effectual and speedy reducing of the Enemy in those Parts, and putting a happy Issue to the Distractions of both Kingdoms, for which the Two Houses are desirous to give you all possible Encouragement; and therefore the Earl of Manchester hath Order, with his Army, to attend the Motions of Prince Rupert's Forces, that they may not disturb you; and the Houses have appointed the Sum of Twenty Thousand Pounds to be sent within very few Days, for the supply of your Army, which for the present they hope will give some Satisfaction, considering the manifold Neccesities which lies upon the Care of the Parliament to supply, and particularly those of Ireland, which they are no less desirous to satisfy and shall suddenly give a real Testimony of,

We have no more to add, but that we are,
Your Excellency's.

Letters written in a similar strain by the House were at the same time addressed to 'the Committee of the Convention of Estates, residing with the Scots Army' and to Lord Fairfax.[34] On 16 May Leven sent this reply :—[35]

Right Honourable,

You have presented to me in your Letter the kinde Expressions of the Honourable Houses of Parliament, for which I am desirous to render all humble Thanks; and hereby do professe, that as the Safty of Religion and Liberty, now so neerly interessted, is allwaies deerest to me, so nothinge could be so powerfull to bringe me and this Army heere, as the great Desires to further the Weele of this Kingdome, and establish the Peace of both Nations, now happily united by Nationall Covenante. Give me therefore

Leave by theise to assure the Honourable Houses of Parliament, that nothinge shall be left undon, which may serve to produce the desired Issue of theise Troubles; and that this Army shall, God willinge, apply itself with constant Care and most effectuall Endeavours for speedy reducinge the Enemy, and helpinge to restore these Nations to a flourishinge Condition, under Truth and Peace; being confident of the Parliament's Care of them, as they are not insensible of that which theise Honourable Houses have formerly don for their Maintenance and Encouragement. My Lord Fairfax and I remaine close aboute this Citty, and have sent Two Thousand Horse and Dragooners for my Lord Manchester's better Assistance, who, I am confident, as they have Orders from us, so will they be most carefull to pursue their best Advantages, either of the Lord Newcastle's Forces, or of any other Forces which shall come from the South; and thus, having nothinge to add, with my heartiest Wishes for the Prosperity of the Honourable Houses of Parliament, and my due Respects to your Lordships, I remaine

Your Lordship's humble Servant

Leven

From the Campe before York,
16th May, 1644.
For the Right Honourable the Speakers of both
Houses of Parliament.

*4th May.   Buttercram yeelded, the souldiers leave their armes, and goe home; the officers of whom Carbraith[36] [is one] remaine prisoners.

Hulls Managing mentions the capture by the Parliamentarians of 'a strong fort at Buttercram' but gives no date. That tract and *Exact Relation* refer to a successful raid on it after this by the Royalists. *Exact Relation* says :—

. . . . the third of June in the night, 60 horse sent by Sir Hugh Cholmley from Scarborough came to Buttercoms [Buttercrambe], where Mr. Henry Darley lodged; and the Draw-bridge being accidentally let down that night they entered, and took him in bed, and carried him prisoner to Scarborough.[37]

*5th May.   Psal. 83. 16, 17.[38]

In a letter[39] dated the same day, John Frechville, a Royalist writing to Lord Loughborough, said '. . . according to the best intelligence we have from York it is not so distressed.' Admittedly Frechville had his tongue in his cheek as he was trying to persuade Prince Rupert to 'take in' Derby in his sweep into Lancashire, (see further p. 78) but this opinion about conditions in York agrees with others forthcoming at this time.

On 9 May the Committee of Both Kingdoms sitting in London ordered its secretary

> To write to the Committee of both Kingdoms residing in the Scottish army near York, to let them know that there is sent to them, by the ship 'Deliverance of London,' a supply of peas, oats, oatmeal, butter, cheese, biscuits, boots and shoes for the Scottish army.[40]

This incident is to be linked with these three entries in Baillie :[41]—

> 3rd May 1644. But are [our] greatest difficulty is want, no penny have we [the Scottish army] gott since we came to England, except it have been a fourtnight's pay at most. The country gives no victuall; our discipline hinders the taking of it; the sojours cloaths are worne; their extremity is great.

> 9th May 1644. Tomorrow there will be shipped twenty thousand pounds sterling for our armie.[42]

> 14th May 1644. This day twentie thousand pounds sterling is shipped for our armie.[43]

Local Yorkshire accounts of the Scots occupation of the districts around York, as might be expected, give a very different picture from that painted above by Baillie under the date 3 May — 'our discipline hinders the taking of it [i.e. food &c. by force].' Here are two examples. The tenants of Acaster Malbis complained that the Scots 'who were quartered there whilst York was beleagured' did damage to the extent of £2,000. They said that they had 'had all their corn wasted, and the sheep, kine and swine eaten by the Scots.' As a result their unfortunate landlord, young Viscount Fairfax of Gilling (distantly related to the Parliamentarians Lord Ferdinando and Sir Thomas) was obliged to forgive them a whole year's rent and to reduce their future rent by half 'for the time to come.' At Walton, on another estate belonging to the Viscount near Scarborough, the tenants complained that the Scots, though not permanently billeted there, had paid three foraging visits and during the last of these 'took all their beans and oats and barley they had left for seed. They left but three sheep about all the town, and when they went away the soldiers at divers houses took away with them the sheets and bedding they had lain in, and kept some of the tenants till the rest ran to other towns to borrow ten pounds to give them for a farewell.'[44]

In Appendix VI is printed *A Remonstrance concerning the Misdemeanours of some of the Scots souldiers in the County of Yorke*. It is dated 1646, two years after the siege of York, at a time when the Scots were in occupation of much of the North of England. The incidents described are such as probably happened in the districts around York during the time of the siege.

> *11th May   Lindsay, General [of] Artillerie[45] and Sir Thomas [Fairfax], goe to meet with Manchester.

Short Memorial confirms this. Dudhope names Sir Thomas only. The meeting was apparently somewhere in East Anglia.

> *12th May   Psal. 83. 18.[46]
>
> *13th May   80 prisoners of the enemy taken in a kirk without Wangate [Walmgate] barr, with a Captain, Lieutenant, and Ensigne.

According to Drake,[47] the church was that of St. Nicholas; Terry [48] says it was St. Lawrence's; *Manifest Truths* says 'My Lord Fairfax his men at Walmegate, where they tooke a church and divers prisoners in it.' It appears that the Royalists had held one or both of these churches and a bastion in advance of their main defence line, that of Walmgate Bar and the adjoining walls.

> *14th May   Little Strouse before Akhame taken from the enemie, and slighted a little, 25 of them killed, 39 taken; none of ours killed or hurt.

The exact site of this defensive outwork is not known (see p. 145). Artillery was mounted by the Scots on this sconce, or on another near it, following the resumption of the siege after Marston Moor.[49]

On 16 May, the Committee with the Scottish army, from their headquarters at Middlethorpe, wrote to the Scottish Commissioners in London :—

> Our armes and ammunition are continually wasting so as wee will have necessity of a supplie: you shall therfor labour to procure 2,000 musquets with bandiliers and als many pikes, to be sent unto Hull for us, and a considerable quantitie of poulder [powder], match and leid [lead].[50]

The request was repeated four days later together with a demand for 1,000 pairs of pistols 'because our horsemen's armes do daylie become unusefull or are lost.'[51] On 27 May the Scots at Middlethorpe did, in fact, receive a fairly large consignment of powder and match via Hull on the 'English Charge'[52] and on 5 June £20,000 'which being to be distribute efter calculation, wee find will‑not amount unto fyfteene dayes' pay to each officer and sojour of this army, which is but a very small releiff efter fyve monethes' patience and receaving nothing.'[53]

*17th May	160 horse fall in at Northallerton, where some of our dragooners out of the regiments lay. A serjeant, with some muscateers, beat them off, kill some, among whom a Lieutenant Collonel, and take some.
*18th May	A serjeant and six our souldiers killed before Akham [Acomb].
*19th May	Isai[ah] 31, 1.[54] Lawood [Cawood] Castle rendred; the souldiers to leave their armes, and goe to their houses; the officers of them, the governor Lumsden a Scot, to remain prisoners.
	Enemy fall out towards Dalhouses quarters;[55] kill 8, take 20 of ours, we kill 9 of theirs, take 4.

Manifest Truths says Sir John Meldrum took Cawood. *Hulls Managing* — 'Cawood Castle [taken], in which were 3 Guns and almost 200 souldiers with their Armes; also Crayke Castle.' Dudhope — 'Since o[u]r comming here wee have cleared ye passage to Hull & taken in Cawood Castell upon Ows [Ouse] & airemouth which is one of ye strongest places in England.'

A month later a party of Royalists attacked the Parliamentarian garrison in Cawood and rescued some of the prisoners. Douglas[56] under 28 June wrote — 'Enemies horse from Pomfred [Pontefract] Castle, rescue 40 prisoners out of Carwood [Cawood], whereof 2 Colonells and one Lieutenant Collonel.' *Exact and Certaine News* dated before 1 July has this entry — 'Cawood Castle had like to have been surprised by a party of horse from Pomfret [Pontefract], but was prevented by the vigilancie of the Guards though some Prisoners escaped.'

20–25 May. In his report dated 8 June to Sir Samuel Luke, a Parliamentarian scout, said[57] that

He was at the leaguer at York from Thursday 20 May until the Tuesday following, during which time there were divers small skirmishes at a windmill within musket shot of the town on the south-east side, which was divers times won and lost with small loss on either side . . . .

24

Our men keep guard in a church which stands by the said mill, out of which they are continually playing their muskets against York, and York likewise at them.

The locality — on the south-east of the city — suggests that the church mentioned was either that of St. Lawrence or of St. Nicholas, which, if Douglas is to be trusted, had been captured from the garrison on 13 May (see p. 23), while the windmill is almost certainly that known to have stood on Lamel Hill, which was later pulled down to accommodate the battery which Fairfax built on the site : this is dealt with in the next chapter.

*21st May   Lieut. Coll. Ballantine shot deadly, whereof he died the nixt day.

Manifest Truths names 'Ballantine,' describes him as 'a gallant Gentleman . . . who not content with a little honour, to gaine more lost his life' and implies that he was killed in a brush with the Royalist horse. Slingsby wrote[58] — 'Our horse guards would be pikering, & now and yn [then] killing, & taking of ye Scots, & among ym [them] one Bellintine (*sic*) a major (*sic*), who they made great moan for.' A Lieutenant-Colonel James Ballantyne was in the Earl of Leven's regiment of Foot[59].

*22nd May   Strouse at Aremouth [Airemouth] yeelded upon the same termes that Carwood Castle.

Manifest Truths says that Sir John Meldrum took the Castle at Cawood and 'the strong Fort of Airmouth . . . which much advantaged our provisions from Hull by water.' *Hulls Managing* — 'and the invincible fort at Ares-mouth [Airemouth], which hath very much conduced to the more easie conveyance of provision to the Leaguer, namely by water, in which fort were taken 5. peeces of Ordnance, 200. Souldiers, 6. barells of powder, with an answerable quantity of Match and Shot ; some other forts have been taken, whose names do not occur.' The entry in Dudhope's *Letter* relating to Airemouth has already been quoted (p. 24).

*26th May   Joel. 2. 12, 13, 14, 15.[60] a fast.

*27th May   Bremham [Bramham] Hall taken.

As mentioned already Bramham Hall is near Boston Spa.

*28th May   L[ord] Manchester cometh to our quarter.

Intelligence No. 2 confirms this date. Dudhope (under the same date) says 'The Earle of Manchester came yesterday to o[u]r leaguer.'

*29th May   Joël 2. 13, 14, 15, 16, 17.[61] fast.

*30th May   Enemy fall out at Dalhousies quarter; are beat in; 5 of them killed and 4 taken.

From another source we learn of a dramatic event which occurred on this day. Under the date 5 June a scout reported[62] to the Parliamentarian Scoutmaster-General that

> A man in woman's apparel came last week into the leaguer on Horse back and by that means passed most of the sentries till coming near the walls, he espying his opportunity, turned over his leg, immediately rode into the town and was followed by several of our soldiers, one of whom was killed in the pursuit.

Three days later — 8 June — another scout gave further details of this incident[63] —

> On 31 May order was given to all the sentinels nearest the town to suffer no woman or others to come out of the town but to examine them and send them in again. A woman that came to sell provision at the leaguer, having passed the guard next to the town, being well horsed rode full gallop into the city: the guards shot at her but missed.

The same account says that about this time 'The Earl of New-castle sent to have the ladies [in the city] come out, but it was not granted.'

*31st May   34 of Waltoun's regiment surprized at Yarid Bridge.

Terry,[64] calls this the East Lothian Regiment, whose com-manding officer was Sir Patrick Hepburn of Wauchton.[65] He hazards no guess as to where 'Yarid Bridge' was: it might have been Yearsley.

*1st June   Enemy fall out againe at Dalhousie quarter, 24 of them killed and 32 taken, 24 horses, 35 kine and oxen.

Exact Relation refers to this same episode thus :—

> The first of June, the Scots forces fetched a great many cattell and horses from the enemy near Mic[k]legate Barre, and kil[le]d many both of horse and foot of the enemy; I heare they left four and thirty dead, and brought away thirty prisoners, but all sore wounded.

26

*2nd June	Isai[ah] 31. 1, 2. [66]
*3rd June	Manchester cometh up to us with 6 regiments of foot and 6 troops of horses.

Manchester's arrival at the siege forms the subject of the next chapter.

| *4th June | Lieutenant Taite killed. |

In the Scottish army there was a Lieutenant George Tait in the Minister's Regiment.[67]

1 Douglas, p. 59; Somervell, p. 53; Fairfax, p. 60b; Rushworth, p. 620; *Extract of Letters: CSP Dom.*, p. 131 dated 21 April; *Short Memorial*, p. 393, Drake. p. 163; *Correspondence*, p. 21.

2 Fairfax, p. 60b.

3 *Ibid.*

4 Douglas, p. 58; cf. Slingsby, p. 107.

5 Douglas, p. 57, under 30 April, says that 'The bridge of Kavie [presumably Cawood] brought up.' However, according to Stockdale, p. 73, there was a 'bridge of botes' at Cawood as late as 2 July, 1644.

6 Hildyard, p. 56.

7 p. 107, Drake, p. 163, endorses this.

8 *Sic.* The figure was probably nearer 20,000 (see p. xi).

9 If the date and locality ascribed to this incident are correct it occurred in the sector taken over by the army of the Eastern Association on the very day that these troops took up their quarters there. No other authority refers to the episode and it must, in consequence, remain somewhat suspect.

10 But for a very different picture of the state of affairs, see p. 22.

11 Warburton ii, pp. 433–4.

12 Rushworth, p. 622; Baillie, p. 176; *Manifest Truths; Correspondence*, p. 21.

13 *CSP Ven.*, p. 100, dated 20 May.

14 p. 54.

15 Douglas, p. 57, presumably refers to this same incident but puts it two days later. He says that the Parliamentarian cavalry, both Leven's and Fairfax's, went via Selby to Ferrybridge to cut off the Royalist horse going thither from Knaresborough where they had spent the first night after leaving York. (The passage, taken verbatim from Douglas' *Diary*, as is quoted on p. 19 under the date 25 April).

16 'or more probably Lord Eythin' — Wedgewood, p. 309. Warwick, p. 307, claims that, during the siege of York, Eythin (General James King) 'showed eminency in soldierly and personal stoutness.'

17 p. 54.

18 A Scottish liquid measure equal to one pint.

19 Some fields in what is now the Mount/Blossom Street area outside the city walls remained in Royalist hands throughout the siege, being shielded by the 'Great Sconce' (for which see pp. 144–5). Cattle for the use of the garrison were pastured in these fields.

20 p. 56.

21 p. 108.

22 All the contemporary authorities are agreed that the city never suffered from hunger during the whole time of the siege. Here are two more:– *Hulls Managing* — 'They are much straitned for flesh, meat & salt, but of corne they have no lack.' *CSP. Dom.*, p. 160, dated 12 May — 'We hear from the north that York is well provided of victuals till the end of this month.'

23 As a result of this one might have expected siege money to be minted: none has been found (see further pp. 115–6).

24 p. 108.

25 Quoted in Appendix IIA, no. 31, p. 164.

26 HMC Luke, pp. 110–1 no. 194 and p. 112 no. 198. There are a number of other passing references to the siege in this publication: two of particular interest are considered in some detail later (pp. 24 and 26).

27 *New-Come Guest*, dated 5 June, 1644.

28 All these forays appear to have been successful.

29 Cf. *Intelligence* No. 2 and No. 3; Douglas, pp. 56–8; *Manifest Truths; Hulls Managing;* Memorials, p. 95. See also p. 41.

30 Psalm 83 v.   14   As the fire burneth a wood, and as the flame setteth the mountains on fire;

v.   15   So persecute them with thy tempest and make them afraid with thy storm.

v.   16   Fill their faces with shame; that they may seek thy name, O Lord.

31 p. 56.

32 p. 280.

33 LJ vi, p. 539

34 LJ vi. pp. 539–540.

35 LJ vi. p. 561. The letter is also printed in Terry, p. 218.

36 'Colonel Galbraith' (Newcastle, p. 163).

37 *Hulls Managing* and *Exact Relation* also mention the capture of Waltham Hall near Wakefield on the same day. The latter reads:–

. . . . in it Sir Francis Wortley, the elder, the first incendiarie in this County, that publikely engaged a party for the King against the Parliament, and 120. souldiers with him, who yeilded themselves prisoners after they had kil[le]d severall of our men.

38 Psalm 83 v.   16   Already printed above.

v.   17   Let them be confounded and troubled for ever; yea, let them be put to shame, and perish.

39 Hastings MS., ii. p. 128. (Royal Manuscripts Commission.)

40 *CSP Dom.* p. 155. There are many references in *CSP. Dom* to 'The Deliverance.' From these — and from *Correspondence*, p. 28 — we learn that the master of this ship during the period of the siege was called George Phillips and the mate John Mace.

41 pp. 176, 179 and 182.

42 This is presumably the money which reached the Scottish army at Middlethorpe on 5 June (see entry under 16 May).

43 Baillie continues — 'We trust God will arise, and doe somewhat by our Scott's armie. We are afflicted, and after so long tyme we have gotten no hitt of our enemie; we hope God will put away that shame. Waller, Manchester, Fairfaxe, and all gets victories, but Lesley, from whom all was expected, as yett has had his hands bound. God, we hope, will loose them and send us matter of praise also.'

44 *Fairfax Correspondence*, i. pp. 210–1.

45 Actually Sir Wm. Hamilton was General of Artillery. (SHS vol. XVI, p. xxiv).

46 Psalm 83 v. 18   That men may know that thou, whose name alone is
                    Jehovah, art the most high over all the earth.

47 p. 164.

48 p. 217.

49 Appendix VII under 10 and 12 July, p. 199.

50 *Correspondence*, p. 29.

51 *Ibid*, p. 30.

52 See Appendix VII, p. 198.

53 *Correspondence*, p. 30.

54 Isaiah c. 31 v.1.   Woe to them that go down to Egypt for help;
                    and stay on horses, and trust chariots, because
                    they are very strong; but they look not unto
                    the Holy One of Israel, neither seek the Lord.

55 The Earl of Dalhousie commanded a Scottish Regiment of Horse which bore his name. (SHS vol. XVI, pp. xxv and xlix). Dalhousie's 'quarter' is mentioned twice more by Douglas under 30 May and 1 June (*q.v.*).

56 p. 60.

57 HMC Luke, p. 664 no. 157.

58 p. 110.

59 SHS vol. XVI, pp. xxv and lvi. He is named in *Carmen*, see pp. 130–1 where it is stated that he was killed by one Donnel (Donnelly?).

60 Joel c. 2 v. 12 Therefore also now, saith the Lord, turn ye even to me with
                    all your heart, and with fasting, and with weeping and with
                    mourning.
          v. 13 And rend your heart, and not your garments, and turn unto
                    the Lord your God: for he is gracious and merciful, slow
                    to anger, and of great kindness, and repenteth him of the
                    evil.

v. 14 Who knoweth if he will return and repent, and leave a blessing behind him; even a meat offering and a drink offering unto the Lord your God?

v. 15 Blow the trumpet in Zion, sanctify a fast, call a solemn assembly.

[61] Joel c. 2 vv. 13–15 Already printed above.

v. 16 Gather the people, sanctify the congregation, assemble the elders, gather the children, and those that suck the breasts: let the bridegroom go forth of his chamber, and the bride out of her closet.

v. 17 Let the priests, the ministers of the Lord, weep between the porch and the altar, and let them say, Spare thy people, O Lord, and give not thine heritage to reproach, that the heathen should rule over them: wherefore should they say among the people, Where is their God?

[62] HMC Luke, p. 663, no. 150.

[63] *Ibid.* p. 664, no. 157.

[64] p. 217.

[65] Cf. SHS vol. XVI, pp. xxv and xxviii.

[66] Isaiah c. 31. v.1. already printed on p. 29.

v. 2 Yet he also is wise, and will bring evil, and will not call back his words: but will arise against the house of the evildoers, and against the help of them that work iniquity.

[67] SHS vol. XVI, p. xl.

Bootham Bar in 1806.　　Artist Henry Cave.

PLATE IV

Chapter Three

MANCHESTER ARRIVES

THE HISTORIAN is indebted to Simeon Ashe and William Goode, who describe themselves either as 'Chaplains' to the Earl of Manchester or as 'Preachers' to his army, for the detailed information which they gave of the part played by Manchester's army in the siege of York and the battle of Marston Moor. This information was sent up to London every few days and was quickly printed in the form of 'Relations' or 'Intelligences' (as the tracts were called: Plate XIX) and became available to the limited reading public of the time. These provide the basis of the narrative which follows. It is unfortunate, however, that this information cannot be corroborated in much detail from other sources, in particular, from Royalist ones. It is clear, too, that all sections of Parliamentarian opinion did not receive these tracts uncritically; this applies especially to their Scottish allies. Robert Baillie, Rector of the University of Glasgow, one of the Scottish delegates at the Westminster Assembly which sat in London from 1644 to 1646 trying to formulate a joint religious settlement for England and Scotland, was particularly outspoken. Writing on 16 July 1644, soon after Ashe's account of the Battle of Marston Moor had been published, he said :—

> Mr. Ashe's relation ... gives us [the Scottish army] many good words .... but gives much more to Cromwell than we are informed is his due .... the Independents have done so brave service, yea, they [are] so strong and considerable a party, that they must not only be tollerate, but in nothing grieved, and in no wayes to be provocked. It seems very necessare, that since none of yow of purpose, and ordinarlie, sends up relations, and Mr. Ashe sends to the presse constant intelligence of your actions, which, for the man's known integrity, are every word believed, your proceedings have a

great influence in all affaires here both of Church and State; I say, it seems needfull that all Mr. Ashe's letters which are sent hither to the presse, should be first seen and pondered by some of yow there.[1]

Ashe and Goode give a detailed account of the advance of the army of the Eastern Association northwards to join the siege.[2] Lincoln was taken on 6 May. Later in the month 'it being common and confidently reported, that Prince Rupert, with great strength gathered from various Counties, was advancing towards York, for the reliefe thereof, and the releasing of his good friends, both Papists and others besieged.' and since it was anticipated that he might try to seize the Parliamentarian stronghold of Manchester on the way, the Earl of Manchester temporarily detached his cavalry from the rest of his army, and sent it to link up with 'two regiments of foote, and some troopes of horse under the command of Sir John Mildrum [Meldrum]' which had been sent from the forces of the 'renowned General Lesley and the worthy Lord Fairfax' who were then besieging York. The news of Rupert's advance into Lancashire proved premature, and some days later the Parliamentarian cavalry returned to Yorkshire and took up semi-permanent quarters in the Barnsley-Sheffield area,[3] making numerous forays (as noted in the previous chapter) to capture isolated Royalist strongholds in the neighbourhood of York.

Meanwhile, Manchester's infantry moved slowly forward from Lincoln.[4] On Friday 24 May they reached Gainsborough but were compelled to leave their 'greatest Ordinance behind . . . the wayes being deep, by reason of great rain which hath been in these parts.'[5] On Saturday they marched into the Isle of Axholme. Here they rested, as the following day was 'the Sabbath.' Nevertheless 'Our Noble Lord [Manchester] in reference to the necessity and importance of publike businesses, did that day travell to mett with some Commanders, who were intrusted with the care of the main body of horse.' On Monday, 27 May, while the army marched to Thorne, 'our much honoured Lord, went unto the Leaguer at York,[6] to consult with Generall Lesley and the Lord Fairfax, about the best way of promoting the publike cause which is deeply settled in all our hearts.' Other matters engaging his attention may have had to do with the commissariat. The accounts of one of the 'treasurers' of Manchester's army covering the period 8 April–12 September 1644 have survived.[7] On 28 May, 156 tents were paid for in London; under the same date is the entry 'Payd Nathanyell Gurry for bringing tents from Hull to York £1. 11s. 6d.' As this account covers the entire period of the siege of York, most of the entries presumably relate to it. Only in a few instances are the city, or identifiable places around it, mentioned, *viz* :–

May 21st	Payd for two mares taken from Yorke, and delivered on[e] to Bennett, on[e] of the liffeguard and the other to [blank]	£4 0s 0d.
July 10th	Payd for two horses at Haslington [Heslington] delivered to two of my Lorde's liffeguard	£2. 5s. 0d.
	Payd him which he payd for bringing armes from Gaynsborough to the Leaguer	£1. 7s. 6d.
July 17th	Payd Mr. Murfett of Lyn [King's Lynn] for bringing of armes and ammunicion from Lyn to Yorke, and other things as by his accompt.	£31. 6s. 0
July 20th	Payd to Mr. Edward Pickering, which he gave to sicke souldyers in their march from Yorke.	10s. 0d
August 16th	Payd Maior Holmes for a suite of armes which Captain Waylet lost of his at Yorke, and for 3 journeys into Essex.	£22. 0s. 0d.

It is clear that Manchester's army had a military store at King's Lynn and that supplies from this were normally brought up to the Leaguer at York by ship. Manchester's army appears to have been the best supplied of the three besieging York: he certainly issued military supplies to his allies.[8] On 26 October, three months after the siege was over, the Committee of Both Kingdomes issued him with a warrant to cover the loss in his accounts of 'two barrels of gunpowder . . . in lieu of so much lent by him to the Scots' army at the siege of York.'[9]

The Earl stayed at the Leaguer over the Monday night, and arrived back in Selby the following evening to find his army had progressed that far north. Here it remained for three days. Wednesday was a public fast: on Thursday 'his Lordship went into the neighbour villages [around Selby] to take notice of the state of his soldiers in their severall quarters' while on Friday he met 'General Lesley, the Lord Fairfax and field-officers, at the

Lord Howards house in Eskrigge [Escrick], to consult for the publike.' It was decided that the army should move forward to York on the following day and, in anticipation of this, 'an Officer is sent to take Quarters on the North side [i.e. somewhere in the Clifton/Heworth area] for his Lordship and those who attend him.'

This ends the first of the five *Intelligences* written by Ashe and Goode relating to the siege. It is dated 1 June from Selby and ends with this pious entreaty — 'Our eyes are towards heaven for the success of our service and we hope that through God's mercy, our next Intelligence will rejoyce the hearts of our faithfull friends.'

Ashe and Goode begin their second report[10] by introducing us to one of the most pernicious practices indulged in by both Royalist and Parliamentarian commanders in the Civil War, that of billeting troops on private citizens. This was inevitable because of the chaotic financial arrangements.

> Such was the forwardnesse and faithfulnesse of the Noble Earle of Manchester to promote and expedite the publick service, that as he would not be detained at Lincolne, through want of money, longer then [than] necessary service there required; so neither would he waste his time in the way to Yorke, though the money to maintaine his Armie, was not brought unto him, while he quartered at Selby and the adjacent villages; for want of present pay Tickets were given to them who were charged with the souldiers, in their severall quarters, and all the scores must be discharged honestly, according to the command of that Religious Lord, so soone as his moneyes (which are now daily expected) shall come to his Armie.

We hear no more about this matter, and are left in doubt as to whether the promissory notes given to the unfortunate folk in and around Selby, on whom the troops had been compulsorily billeted, were ever honoured.

This *Particular Relation* contradicts the preceding *Intelligence* on a matter of detail in saying that 'Upon Saturday (being the first of June) some of the Earle of Manchester [and] his Forces marched from their Quarters towards the Leaguer to facilitate Mundaies march.' This advance-guard — if such it is to be called — seems to have reached the Osbaldwick/Heslington outskirts of York before nightfall on 1 June, having crossed the Ouse south of the city[11]. By this date the boat bridge at Cawood had been dismantled and probably re-assembled nearer the City in the Fulford/Middlethorpe area.[12] The other boat bridge built by Fairfax and the Scots on 23 April at Acaster Malbis[13] may still have been in use. It was by one or both of these bridges that Manchester's advance-guard and later the whole of his army,[14] crossed the Ouse to take up their position opposite the northern defences of the city in the first week of June.

Ashe and Goode continue :–

[3rd June]   Having rested the Sabbath, the Earle himselfe with his whole bodie of foote and Artillerie, advanced upon Munday morning early, and though the morning was discouraging by reason of long and strong showers, and although the wayes were tedious and tiring, yet respect to the worke, and the commands of their much honoured Commander, carried the poore souldiers forward without murmuring, with much chearfulnesse, and the rather, because the Earle himselfe, for their encouragement, marched along with them the greatest part of the way. This dayes march (considering divers diversions by waters and deepe waies) was little lesse than 12. Northerne miles, which was more longsome then [than] 20 miles at another time, and else-where would have been accounted.

[4th June]   Upon Tewsday the tired souldiers tooke some rest though some of them upon their owne accord went up to the walls of Yorke, and fetched out of the Pastures there oxen, kine, and some horses. That day the three worthy Commanders, with some of their field Officers, met as a Councell of Warre, to consult in what manner to carry on their intended assault against the City. All this day and the next, there were some sleight encounters between our souldiers and theirs, the greatest losse by farre falling on their side, and all this while the Cannon from Cliftons [Clifford's] Tower and another Fort Eastward[15] in the City played frequently upon our men, as they espied any advantage, yet through God's good providence there were not any one of ours slaine.

The arrival of Manchester's troops presented problems to the besiegers as well as to the besieged. Baillie[16] touches on one of these :–

We are advertised, that much more than the most part of my Lord Manchester's armie are seduced to Independencie and very many of them have added either Anabaptisme or Antinomianisme, or both . . . . We all conceive, that our silly simple lads are in great danger of being infected by their companie; and if that pest enter in our armie, we fear it may spread.

One of the first things the Earl of Manchester did after he took up his position on the northern side of the city was to construct (in conjunction with the Scots) a bridge of boats across the river to link the two armies together. This bridge, which was to play an important part in the events immediately preceding the Battle of Marston Moor (see further p. 78f), is referred to in many contemporary documents. It is variously described as being 'on the west side of the city'[17] 'at Poppleton'[18] 'Poppleton Ferry'[19] 'over the Ouse'[20] and 'in Clifton Ings.'[21] Its precise location is conjectural, though there are reasons for supposing it was in the Clifton area (see pp. 146-7) on, or close to, the site of the new (1963) bridge.

A reference to this bridge — or to the one already constructed at Fulford between Fairfax's army and that of the Scots — is contained in the following petition dated 6 August 1651: —[22]

> Petition of Elizabeth, wife of John Coole, seaman of York, to the Committee for Compounding. Petitioned the county committee, for allowance of 6*l* for weighing and trimming a boat of her husband's, which was sunk with others to make a bridge over the Ouse, when York was beleagured, and 6*l* for hay for Lord Fairfax's horses; but they cannot relieve, though they recommend her, as does Lord Fairfax. Her husband has been in arms through the war, and now serves in Scotland. Begs an order for payment. Noted that the Committee for Compounding have no power to relieve her.

Elizabeth Cole (or Coole) seems to have had a propensity for petitioning royalty. In 1662 she petitioned Charles II concerning a matter affecting her father and his boat relating to an event which occurred in the year 1640 — twenty-two years earlier![23] Although this has nothing to do with the siege of 1644, it is such a colourful and hitherto unnoticed episode in York history, and throws so much light on Elizabeth's family and character, that no apology seems necessary for including it in Appendix V of this work.

Ashe and Goode continue their narrative thus :—

> [5th June]   Upon Wednesday most of the Scotts Regiments, and all the Earle of Manchesters were drawne forth in nearer

approaches towards the Towne to amuse the Towne, whilest the Lord Fairfax with his Forces[24] raised a battery within lesse than Musquet shot of the Towne upon an hill westward, where a wind-mill stood heretofore: They quartered all night in the field, the enemy from the Towne spent upon them with their Canon in the night, and the next morning (as 'tis thought) about two hundred shot, and yet not above 5 or 6 slaine, and about so many hurt.

The hill on which this battery was erected is in what are now the gardens of The Retreat. It is called Lamel Hill, a name which it seems to have acquired about a century after the siege was over. The battery is mentioned in many contemporary and near-contemporary accounts of the siege;[25] archaeology has also contributed to our knowledge of it (see pp. 147-8). The first three of these accounts are quoted :—

Slingsby :—

W[he]n ye enemy had thus besieg'd us he began to make his approaches, & rais'd a battery upon ye Windmill hill, as ye way lyes to Heslington, plants upon [it] 5[26] peices of Canon & playes continually into ye town, they come nearer to us & takes ye Suburbs w[i]t[h]out Waingate [Walmgate] barr, plants 2 peices in ye street against ye barr.

Exact Relation :—

. . . . and yesternight being June the fifth, they have caused a work to be raised for a battery, upon a hill neer Walm-gate, where there are four[27] pieces of battery already planted, that have played all this afternoone upon the Castle, Tower and Towne; and they from the Tower have sent us at least an hundred Bullets from severall Platforms in the Towne, but they have done us very little hurt, not above one man killed, and what execution our Ordnance do in the City we cannot yet tell; But we are getting more pieces up to our new worke, which we know hath already put them into very great fear.

Hildyard, who got his information from Royalist sources, underlines the difficulty that the besiegers had in getting their guns into position on Lamel Hill. He wrote :—

It is remarkable, That when the Enemy advanced with their whole Cannon (which carried a sixty pound Bullet[28]) from Gate-Foulford [Fulford], to plant it on Heslington Hill [another of the names given to what is now called Lamel Hill]; the Lieutenant Collonell of the Tower [Clifford's Tower],[29] being then upon the Platforme, commanded David Guillome, a

Loyall Citizen, the Cannoneers Mate, to travers the Guns, and to Levell them according to Art, and giving Fire to a Demy Culveren, did that Execution, which made the Enemy run all from their Cannon, where she lay all that day betwixt Foulford and York.

This demi-culverin was a famous gun in the Civil War known as 'The Queen's Pocket-Pistol.' It had originally belonged to the Marquis of Newcastle but was captured by the Parliamentarians at Hull on 11 October 1643. *Hulls Managing*[30] records :— 'The Guns we tooke were these, viz. a *Demi-Cannon* in weight 5790 [lbs] which shoots 36 pound bullet of which size they have one more, which we broke in the mussell on the North side of the Towne; these two they called the Queenes pocket pistolls, or their Gog and Magog.' It would seem that the gun remained in York after the siege ended. Rushworth[31] recorded that on 1 August 1644, to attack Sheffield Castle, the Earl of Manchester had to 'send to *York* for an Iron Demicannon and that great Piece, commonly call'd *The Queen's Pocket-pistol.*'

Hulls Managing says that the day after the battery was put in position it 'made a breach in Clifford Tower, where they have planted two pieces of Ordnance.'

Soon after the erection of this battery and the capture of the suburbs outside Walmgate Bar, referred to above by Slingsby (see p. 37), Fairfax's forces started to mine under the Bar. If *Exact Relation* (12 June 1644) is to be trusted, soon afterwards they also erected another battery in this area even closer to the City than Lamel Hill. The appropriate entry reads :—

.... another battery was yesterday got at S. Laurence Church, made within the Churchyard next Wombgate [Walmgate], about fifty yards from the gate, and here, and in the Church, and houses, there are about 3000 of our men.

Hildyard[32] gives the fullest account of the mining under Walmgate Bar and of its subsequent discovery and neutralisation by the defenders :—

After this long Siege, during which, some Houses in Walmegate neer the Gate were pulled down, by reason the Enemy had Mynded [mined] to the middle Jaume [jamb] of that Barr; which was discovered by one that the Perdues in Saint Georges Close (then under the Command of the Governour of Cliffords Tower) took, who brought him to the Tower, and being strictly examined by the Lieutenant Collonell in Cliffords Tower, confessed, That they were Mynding [mining], and that they had Mynded to the middle of the Barr, and shewed where they began to Mynde, being at a little House on the North of the said Gate, which Sir Thomas Glemham, that Gallant and Vigilant Governour prevented, by Mynding above them, and powring water in upon them. He also caused a new Wall of Earth to be made crosse the Street, a good distance within the Gate, for the better security of the City.

The mine was roughly filled in at the time of the siege : it was not until October 1645, over a year later, that this was done carefully and the nearby roadway made up[33]. The barbican of Walmgate Bar now bears the date 1648 which may be interpreted as meaning that the gateway was so badly damaged in the siege that it had to be practically rebuilt four years later[34]. Cooper[35] says that this was probably done with stones obtained from the ruins of the nearby church of St. Nicholas, which stood just outside the Bar and which was destroyed in the siege. He adds that 'fragments of inscriptive tombstones built into the walls are observable though time has almost obliterated the letters, making them now indecipherable.' Cooper wrote in 1904 : the writer cannot identify any of these stones now. Cooper[36] is the sole authority for the statement that 'some relics of the [1644] bombardment were unearthed in April, 1836, whilst excavating for a drain near the bar, two unexploded bombshells being found, still filled with gunpowder.' He does not say what happened to them. Bullet holes can still be seen in the stonework of the gateway (Plate V).

Ashe and Goode again take up the story :–

[6th June]   The Earle of Manchesters Forces on Thursday morning ent[e]red the suburbs on the north side, and maintaine what they have got, with the losse of 5 or 6 men at the most, and so many wounded.

About 27 of the Earle of Manchesters Regiment being voluntarily led on by a Corporall of Horse into the east suburbs, killed 5 men, took some goods, and retreated without any losse.

Yesterday the Cannon played on both sides, very often; we know not with what damage unto the enemy, but only one of our souldiers was slaine, who as he was asleepe, by a bullets grazing was struck through his body, yea through his heart, as it was imagined by that which appeared.

[7th June]   About midnight, a commanded Company of the couragious Scots, assaulted fiercely and bravely the three Forts on the west side of the City,[37] and after a very hot service, for the space of two houres, (whereof many of us, with deepe affections were eye witnesses at a distance) they became possessors of two of them. The one of the Forts (which was the nearest to the Towne) was strengthened with a double ditch, wherein there were 120 souldiers, above 60 were slaine, and all the rest taken prisoners. The other Fort taken, had only 50 men to maintaine it, who were all either killed, or taken prisoners desiring quarter. And the 3[r]d. Fort had been possessed by the Scots also, if that a strong party of both Horse and Foot, had not come out of the Towne[38] for the reliefe thereof. In this brave and bold service the Scotts lost 3 Captaines and some others (whether 6, 7, or some few more as yet is not manifested) were killed, one Lieftenant-Collonell and 2 Captaines deadly wounded, with many others wounded, but (as its hoped) not in danger of death. The Earle of Manchesters Army is possessed of the suburbs on the north side of the City, where the souldiers have fortified themselves, and are come up to the gates of the City.

         Yesterday morning the enemy began to fire the suburbs, and in the beginning of the night, there was a lamentable fire in those places, most dolefull and dreadfull to many of us, who with sad hearts saw that fearfull fruit of wasting wars.

Baillie[39] refers to this incident thus :–

         On Wednesday last they drew near the walls: they within put all the suburbs in a fyre; we were favoured by the wind to quench the fyre. We are now within pistoll-shott of the walls, and are making readie to storme it; for they have much more victuall within than was thought: it cannot but be a bloodie business.

Exact Relation gives further details :–

         . . . . this day they [the garrison] have fired most part of the Suburbs, and drawne their people into the Town; our men fall into the Suburbs and beat them in when they sally out either to fire houses or fetch in goods; but whilest they skirmish the fire consumes the houses, they will not suffer our men to quench it, for if the houses could have been saved, they would have been a great shelter for our men in their approaches.

         And the Suburb without Bowdom [Bootham], where there were many faire houses, being fired, the E[arl] of Manchesters men neverthelesse

40

entered, and beat in the enemy this morning, and saved much of the houses from the fire, and doe gallery through them close to the walls.

Douglas[40] is presumably referring to this episode when he writes :

> 8 [June] Lumsdan [Lumsden] breakes the port fires, the punchoons[41] filled with earth, and breaks some of the iron gate within.

Hildyard[42] says that during the siege 'Most of the Suburbs of the City was burnt down, except a few Houses without Micklegate Barr, which was preserved by the Royall Fort. Moncke Bridge and the Bridge at Lathropp [Layerthorpe] Postern were broken down.'

Ashe and Goode continue :—

> There were some remarkable providences of God since our more nigh approaches towards the Towne, within the reach of the enemies Cannon, wherein we desire that our selves and freinds may thankfully acknowledge his hand. A Cannon bullet was shot through the Tent wherein Generall Lesley, some Scots Commanders and others were, yet no one killed or hurt. A Cannon bullet took off the crowne of a Souldiers hat and the man preserved. Another lying on the ground, the bullet of a Cannon grazeing, took off the heele of his shooe, skratched his foot, and did no more harme. Also there was a souldier whose sleeve was torne with a Cannon bullet, and yet his arme neither broken nor wounded. A Lieutenant was beaten downe with the wind of a Cannon shot, but received no harme; and two Cannon bullets fell downe in the midst of two of our Regiments, and no one hurt thereby in the least measure.
> [43]The body of Horse (which all this while hath been at and about Wakefield, expecting Prince Ruperts motions, and desiring to meet with him) hath neither been altogether idle nor successelesse; they have possessed themselves of Mr. Elmers house within a mile of Barnsley,[44] wherein they tooke himselfe, with above 40 more prisoners, where also they had 20 Horses, and the souldiers found good pillage; Upon our approach Wortley Hall was quitted by the enemy.
> On the third June, Waltham House was delivered up, on condition that all persons in it should be yeelded up to our mercy; Sir Francis Wortley with 120 more were taken prisoners, but none were slaine; the souldiers had there a 100 Horses and other pillage, worth 5,000 pound, most of the goods being sent or brought thither by Papists for better security; this house was deeply mo[a]ted, there was no approach but over one bridge, which being gained with the losse of 12 men, the house was yeelded.
> They took also 12 Horses which issued out of Landall [Sandal] Castle, intending to have gone unto Sheffield; And they have left there a party of Musketieres to block up the passage from the Castle that they may not issue

forth thence to plunder the countrey. Now the body of Horse is removed to Witherby [Wetherby], and places adjacent, upon intelligence that Prince Rupert is on motion, there our Horse now quarter, that they may be in a capacity to check the enemies approach unto Yorke, which is his designe as our common intelligence doth report.

The tract concludes with this note headed "M[r] Ashes Letter to his Friend" :—

Beloved:

Had thine eyes yesternight with me, seene Yorke burning, thy heart would have been heavie. The Lord affect us with the sad fruits of wasting warres, and speedily, mercifully end our combustions, which are carried on with high sinnes and heavie desolations. Truly, my heart sometimes, is ready to breake, with what I here see, and the thoughts, which thereupon take hold upon my spirit. If God would, with the peace of the Kingdome, upon Gospel termes, restore me to such a condition of life, as I have heretofore enjoy'd, I hope, that with more thankefulnesse, I should endeavour the improvement thereof. Tell my Christian friends (with the remembrance of respects) that they at London, cannot sufficiently esteem their tranquility with Gospel liberties. O know, know the things of your peace, in this your day, that your peace and the companions thereof may never be removed. Pitie, pitie, and praye for poore people, oppressed with the pride and cruelty of the inhumane prevailing souldier. My heart is full of warm workings: the best emptying of the full heart, is before God, in humble, holy, hopefull prayers.

I am in health through Gods patience, and my hardship is nothing, nothing to that which thousands here suffer; the Lord sanctifie every condition to his poore people.

Alas, alas, I know not when to hope my returne to London! Our God give us to enjoy himselfe sweetly and spiritually every where: In his presence is life, in his fulnesse is happinesse; and we may enjoy it, possesse it through Christ.

I am &c

S[imeon] A[she].

---

[1] Baillie, p. 209. An early hint of military censorship!

[2] *Intelligence* No. 2. Unless otherwise stated all quotations are from this tract.

[3] HMC Luke, p. 662 no. 150.

[4] At a later stage in Manchester's march northwards the Venetian Ambassador commented unkindly thus — 'The Earl of Manchester has advanced to Selby and has orders to join them [the besieging armies at York], but whether from reluctance to go far from the Associated Counties or for lack of courage, he has

always shown himself very slow to carry out his orders.' *CSP.* Ven., p. 110, dated 24 June.

5 A number of contemporary references to the weather during the period of the siege makes it clear that at least until the second week in June it was particularly wet. Writing on 8 June Manchester commented on 'the tempestuous rainy weather.' *CSP.* Dom., p. 216.

6 According to Dudhope he arrived there the previous evening.

7 PRO State Papers 28/139, printed by A. Everitt, *Suffolk and the Great Rebellion* 1640–1660. Suffolk Record Society III, pp. 89–93.

8 See Appendix VII.

9 *CSP Dom.* 1644–1645, p. 73.

10 *Particular Relation.* Unless otherwise stated, all quotations in the remainder of this chapter are from this tract.

11 Terry, p. 219 (footnote), summarises the evidence for this. Hildyard, p. 56 is clearly incorrect in stating that Manchester's army arrived as early as 29 *April* (my italics). He presumably meant 29 May, a date which is confirmed from a Scots source (Appendix VII under 29 May). On that day the Scots loaned to Manchester guns capable of firing 18-lb ball. The guns must have been culverins.

12 Douglas, p. 57; Appendix VII, p. 199 under 11 July.

13 Douglas, p. 56: see p. 13.

14 *Exact Relation* says that this consisted of 'about 6,000 foot and a thousand horse, and twelve field pieces.' Baillie puts the figure higher — 'more than eight thousand' (p. 181); 'above twelve thousand very well appointed men' (p. 188).

15 The site of this is not certain; but it was probably Baile Hill (see further p. 149)

16 p. 185.

17 *Letter from Generall Leven. CSP.* Dom. 1644, dated 5 July; Thurloe, p. 38; Cholmley, p. 347.

18 Slingsby, p. 112; *Short Memorial*, p. 394.

19 Drake, p. 167.

20 Rupert's *Journal*, p. 737.

21 *Exact Relation*, viz:–'There is a bridge made of boats over the Owse at Cliftonings that the armies may on a sudden send succour one to another.'

22 *Calendar of the Proceedings of the Committee for Compounding.* 1643–1660, pt. i, p. 473.

23 *CSP.* Dom. 1661–2, p. 501.

24 Fairfax's army was strengthened by some Scottish Regiments under the command of Sir James Lumsden (Douglas, p. 58; *Manifest Truths* and *CSP. Dom.*, pp. 223–4). The former says there were four regiments involved, the second 'a Regiment or two of Foote.' while the third mentions no number. As early as 3 May (unless the date is quoted wrongly) guns from the Scots ordnance depot had been supplied to 'Fairfax Leagour' (Appendix VII under 3 May): gunners were doubtless loaned with them.

General Sir James Lumsden commanded the Scottish foot at Marston Moor. On 5 July he wrote an important letter to Lord Louden describing his experiences there to which he appended a plan showing the Parliamentarian battle order. (See Ridsdill Smith, pp. 77 and 179–181).

25 Slingsby, p. 108; *Exact Relation;* Hildyard, p. 56; Rushworth, p. 622; Douglas, p. 58; and Drake, p. 163.

26 *Exact Relation,* Rushworth, p. 622 and Drake, p. 163 say the battery mounted four guns, the other accounts specify no number.

27 Later in this tract the number is given as five.

28 If Hildyard has given this weight correctly the cannon on Lamel Hill must have been culverins (Cf. B.H.St. J. O'Neil, *Castles and Cannon, A Study of Early Artillery Fortifications in England,* 1960, p. xix.) It is perhaps to this gun that Sir Henry Vane was referring on 16 June when he wrote ' . . . the best battering piece which carries 64lb. bullet is now upon carriages again.' *CSP. Dom.,* p. 241.

29 Sir Francis Cobb.

30 See also B. N. Reckitt *Charles the First and Hull,* 1952, pp. 84, 94, 97, and Appendix I, pp. 117–8, a letter of Lord Fairfax to the Earl of Essex: 'we have drawne into the Towne their great Demi-canon, one Demi-culverin, one sacra.'

31 V, p. 642.

32 pp. 58–9.

33 YCHB, 11 October 1645. Appendix II, no. 65, p. 171.

34 See Raine, p. 16.

35 p. 303.

36 p. 302.

37 *CSP. Dom.,* pp. 223–4, *Hulls Managing, Manifest Truths,* and Slingsby, p. 110, refer to this episode; Douglas, p. 58, has this to say about it:–

    7 [June] Strouse on the right hand taken by storme, 50 of them killed, 85 taken. Lieut. Col. Carmichael deadly shot, whereof he dieth the nixt day. Captain Campbell killed, and 10 souldiers. Strouse on the left hand assaulted, but not taken; 18 of theirs killed, 33 taken; we losse Captain Panther and 10 souldiers.

For the siting of these and other outworks see pp. 143-9 Lt. Col. William Carmichael was the second-in-command of the Clydesdale Regiment (SHS. Vol. XVI, pp. xxiv and xxvii); Captain Campbell cannot be identified. There was a Captain Panter in the Angus Regiment (SHS. Vol. XVI, p. xxvi).

38 Doubtless through Micklegate Bar which, according to Slingsby, remained open throughout the siege.

39 p. 193.

40 p. 58.

41 A Scots word meaning 'barrels.'

42 p. 59.

43 This paragraph and the following one are to be read in conjunction with the latter part of the previous chapter (see pp. 18f).

44 Referred to already on p. 18.

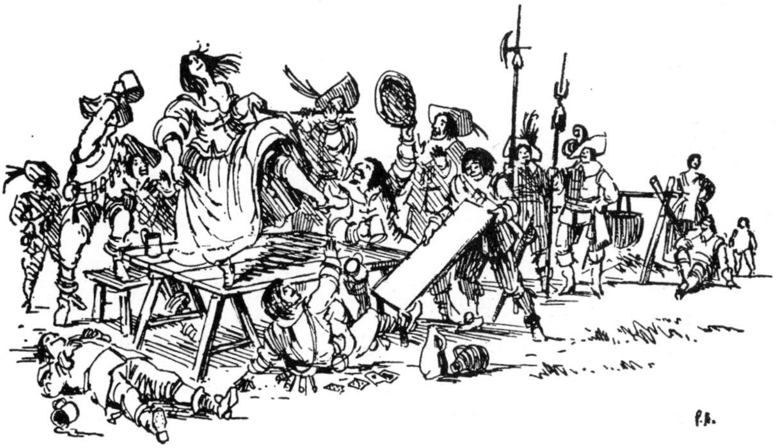

Chapter Four

PARLEY: 8–15 JUNE

> June the eighth, being Whitson Eve, a Cannon Bullet weighing sixty pound shot from the Mill Hill above Saint Lawrence Leyes [Lamel Hill] without Wolmegate Barr, was shot through Saint Sampson's Church Steeple, and there taken up: And also in the time of the Siege, the Spire of Saint Dionis [Deny's] Church was shot through with a Cannon Bullet.[1]

Writing in 1818, William Hargrove[2] said that the 'perforation' (as he described it) made by this cannon ball was then still visible in St. Sampson's steeple. This church was badly burned in 1848 and the subsequent rebuilding has destroyed all traces of this damage.

It appears that even as late as 8 June there were still buildings standing sufficiently high in the suburbs to cause anxiety to the defenders. Ashe and Goode[3] constitute the sole authority :–

> Upon Saturday the 8 day in the morning, a souldier of the Marquess of Newcastle was taken in the Earl of Manchesters leager: he was in a red suit,[4] he had pitch, flax, and other materials upon him for the fiering of the suburbs there, as yet free from the wasting flames. Some more of the Marquesse his souldiers were taken prisoners also; they had white coats (made of the plundred cloath taken from the Clothiers in these parts) with crosses on the sleeves, wrought with red and blew silk, an ensigne as wee conceive of some Po[p]ish Regiment. Divers Granadoes were cast from the Citie into the Suburbs, when the Earle of Manchesters men were about the fiering of the gate, to make passage into the Citie.

The 'suburbs' and 'gate' referred to could equally well have been Bootham or Monkgate, both of which lay within the Earl of Manchester's 'leaguer.' Some of the prisoners taken were obviously members of Newcastle's 'White-coats', the regiments

46

Walmgate Bar in 1970, showing the
scars of bullets and cannonballs from
the Siege of 1644.

PLATE VI

Laverthorpe Postern in 1806.   Artist Henry Cave.

which a month later, were to fight and die so gallantly on Marston Moor. It is possible that the 'crosses on the sleeves, wrought with red and blew silk' were, in fact, unit signs or even distinctions for valour rather than Popish 'ensignes' as the *Intelligence* supposed. One of the main propaganda themes running through the contemporary Parliamentarian tracts relating to the Civil War in general, and the siege of York in particular, concerns the alleged numbers and influence of Papists in the Royalist forces. Another well-exploited piece of Parliamentarian propaganda had to do with the bringing of Irish troops into England to help the King. While some Irish troops were unquestionably brought over, their numbers were grossly exaggerated in Parliamentarian tracts.[5] (The great majority of the troops brought over from Ireland were English regiments which had been sent there in 1641. These were troops originally raised for the Second Scots War. Lord Inchquin's regiment is perhaps the chief exception to this rule). These tracts, published by both sides, constituted the main sources of information about the course of the war. They were the only 'official' sources of news available to the public.

Since the arrival of the Earl of Manchester's forces on 3 June the siege had been pressed on with vigour, and the Marquis of Newcastle realised that his sole chance of succour lay with Prince Rupert and his hoped-for relieving army. As Robert Baillie[6] in London put it :–

> .... their confidence is in Prince Rupert's secours. He is ane ubiquitarie; he holds both York and Oxford in full expectation of his coming daylie: yet where he is, and what are his forces no man certainlie can tell.

Clearly Newcastle's policy was to hold out as long as possible and, whenever he could, to play for time. Drake[7] expressed it thus – '. . . to amuse the commanders of the rebels with specious shews of treaty about the rendition of the city.' The Venetian Ambassador was perhaps attributing too much subtlety to Newcastle when he reported home :–

> The Marquis of Newcastle is not only holding out in York, but having discovered an understanding between the aldermen of the city and the Scots he feigned ignorance and used the conspiracy to their own hurt . . . .[8]
> The Marquis of Newcastle scores off the besiegers by various military ruses, feigning weakness, and he cut up about 4000 (*sic*) after pretending to

47

parley. He caused false letters to fall into their hands, which he sent to Prince Rupert, urging him to come, describing the perilous state of the city, so the others weakened their forces to send some troops to block the prince's passage.[9]

There may be some truth in this 'alderman' incident. On 17 September 1644, three months after the end of the siege, the Parliamentarian Committee then governing York under Lord Fairfax ordered[10]

> That James Brooke [Alderman of York][11] whilst the Citty of Yorke was held a garrison against the Parliament did frequently traffique and trade thence and from other garrisons and quarters held against the parliament.

Further, an order made by the Committee of Both Kingdoms,[12] dated one day earlier than the above, emphasises the influence that this particular York alderman had in the highest Parliamentary councils :–

> That the goods of James Brook, Alderman of York, may pass into Amsterdam or Rotterdam without interruption according to the engagement and warrant of the Earl of Callender.

Newcastle's opening gambit in a series of exchanges which occupied the next week was the following letter delivered[13] to the Earl of Leven on the evening of 8 June, in which he reproached the latter for having broken the normal procedure of siege warfare by not signifying his intentions to the besieged.

> My Lord,[14]
>> I cannot but admire that your Lordship hath so neere beleaguered the Cittie on all sides, made batteries against it, and so neere approached to it, without signifying what your intentions are, and what you desire or expect, which is contrary to the rules of all military discipline and customes; therefore I have thought fit to remonstrate thus much to your Lordship, to the end that your Lordship may signifie your intentions and resolutions therein, and receive ours, and so I remain my Lord,
>> Your Lordships humble servant
>> Will[iam] Newcastle.
> York 8, Iunii 1644
> For his Excell[ency] the Earle of Levin [Leven].

A letter to the same effect was, at about the same time, delivered to Lord Fairfax; no corresponding letter was, however, sent to the Earl of Manchester as the Marquis was, or affected to be, ignorant of the latter's arrival at the siege. (Terry[15] has suggested that this discourtesy was deliberate because, four months earlier, when Leven had arrived to besiege the city of Newcastle he had been, or had feigned to be, ignorant of the Marquis' presence within it). Leven replied as follows :–

My Lord,

At this distance I will not dispute in points of militarie discipline, nor the practice of Captains in such cases; yet to give your Lordsh[ip] satisfaction in that your letter desires from me, your Lordship may take notice, I have drawn my forces before this citie with intention to reduce it to the obedience due to the King and Parliament, whereunto if your Lordship shall speedily conforme, it may save the effusion of much innocent blood, whereof I wish your Lordship to bee no lesse sparing then [than] I am, who rest,

Your Lordships most humble servant

Leven

From Fowforth [Fulford] 8. June 1644

For his Excell[ency] the Lord Marq[uis] of Newcastle.

When Generall Lesley and the L[ord] Fairfax understood that the Earle of Manchester had received no letter from the Marq[uis] of Newcastle, they signified that seeing the Earle of Manchester was equally concerned in the businesse with themselves, except hee also might bee called to consider thereof, they neither could nor would admit of any parl[e]y with him about it. Hereupon the next day following, this letter was brought to the E[arl] of Manchester, with the transcript of what had been sent unto the E[arl] of Leven and the L[ord] Fairfax, inclosed.

My Lord,

The inclosed is the effect of two letters I writ yesterday, one to the Earle of Leven and the other to the Lord Fairfax, and I had done the like to your Lordship then, if I had had any assurance of your Lordships being in these parts in your own person. But since I am now satisfied of your Lordships being here, I have thought fit to present the same to your Lordships consideration with this desire that I may receive your Lordships resolution therein, and so I remain,

My Lord, Your Lordships

most humble servant

Will[iam] Newcastle.

York June 9. 1644

To the right honourable the Earle of Manchester.

Suddenly upon receit hereof the Earle of Manchester dispatched this following answer, being unwilling to be seemingly guilty of the least delay, in promoting the publick service, especially in wayes which may in appearance promise to prevent the effusion of guiltlesse blood.

49

My Lord,

By favour of his Excellencie the Earle of Leven, and the Lord Fairfax, I was no stranger to your Lordships former letters, and your Lordship having now with civility put me in a conjuncture with them, I shall desire your Lordship to beleeve that my heart is the same with theirs in this business, and their expressions in their letter to your Lordship, are fully owned by me, as my sense; and therefore if your Lordship will please to read the first letter from the Earle of Leven, and the Lord Fairfax, you shall by that clearly see the resolution of

Your Lo[rdship's] most humble servant

Manchester

Leaguer before York

June 9, 1644.

The same day (being the lords day) Generall Lesley, Lord Fairfax, and the Earle of Manchester met, and that evening upon consultation, reported their readinesse to treate about the surrendering of the Citty in such sort, that mens lives and estates might not bee exposed to ruine unnec[e]ssarily. Generall Lesley nominated for Commissioners, the Earle of Lindesay, Lord Humbey, Leiftenant-Generall of his Army. The Lord Fairfax, named Sir William Fairfax, and Colonell White. The Earle of Manchester propounded Colonell Russell, and Colonell Haword;[16] And they expressed an unwillingnesse to yeeld unto cessation of Armes in any part of the Citty, but the places appointed for the Treaty,[17] the Marquesse deferred his answer untill Tuesday,[18] and then his Letter was as followeth.

My Lord,

I Have received your Lordshipps Letter with the names of the Commissioners appointed by your Lordshipps, But since your Lordshipps have declared in your Letter to allow a Cessation of Armes only on that side of the Towne during the time of the Treaty, I finde it not fit for me to incline to it upon those conditions, and had returned your Lordshipps this answer long before this tyme if some weighty affaires had not retarded my desires in that particular, I am

My Lord

Your Lordshipps most humble servant

W[illiam] Newcastle.

Yorke 11. of June 1644

To the Right Honorable the Earle of Leven, the Lord Fairefax and the Earle of Manchester.

The three Noble Commanders having in the Evening received this Letter, they unanimously resolved, the next day to send unto the Marquesse of Newcastle these Summons,[19] which was done accordingly.

We the Generalls of the Armies raised for the King and Parliament,

and now imployed in this expedition about Yorke, That no further effusion
of blood be done, and that the City of Yorke and Inhabitants may be preserved from ruine; We hereby require your Lordship to surrender the said
City to us in name and for the use of King and Parliament within the space
of 24. houres after the receit hereof, which if you refuse to doe, the incon-
venience ensuing upon your refusall must bee required, at your Lordships
hands, seeing our intentions are not for blood or destruction of Townes,
Cities, and Counties, unlesse all other meanes being used, we be necessitated
hereunto, which shall be contrary to the mindes and harts of

              My Lord
      Your Excellencies humble servants
         Leven, Fairefax, Manchester.

12. June, 1644.

These summons, being received, was the next day answered as followeth:
And then Answer was directed unto all the th[r]ee Noble Lords who sent the
Summons.[20]

My Lords,
    I Have received a Letter from your Lordships dated yesterday about
four of the clock in the afternoon, wherein I am required to surrender the
City to your Lordships within 24. hours after the receipt; but I know your
Lordships are too full of honour, to expect the rendring the City upon a
demand, and upon so short an advertisement to me, who have the kings
Commission to keep it and where there is so many generall persons, and men
of honour, quallity and fortune concerned in it. But truly I conceive this said
demand high enough to have been exacted upon the meanest Governour of
any of his Majesties Garrisons: And your Lordships may be pleased to know,
that I expect Propositions to proceed from your Lordships, as becomes
Persons of honour to give and receive one from another; and if your Lordships therefore think fit to propound honourable and reasonable terms, and
agree upon a generall cessation from all acts of hostility during the time of a
Treaty, then your Lordships may receive such satisfaction therein, as may be
expected from persons of honour, and such as desire as much to avoid the
effusion of Christian blood, or destruction of Cities, Towns and Counties as
any whatsoever, yet will not spare their own lives, rather then [than] to live
in the least stain of dishonour, and so desiring your Lordships resolution,

           I remain my Lords,
      Your Lordships most humble Servant
         Will[iam] Newcastle

York, 13 June 1644

    This letter moved our three worthy Commanders to meet speedily, that
they might without losse of time, consider what answer to return unto this
motion, and lest they should seem averse unto any proposition; which carrieth

the colour of any good accord, they yeelded unto a cessation from all acts of hostility, from all sides of the City, both during the time of treaty, and three hours before and three hours after it. Hereupon the names of the Commissioners appointed by the Marquess, were sent out of the town, viz. Lord Withrington [Widdrington], Sir Thomas Glemham, Sir Will[iam] Wentworth, Sir Richard Hutton, Sir Thomas Mattam [Methem], Sir Robert Strickland and Mr. Rockley[21], their meeting to treat with our Commissioners, was resolved, to be the next day, about 3. of clock, and a Tent was set up for them betwixt two Forts, one of ours, lately taken from them, and one of theirs:[22] Each party of Commissioners had 100 Musketiers to attend them. The Commissioners continued together from 3. a clock till 9. Mr. Botelor the Marquess of Newcastles Secretary attended on their party, and Mr. Primrose Secretary to the Scots Army,[23] and Mr. Weaver as Secretary on our party, what passed betwixt them by way of debate amongst themselves, cannot be expected in this generall relation of occurrences. The result of that which the Commissioners from the City pleaded, appears in these five following Propositions which they tendered.

June 15 (sic[24]) 1644

Propositions made to the three Generalls by the Earl of Newcastle, concerning the render of the City of York, entitled *Propositions to be tendered to the Enemy*.

I.   That the Town shall be rendered within twenty dayes, in case no relief come to it by that time from the King or Prince Rupert, upon these conditions:

> That the Marquess Newcastle, with all officers and souldiers therein have free liberty, to depart with colours flying and match light, and to take with them all Arms, Ammunition, Artillery, Money, Plate, and other goods belonging to them; for which end, that carriages be provided them, and victualls and other provision for their march.

> That they be convoyed with our Troops to the King, Prince Rupert, or any other garrisons of the Kings where they please; And that they be not forced to march above 8. miles a day.

> That they shall have liberty to stay or appoint others to stay 40 dayes in the town for sale of such goods, or for conveying of them to other places which they shall not be able to carry away with them.

> That no Oath, Covenant, or Protestation be administered to any of them, further then [than] is warranted by the known lawes of the land.

II.   That the Gentry therein have liberty to go to their houses, and there be protected from violence, and not questioned for what they have done to the other partie: that no Oath or Covenant be tendered to them as abovesaid.

52

III.   That the townes-men injoy all their priviledges and libertie of trade and merchandice, as before and not to be questioned for any thing they have done against the Parliament; and that no Oath be tendered to any of them, &c.

That the Garrison to be set into York, be only Yorkshire men.

That all the Churches therein be kept from prophanation, and no violation offered to the Cathedrall Church.

That the service be allowed to be performed therein, as formerly had bin.

That the Revenues of the Church remain to the Officers thereof as hath done; and that the Prebends continue their Prebendaries and other Revenues as formerly according to the Lawes.

IV.   That all Ministers and other Ecclesiasticall persons therein, of what countrey soever, have liberty to depart with the army, or to their owne livings, there to serve God and to enjoy their estate without disturbance.

That no oath or covenant be proffered them as aforesaid, nor they questioned hereafter for what they have done to the King's party.

V.   That good Hostages be given, and to remain in their custodie: And that Cliffords Tower (the chiefe Fort in Yorke) be still kept Garrisoned by them, untill the Articles abovesaid and some others then offered with them, be punctually performed. And then the said Garrison, and all Armes, Ammunition and Cannon therein, be safely conveyed to what Garrison of the Kings they pleased.

It is needless here to tell you, how strange and displeasing these Propositions were to our Commissioners, as some of them did not spare to discover, after some words used concerning the unreasonableness of these demands; our Commissioners moved, that the copy of these their Articles might be sent to the Noble Lords, who assigned them unto this service; and also their copy was denied, yet three of our Commissioners and Secretaries had leave to goe unto the three Lords who imployed them, and to impart the sum of what had passed amongst them. After an hour and an half they returned to the Tent, with a paper containing the particulars following, being signed by Generall Lesley, and the other two religious Lords then with him.

That the City of York and all the Forts together with all Arms, Ammunition, and other warlike provisions whatsoever in and about the same to be rendered and delivered up to us for and to the use of King and Parliament, upon the Conditions following, viz.

That the common souldiers shall have free liberty and licence to depart and go to their own homes, and to carry with them their clothes and their own money (not exceeding 14. days pay) And shall have safe conduct and protection of their persons from violence, they promising that they will not hereafter take up Arms against the Parliament or Protestant Religion.

That the Citizens and ordinary inhabitants of the said City shall have their persons and houses protected from violence; and shall have the same free trade and commerce as others under obedience of King and Parliament; And that no Regiments or Companies shall be admitted or quartered in the Town of York, except those that are appointed for the Garrison thereof.

That the Officers of all qualities shall have liberty to go to their own homes with swords and horses, and shall have licence to carry their apparell and money along with them (the money not exceeding one moneths means for every severall officer).

Any officer who shall be recommended by the Marquess of New-castle shall have a pass from one of the Generalls to go beyond seas, they promising not to serve against the Parliament and Protestant Religion.

That the Gentry and other inhabitants of the County of York, now residing in the City of York, shall have liberty to go to their own homes, and shall be protected from violence.

That a positive Answer be returned to these Propositions by 3. of the clock tomorrow afternoon, being the 15. instant; And in case they shall not be then accepted, we shall not hold our selves bound to them, and in the mean time we declare there is no cessation after the 3. hours already granted.

Upon the reading of these propositions, the Commissioners from Yorke fell into exceeding great passions, using many bloody oathes and and fearefull Execrations, desiring that Gods veng[e]ance might bee upon them, if ever they gave up the Towne upon such conditions. Their heate and indignation was such, that they refused to take the Coppie unto the Marquesse: but the next morning early, Generall Lesley sent it to him by a Drummer. The answer of the Marquesse, was as followeth,

My Lord,

I Have perused the Conditions and demands your Lordship sent, but when I considered the many professions made to avoide the effusion of Christian blood, I did admire to see such propositions from your Lordshipps, conceiving this not the way to it for I cannot suppose that your Lordshipps doe imagine that persons of honour can possibly condiscend to any of these propositions, and so I remaine,

My Lord,

Yorke   Your Lordshipps most humble Servant
15 of June. 1644   William Newcastle.
For his Excellencie the Earle of Leven

The Souldiers in City and Leagure, Musketteers and Canoneers, who all the weeke before both day and night had answered each other, with many fierce oppositions. After this Letter was received, and time of Cessation expired, did renew and increase their assaults upon all seeming advantages against one another; which were frequent all the day and night following.

1 Hildyard, pp. 56–7.
2 *History and Description of the Ancient City of York* . . . 1818, i, p. 164.
3 *Intelligence* No. 4. Throughout this chapter, unless otherwise stated, the text quoted is from this tract.
4 At Marston Moor in the Royalist armies there were, according to *Full Relation*, 'a Regiment of Red Coats;' 'the Earle of Newcastles brigade of White-coats' and 'a brigade of Green-coats.'
5 For examples of such propaganda from two contemporary tracts, see Appendix IV. Another scaremongering piece of propaganda (in this instance on the Royalist side) — which has a very modern ring — is the allegation that the Parliamentarians were using poisoned bullets! (see p. 60).
6 p. 188.
7 p. 164.
8 *CSP. Ven.*, p. 108, dated 17 June.
9 *CSP. Ven.*, p. 112, dated 1 July.
10 *A Booke of all the Ordrs. Warrants and p'cedinges maid by the Comitie of the Cittie of Yorke.*
11 For his biography see R. H. Skaife, *Civic Officials of York and Parliamentary Representatives* (MS. in York Public Library), pp. 121–3, no. 454.
12 *CSP. Dom.*, p. 508.
13 Like the similar one delivered to Lord Fairfax it was despatched by a trumpeter. *Hulls Managing* and Rushworth, p. 624.
14 The text of this letter, like the other five and the 'Propositions' which follow, is that given in *Intelligence* No. 4. Some, or all, of these letters, etc., with slight differences in spelling and punctuation are given in *Hulls Managing;* Rushworth, pp. 624–31; Drake, pp. 164–6; Terry, pp. 222–6.
15 p. 222.
16 Except for the last named, this list agrees with that of Douglas, Rushworth and Drake. Douglas, p. 60, gives the last name as 'Hawoodhouse,' while Rushworth, p. 626, and Drake, p. 164, give it as 'Hammond.' *CSP. Dom.*, p. 224, dated 11 June, has 'Lieut-Gen. Bagliff [Baillie]' instead of Humbey, while Hammond is described as 'Lieut-Gen. of Ordnance.' Hammond is possibly a mistake for Hamilton who was Lt. General of the Scottish Ordnance. (*SHS. vol* XVI p. xiii *passim*).
17 It was clearly to the advantage of the besiegers to press on with their assaults on the city except in the particular locality where, and during the short period while, the actual parleying took place. Newcastle, on the other hand, playing

for time, wanted a complete cessation of hostilities around the whole of the city for as long a period before, during and after the discussions as he could obtain.

18 i.e., two days later, a further illustration of his delaying tactics.

19 Douglas, p. 58, briefly mentions this and confirms the date. Slingsby makes no mention of either the summons or the parley.

20 According to Douglas, p. 58, nine Royalist horsemen tried to break through the lines of the besieging forces on the west side of the city during the course of this day (13 June), see p. 77.

21 Apart from differences in spelling this list agrees with that of Douglas, p. 60, except that he names 'Sir Robert Lintoun' instead of Sir Richard Hutton. Rushworth, p. 628 has Hutton but does not include Rockley.

22 Douglas, p. 60:— 'Parlee in a tent betwixt the great Strouse and ours in the right hand.' The site of the meeting place must therefore have been somewhere in what is now the central sector of Scarcroft Road (shown on front end paper as no. 7).

23 Mr James Primrose, 'Clerk to the Committee of the Scots Army',— to give him his correct title (SHS, vol XVI–XVII, pp. 247, 348 and 607).

24 This is the date as given in *Intelligence* no. 4. It is surely a mistake for 14 June, the time sequence being as follows:— the letter from Newcastle dated 13 June (p. 51) followed by *Intelligence* which says 'meeting . . . . was resolved to be the next day [14]' (p. 52). This meeting was held from 3 p.m. to 9 p.m. on that day. Sometime during this period (presumably in the late afternoon or evening) the Parliamentary counter-proposals were issued, the last paragraph of which says ' . . . . tomorrow afternoon, being the 15th instant' (p. 54). Still writing on the day of the parley Ashe and Goode in *Intelligence* refer to 'next morning early' [?15] (p. 54), to which Newcastle replies over the date 15 June (p. 54).

Chapter Five

ATTACK ON THE MANOR, 16 JUNE

THE PARLEY ENDED ON 15 June. On the following day — Trinity Sunday — occurred the most dramatic episode in the siege, the exploding of a mine under St. Mary's Tower[1] and the assault on the Manor (now called the King's Manor). This great house, originally the residence of the abbots of the monastery of St. Mary, one of the richest Benedictine foundations in the north of England, had, after the Dissolution, become the headquarters and home of the Lord President of the Council of the North. Thomas Wentworth, Earl of Strafford, lived there from 1628 until 1633, when he went to Ireland. The Manor, Bootham Bar and the Minster[2] constituted the strong points in the north-western defences of the city. St. Mary's Tower, (Plate IX) situated at an angle in the salient of the defences projecting into the lines of the Earl of Manchester, was an obvious point against which the besiegers might be expected to concentrate their attention. The extensive grounds of the Manor, which included all the area now covered by the Museum Gardens, Yorkshire Museum, Art Gallery, York School of Art and Marygate Centre of Adult Education, had a garden, orchard and bowling green[3] situated somewhere between St. Mary's Tower and the Manor, all three of which played an important part in the day's events.

Following the arrival of Manchester's army on 3 June when the city had been closely beleagured, tunnels for mines had been dug by the besiegers under the defences at Walmgate Bar and St. Mary's Tower. Contemporary and near contemporary accounts are as follows :–

Drake[4]

'Manchester's forces had undermined St. Mary's Tower.'

Hulls Managing

'. . . . there were two mines ready to be sprung.'

Douglas[5]

'Mine sprung. At Bouden [Bootham] Barr.'

Rushworth[6]

'Undermined a Tower belonging to the Mannor neer Bootham Bar.'

Exact Relation

'Manchester's men . . . . doe gallery through them [i.e. houses saved from the burning of the suburbs in Bootham] close to the walls.'

Hildyard[7]

mentions both the mine under Walmgate Bar and the one under St. Mary's Tower.

Particular Relation

'. . . . there were two mines ready for springing, one at the Mannour House and the other at Womb-gate [Walmgate].'

Intelligence No. 4

'. . . . undermined a Tower belonging to the Mannour neere Bootham Barre.'

Short Memorial[8]

'. . . . approaches were made to St. Mary's Tower; and soon came to mine it.'

CSP. Dom.,[9]

Sir Henry Vane reported (16th June) — 'there are now two mines ready to play.'

Dodsworth[10]

'Quae omnia penitus igne absumerentur, ... cum per cuniculus subterraneos, turris, et per tormenta bellica muri funditus eversi sunt.' [All of which were utterly consumed by fire . . . . when the tower was destroyed by underground burrowing and the foundation of the wall by engines of war].

The *Weekly Account* (25 June) says there were *'Three* (my italics) Severall Mines' and Markham[11] says that there were mines under Micklegate Bar and St. Mary's Tower. The 'three' should be 'two' and 'Micklegate Bar' is clearly a mistake for 'Walmgate Bar.' Markham's error may well be due to a misreading of the Slingsby extracts[12] which follow.

> [Fairfax] works under ground close by ye [Walmgate] barr, & makes
> his mines in 2 severall places, likewise Manchester .... works his mines
> under St. Mary's Tower w[i]th[out] Bo[o]tham barr.
>   .... ye Scots were all ye while busie about ye mine, & we as busy in
> countermining, but at length both give over being hinder'd by water; they
> had beaten down ye top of ye barr as low as ye gate. w[hi]ch we had barri-
> caded up w[i]th earth & besides had made a travers against it, & pull'd down
> some houses near ye gate.

From the context, the second of these entries might be
taken to apply to Micklegate Bar as that was the only gateway in
the sector controlled by the Scots though it fits perfectly with the
facts as we know them concerning the mine, countermine and
damage to Walmgate Bar (pp. 38-9). Shielded as it was by the
Royalist battery on The Mount (pp. 144-5) the Scots could
never have got close enough to Micklegate Bar to undermine it.
Slingsby's references to 'ye Scots' must be to the regiment of
Scots under General Lumsden which was seconded from Leven's
army to assist Fairfax (p. 43n).

Elementary strategy required that these mines should be
sprung simultaneously accompanied with the maximum of
alarms and of real or feigned assaults at numerous other points
around the defences. If the *Weekly Account* (25 June) is to be
believed this is exactly what had been planned — 'Three (*sic*)
Severall Mines were appointed to be sprung this day [16 June],
and at the same time when these mines were sprung, it was
agreed that the City should be stormed on all sides.' As will be
seen later only one was sprung, and that in complete isolation
from any other aggressive act elsewhere by the besiegers; consequently it proved a failure.

Besides tunnelling beneath St. Mary's Tower, Manchester[13]
had raised a battery[14] somewhere in the Bootham/Clifton area
(a likely site would seem to be somewhere in the vicinity of St.
Peter's School). According to Slingsby[15] early in the morning
Lieutenant-General Laurence Crawford, one of Manchester's
divisional commanders

> .... begins to play w[i]th his Cannon & throws down peice of ye Wall.
> We [Royalists inside the city] fall to work & make it up w[i]th earth and sods;
> this happn'd in ye morning.

The 'peice of ye Wall' shot down must have been somewhere in

Marygate between St. Mary's Tower and St. Olave's Church. Slingsby[16] implies that there was a lull after this breach until noon when the mine under the tower was fired. Markham[17] also thinks that the breach and the blowing-up of the tower were isolated events but Hildyard,[18] the only other contemporary or near-contemporary commentator, says that the two events occurred about the same time.

A number of descriptions of the actual explosion have come down to us; three are reproduced here, the first two by Royalists (Sir Henry Slingsby and Christopher Hildyard) and the third by Ashe and Goode who were with Manchester's forces.

(i)

.... at noon they spring ye mine under St. Mary's tower, & blows up one part of it, w[hi]ch falling outwards made ye access more easy; Then some at ye breach, some w[i]th Ladders, getts up & enters, near 500.

S[i]r Philip Biron yt [that] had ye guard at yt [that] place, leading up some men was unfortunately kill'd as he open'd ye doors into ye bowling green whither ye enemy was gotten; but ye difficulty was not much, we soon beat ym [them] out again, having taken 200 prisoners & killed many of ym [them], as might be seen in ye bowling green, Orchard and Garden.[19]

(ii)

The Sectarian Army thinking to abolish the Service of the Common-Prayer in a Military way, which by Disputation they were not able to performe, made choice of Trinity Sunday, being the 16th. June, to put in Execution their Hellish Designe, and in time of Common-Prayer at the Minster, did blow up Saint Maries Tower at the North-East Corner of the Mannor; and at the same time, they made a Battery, and a Breach in the Wall lower down in Saint Maries Gate, whereat they endeavoured to enter; but by the Valour of the Citizens, and White-Coats of the Marquesse of New-castles own Regiment, being led on by their Commanders,[20] above forty of the Enemy were slain in the Garden and Bowling green, and about two hundred and fifty taken Prisoners. In which Conflict, that Valiant Citizen Master Samuel Brearey (third Sonne of William Brearey Alderman Deceased) and Leiutenant Coll[onel] of a Company of 250. stout Volunteer Citizens, being shot with a poysoned Bullet into one of his Armes, foure dayes after dyed. At the same time was Collonell Sir Phillip Byron, and Collonell Huddlestone,[21] two Valiant Commanders slain. After this Defeat, the Enemy was much daunted. (Cromwell, that monster of men, being a Collonell in that quarter:) Upon this Defeate our Souldiers would jeare the Enemy, and tell them, They were stealing the King's Apples, but they were taken in the Mannor.[22]

Upon the sixteenth, the Earle of Manchesters men (having by many dayes labour undermined a Tower belonging to the Mannour neere Bootham Barre) were compelled to spring the Mine, for that worke could not be longer delayed, in regard of waters which increased upon them, in the chamber of the Mine. The Tower being blown up, the bold Souldiers adventured too farre through inconsideratenesse, and hope of plunder, many of them having scaled two or three inner walles, possessed themselves of the Mannour. But the enemy coming from all parts of the City suddenly and unexpectedly surrounded them,[23] yea they blocked up the breach, the only way of retreat. Hereupon they having spent all their powder and shott, and fresh assistance not getting over the walles to their reliefe soone enough, we receved some losse, both of men and arms, As it is supposed betwixt 12. and 20. men were slain and 200. taken prisoners, whom we expect to have restored unto us again ere long.[24] Some who were in the service, say that many more of the enemies then [than]of our souldiers were killed in the skirmish, but they are too wily to suffer us to know what loss they in the City received by our assaults.[25]

The account which Drake[26] gives of the explosion is based on that of Hildyard. He embroiders a little — pointing out that it occurred 'when most of the commanders of the city were at the cathedral' but 'the violent blow . . . sufficiently alarmed them, and each man ran to his post to watch the consequence' and he adds one new piece of information. He says that a party of the garrison went out by 'a private sally port in the city walls, entered the Manor and cut off the only way the enemy had to retreat.' Ashe's remark, already quoted, that 'they [the garrison] blocked up the breach, the only way of retreat,' lends support to this.[27]

Opinions on Crawford's action in prematurely springing the mine fall into two categories.[28] The first, illustrated in the passage quoted above from *Intelligence* no. 4, takes the view that it was forced on him by the imminence of the tunnel becoming flooded[29]

Sir Thomas Fairfax and Robert Baillie express the other, more widely held, view :—

(i)

Colonel Crawford, a Scotsman, who commanded that Quarter, (ambitious to have the honour alone of springing the mine undertook, without acquainting of the other two Generals with it, for their advice and concurrence); which proved very prejudicial. For, having engaged his party against the whole strength of the town, without more force to second him, he was repulsed with a loss of 300 men. For which he had been surely called to account; but that he escaped the better by reason of this triumviral gover[n]ment.[30]

(ii)

The foolish rashness of Major (*sic*) Crawford, and his great vanitie to assault his alone the breach made by his myne, without acquainting Lesley or Fairfax with it, and the killing of so great a number of his men . . . . will force us to look on these walls till hunger make them fall, whereof as yet we hear not much.[31]

In the accounts of this exploit sent to the Committee of Both Kingdoms in London the damage to the Parliamentarian cause was played down. The Earl of Manchester generously took upon himself the sole responsibility for the failure and offered only the slightest implied criticism of Crawford's action.

Sir Henry Vane wrote :–

Since my writing thus much Manchester played his mine with very good success, made a fair breach, and entered with his men and possessed the manor house, but Leven and Fairfax not being acquainted therewith, that they might have diverted the enemy at other places, the enemy drew all their strength against our men, and beat them off again, but with no great loss, as I hear; this opportunity being thus missed it may possibly occasion some retardment in this work, though I hope it will not be very long.[32]

The Earl of Manchester wrote :–

Yesterday within my quarters I sprang a mine, which did great execution upon the enemy, blowing up a tower which joined to the Manor-yard, and this mine taking so great effect my Major-General commanded 600 men to storm the Manor-house, who beat the enemy and took 100 prisoners, but, being over confident, 2,000 of the enemy's best men fell upon them and beat them back. I lost near 300 men, but still maintain the breaches and the enemy dare not make any sally out; we are now so near them that we are very ill neighbours one to another.[33]

Lord Fairfax dismissed the matter in a very few words, giving no details whatsoever :–

. . . . upon Sunday last Manchester's men sprang a mine and entered into the Manor, which was hotly disputed with loss on both sides.[34]

The Venetian ambassador in England, reporting home,[35] succinctly summed up the effect of the action in this simple

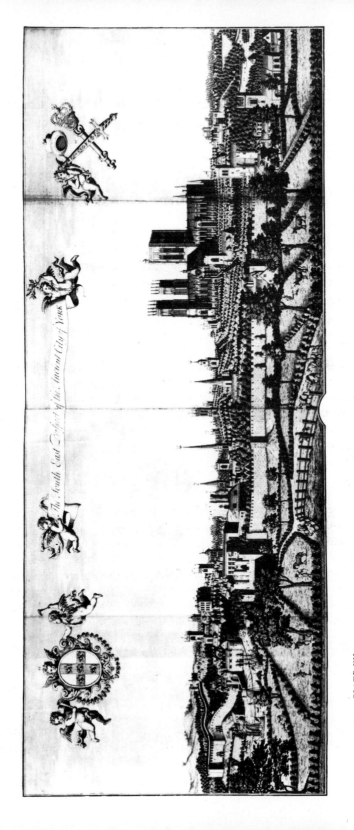

PLATE VII

South East Prospect of York in 1718.   Artist E. B. (Full name unknown)

PLATE VIII

William Cavendish, 1st Marquis of Newcastle.   Artist A. van Dyck.

sentence — 'this incident has not increased their [the Parliamentarian] hopes of taking the place soon.'

In the contemporary accounts which have survived, the numbers taking part, and the losses suffered by both sides, vary considerably, as is to be expected. These are summarised in the following table. It would seem from this that between 500 and 600 of Crawford's men entered the breach and that about 300 of them were lost or slain, wounded or taken prisoner. The only figure which deserves attention is Manchester's 2,000 for the number of the garrison taking part, although this is probably too high : the Duchess of Newcastle's 80 is nonsensical. The Royalist losses were probably not high numerically but they did involve at least four dead of officer rank.

Tucked away in a volume of the *Calendar of State Papers*[36] is a curious passage which not only supplies the name of one of Crawford's soldiers taking part in this assault, but also gives an illuminating account of his military career from the time he joined the army of the Eastern Association at Christmas 1643 until September of the following year when he was incapacitated through illness (or wounds). The passage is self-explanatory and reads :–

> Petition of George Hancock, a sick soldier, clerk to the company of Captain Dennys Taylor under the command of Colonel Montague, to the Committee for the town of Cambridge. Petitioner has been engaged in the service of the Parliament ever since Christmas last as a clerk to the company, and has been upon all designs undertaken since his going forth, as at the taking of Lincoln, the scaling of the walls of the manor-yard at York, the battle against Prince Rupert [Marston Moor], the taking of Sheffield Castle, Tickhill Castle, Welbeck House, Bozer [Bolsover] Castle, Stayley [Staveley] House, and Wingfield Manor. Ever since August he has been carried with other sick soldiers on a cart after the army, and now lies both lame and sick at Cambridge, not having wherewithal to relieve himself. He has 18 weeks' pay due to him at 10s. 6d., the week allowed by the Earl of Manchester, out of which he prays to be advanced some mean to relieve him in his sickness until his captain shall come to town.

> Note authorising Mr. Leeman to pay petitioner 20s. upon his captain's account; Manchester's and five other signatures.

> Mem. 20s. paid the 20th September 1644.

Authority	NUMBERS TAKING PART		LOSSES	
	Besiegers (Parliament)	Garrison (Royalist)	Besiegers (Parliament)	Garrison (Royalist)
Short Memorial p. 394. Douglas, p. 60.	— —	— —	"loss of 300 men" "40 of them killed, and near 200 prisoners, and arms taken by the enemy."	— "500 prisoners"
Slingsby, p. 109.	"near 500"	—	"200 prisoners & kill'd many of them."	"Sir Philip Biron."
Rushworth, p. 631.	"about two hundred of the Besiegers entered"	—	15 killed, 60 wounded, "about a 100 more" prisoners. Also killed before they entered breach "about 20" and 40 wounded. Total "near 300 men."	"many Townsmen and women kill'd."
Weekly Account for 25th June	—	—	"about 200 of them slaine, and taken prisoners"	"uncertaine, but Colonell Hurlstone [Huddlestone], Captain Hackworth, an Irishman and Lieutenant Col."

Drake, p. 166.	—	—	50 killed, about 250 prisoners	Berry were slaine; we also tooke some prisoners, and killed and wounded many of their men"
Hildyard, p. 107.	—	—	"Above forty .... slain .... and about two hundred and fifty taken Prisoners"	"Buried a great many men and women in the ruins.... slain Sir Philip Byron and colonel Huddlestone, with Mr. Samuel Brearey" / Sir Philip Byron, Col. Huddlestone and Samuel Brearey.
CSP. Dom. (Vane) p. 241.	—	—	"no great loss"	—
CSP. Dom. (Manchester) p. 246.	2000	600	"near 300"	"Did great execution .... 100 prisoners" but saved by the garrison.
CSP. Dom. (Fairfax) p. 246.	— —	— —	"blowing up about 300 of Manchester's men"	"loss on both sides"
CSP. Ven., p. 114.	—	—	"supposed betwixt 12 and 20 men were slain and 200 taken prisoners"	—
Intelligence No. 4.	—	—		"Many more of the enemies then [than] of our souldiers were slain"

Intelligence No. 5.	—	—	Slain — inside city "about 15" and outside "20 at the most". Wounded — inside "about 60", without "well nigh 40". 100 prisoners	"4 Colonels, one Major were slain with divers Captains and other commanders . . . . their loss was greater than ours"
Margaret, D. of Newcastle, p. 72	—	"80 of. . . . . [the] regiment of foot, called the White Coats"	"killed and took 1500 of them"	—
Baillie, p. 195	—	—	"the killing of so great a number of his [own] men"	
Thomas Gent, pp. 224–5	—	—	"40 slain 216 taken"	As Hildyard.

The aftermath of the blowing up of St. Mary's Tower is described by Ashe[37] in these words :—

> In the fall of the Tower many were slain, and found dead on the ground, the most of them were Townsmen and women. While the skirmish was betwixt our Souldiers and the enemy, some barrels of Gun-powder were fiered in the Town, whereby many were slain and wounded.
>
> About 15 of our men were slain within the Citie, and 20 at the most without the walls; well nigh 40 were wounded without the Town, and about 60. (as we heare) within, who together with an hundred more were taken prisoners. We cannot get a full account of the loss sustained in the Cittie by that dayes skirmish; but this we are assured of, that 4 Colonels, one Major, were slain, with divers Captains, and other commanders. Some who are since come out of the Towne, tell us, that their loss was greater then [than] ours, and that they rather lament then [than] glory in the successe of that dayes service.
>
> On Munday morning (being the day following) some of our Souldiers betwixt nine and ten a clock, approaching towards the place where the Tower stood, heard in the rubbish a very dolefull cry, some calling, Help help; others, Water, water. Their lamentable complaints moved our men to resolve their relief; so they digged one out dead in the rubbish, & brought two alive; but from the Town such fierce opposition was made by the merciles[s] enemy against our Souldiers while they were labouring to save their friends lives, that they were compelled to leave many poore distressed ones dying in the dust.
>
> Upon Wednesday or Thursday we obtained an hours time to bury our dead.
>
> From this time till June twenty four, the Munday following, there was nothing of any speciall consequence done amongst us, though there were daily small skirmishes, with some losse on both sides: Cannon also playing frequently both night and day.

Although the sermon preached in the Minster on Trinity Sunday (when the explosion under the tower took place) is not extant, another one preached there during the siege, has come down to us. It may be taken as typical of the length, form and content of those preached in the Minster during these months. It was delivered four Sundays previously and was published in a tract — the full title of which is given in the bibliography (p. 222) — printed at York by Stephen Bulkley.[38] It consists of two parts :—

(i) 'The Forme of bidding the Prayer prescribed before the Sermon.' After praying for the King, the Queen, the Royal

Family, the Archbishops, clergy, schools, and 'two famous Universities' it continues :—

> And especially let us beseech God to be neere unto him with his gracious assistance, whose affaires have a neerer and more immediate influence upon us here, his Excellencie, William, Marquesse of Newcastle, Lord Generall of his Majesties Forces in these Northerne parts, and many other Counties of this Kingdome; That his hands may be strong and his designes prosperous against every enemy which hath lift up his hand against the Lords Anointed, or done wickedly in his Sanctuary; and that hee and all that are Commanders under him, in particular, the Vigilant and Worthy Governour of this City, Sir Thomas Glemham, may wade through the throng of their great employment with Wisdome, Courage, Innocence and Honour, and live to see happy dayes, and Peace upon Israel. Pray we in like manner for the Honourable the Lord Maior of this City, for the Aldermen and Sheriffes, and all the loyall Citizens; that God may preserve them, and us with them from the violence of the Wicked; and for his Name's sake preserve this great City, and this famous Church, wherein he hath put his Name from the spoyle and profanation of evill doers.

(ii) The Sermon. This contained no direct allusion to the siege. The text, from *Judges 5*, verse 23, reads :—

> Curse ye Meroz, said the angel of the Lord, curse ye bitterly the inhabitants thereof; because they came not to the help of the Lord, to the help of the Lord against the mighty.

The Bidding Prayer consisted of no fewer than 1,500 words, and the sermon itself of 13,000 !

Thomas Mace, a clerk of Trinity College, Cambridge, who was in York during the siege, has left a vivid account of the fervent singing in the Minster at the time. Extracts from his work[39] are printed here :—

Concerning the great Excellency and Eminency of a Psalm well sung.

Where and when has been the Best singing of Psalms that ever the Author heard.

I will now in the Conclusion of this Discourse, adde only one Chapter more, in making mention, both of the Time and Place, when and where was heard (I believe) the most remarkable, and most excellent Singing of Psalms, that has been known or remembred any where in These our latter Ages.

But most certain I am, that to my self, it was the very best Harmonical-Musick that ever I heard; yea far excelling all other either private, or publick Cathedral-Musick; and infinitely beyond all verbal expression or conceiving.

The Time when, was in the year 1644, the Place where, in the stately Cathedral Church of the Loyal City of York.

And because by the occasion of it, you may the better apprehend, and the more easily be brought to believe the gloriousness and illustriousness of that performance; I will here (in a Short Seeming-Digression) declare it unto you; As also something or more then [than] ordinary remark relating to that Time and Place.

The Occasion of that Singing.

The occasion of it was, the great and close Siege which was then laid to that City, and strictly maintain'd for eleven weeks space, by three very notable and considerable great Armies, viz. The Scotch, the Northern, and the Southern; whose three Generals were these, for the Scotch the old Earl of Leven, viz. David Lesley (alias Lashley); for the Northern, the old Ferdinando Lord Fairfax; For the Southern, the Earl of Manchester; And whose three Chief Commanders next themselves, were, for the Scotch, Lieutenant-General [   ]⁴⁰ for the Northern, Sir Thomas (now Lord) Fairfax; and for the Southern, Oliver Cromwell, (afterwards Lord Protector).

By This occasion, there were shut up within that City, abundance of People of the best Rank and Quality, viz. Lords, Knights, and Gentlemen of the Countries round about, besides the Souldiers and Citizens, who all or most of them came constantly every Sunday, to hear Publick Prayers and Sermon in that spacious Church.

And indeed there Number was so exceeding great, that the Church was (as I may say) even cramming or squeezing full.

A good Custom, not commonly used in Cathedrals.

Now here you must take notice, that they had then a Custom in that Church, (which I hear not of in any other Cathedral, which was) that always before the Sermon, the whole Congregation sang a Psalm, together with the Quire and the Organ; And you must also know, that there was then a most Excellent-large-plump-lusty-full-speaking-Organ, which cost (as I am credibly informed) a thousand pounds.

This Organ, I say, (when the Psalm was set before the Sermon) being let out, into all its Fulness of Stops, together with the Quire, began the Psalm.

The unutterable Excellency

But when That Vast-Conchording-Unity of the whole Congregational-Chorus, came, (as I may say) Thundering in, even so, as it made the very Ground shake under us; (Oh

69

the unutterable ravishing Soul's delight!) In which I was
so transported, and wrapt up into High Contemplations,
that there was no room left in my whole Man, viz. Body,
Soul and Spirit, for anything below Divine and Heavenly
Raptures . . . .

A Strange
piece of
Heathenish
Incivility
of the
Enemy in
time of
Divine
Service.

Because that at That time, the desperateness and
dismaidness of their Danger could not but draw them unto it,
in regard the Enemy was so very near, and Fierce upon them,
especially on That side the City where the Church stood;
who had planted their Great Guns so mischievously against
the Church, and with which constantly in Prayers time they
would not fail to make their Hellish disturbance, by shooting
against and battering the Church, in so much that sometimes
a Cannon Bullet has come in at the windows, and bounc'd
about from Pillar to Pillar, (even like some Furious Fiend,
or Evil Spirit) backwards and forwards, and all manner of
side-ways, as it has happened to meet with square or round
Opposition amongst the Pillars, in its Returns or Rebounds,
untill its Force has been quite spent.

And here there is one thing most eminently remarkable
and well worth noting, which was, That in all the whole
time of the Siege, there was not any one Person (that I
could hear of) did (in the Church) receive the least Harm
by any of their Devillish Canon Shot: And I verily believe,
there were constantly many more then [than] a thousand
Persons at That Service every Sunday, during the whole
Time of that Siege.

One incident connected with the mining of St. Mary's
Tower remains to be recorded.[41] After the Dissolution this tower
had been the depository of the records of the religious houses of
northern England; in 1644 they were 'remaining [there] in
sundry large Chests.'[42] Before the siege, Roger Dodsworth, the
Yorkshire antiquary,[43] had been busy in the tower transcribing
hundreds of the documents which were soon to be scattered far
and wide. Joseph Hunter[44] says Dodsworth was working there
in 1635 and 1636, his labours being made possible because of an
annuity of £40 which Sir Thomas Fairfax gave him.[45] He seems
also to have been there in 1639.[46] Many of the documents are
known only through Dodsworth's transcripts, the originals
having been burnt or lost. These transcripts, consisting of 16
folio and quarto volumes, came into the possession of Sir Thomas

Fairfax who presented them to the Bodleian Library, Oxford, where they are now.

Soon after the explosion some intrepid folk searched the ruins to recover what manuscripts they could, spurred on, according to Roger Dodsworth,[47] by the offer of a reward from Sir Thomas. One of these searchers was Thomas Tomson who recovered no less than thirty bundles. He was described as

> extremo mortis periculo . . . . homo integerrimus maximam eorum partem ad Archiva publica Archiepisc. Ebor. adduxisset [= a man of the highest integrity who, at the utmost peril of his life, returned the greatest part of them to the public archives of the Archbishop of York].

Dodsworth and Charles Fairfax of Menston, an uncle of Sir Thomas, were themselves searching in the rubble on 1 September 1644[84].

The documents retrieved by Thomas Tomson did not remain in the Archbishop's 'public archives.' The story of their subsequent wanderings and of the original depositing of all these documents in St. Mary's Tower forms the substance of two long articles in the *Yorkshire Archaeological Journal*.[49]

Two documents from the explosion, showing signs of burning and other damage, have found their way into the Minster Library. Both are mediaeval cartularies of St. Mary's Abbey, York. One[50] has this note written on the inside front cover :–

> Decembr. ye 13th 1698.
>
> This Register of ye lands formerly given by [?generous]ly disposed people to ye Abbey of St. Mary's, York, having passed through Severall hands & at last coming to ye hands of Francis Hildyard Bookseller is by him presented to ye Library of Ye Cathedrall [of] St. Peter's in York as ye fittest Repository for ye same.

The other[51] has this inscription in gilt on the outside front cover :–

> J: Lewis / A. M. de Margate / in Com. Cant.[52]

and this on the outside of the back cover :–

> Bibliothecae / S[anc]ti Petri / Ebor. d[ono]. d[edit] / 1743.

It is curious that none of the contemporary tracts relating to the blowing up of the tower mentions the destruction and collection of these documents. In one (quoted earlier, p. 67) Ashe and Goode do refer to people searching in the ruins on the day after the explosion but they are described as trying to rescue victims trapped in the debris.

An echo of the explosion was heard in a law case in York as late as eighty years after the siege. In a tithe dispute, dated 1727, concerning '3 acres of meadow at the Bowtham [Bootham] end of Clifton'[53] the following passage occurs :—

> The defendant was alleged to have attempted to take advantage of the loss of records during the siege of York. The tower where many records of estates in and about the City were kept was blown up and burned; the houses in Clifton near the said 3 acres of land, the houses where Mr. Oxlier lived and all the houses on that side of the City were blown up and demolished or plundered; Alderman Robinson's records were lost (being one of the King's party he was obliged to abscond and was plundered and his home rifled by the Parliament army); the owners of the lands in question had suffered the loss of their documents.

[1] Wedgwood, p. 332, errs in stating it was Bootham Bar that was mined on this occasion.

[2] No guns were mounted on the Minster during the siege and consequently it was never a military objective. But see further p. 77.

[3] There are now two bowling greens in use — the Exhibition Green and that of the Museum Gardens — which must be on, or near, the site of the 17th century one.

[4] p. 166.

[5] p. 60. If 'at' is interpreted as 'near' this statement is correct.

[6] p. 631.

[7] pp. 57–9.

[8] p. 394.

[9] p. 241.

[10] Quoted in Bernard, p. 189a.

[11] p. 147.

[12] pp. 108 and 109.

[13] More specifically Lieutenant General Laurence Crawford, a Scotsman, and one of Manchester's divisional commanders who commanded this sector of the leaguer. *Short Memorial*, p. 394.

[14] Slingsby, p. 108 — '. . . . rais'd a battery against ye mannor Wall yt [that] ly'd to ye orchard.'

[15] p. 109.

16 *Ibid.*
17 p. 147.
18 p. 107.
19 Slingsby, p. 109.
20 The Duchess of Newcastle (Newcastle, p. 72) implies that her husband, the Marquis, led the soldiers of the garrison in person. This is unlikely. Her account of the episode is coloured, biased and quite untrustworthy.
21 According to *Weekly Account* (25 June) Captain Hackworth 'an Irishman' and 'Lt. Col. Berry' (Hildyard's 'Brearey' and *Carmen's* 'Brierus') were also killed in this action. Biron and Huddlestone were both buried in the Minster on the day following their deaths (see p. 133) while Brearey was buried in the cemetery adjoining St. John's Church, Ousebridge on 22 June (see p. 135).
22 Hildyard, pp. 57–8.
23 Lead bullets, doubtless fired by the garrison at this juncture in the attack, were extracted from the *interior* face of the Manor Wall in 1937 and presented to the Yorkshire Museum. (YPSR for 1937, p. 34, no. 11).
24 The figures of the casualties as given by Ashe in *Intelligence* No. 5. differ from these. See pp. 64-6.
25 *Intelligence* No. 4. The tract concludes with this paragraph:–

> Although we desire to be truly sensible of any check received by divine Providence, and to bewalle Christianly the shedding of mans blood by violence: yet God doth, and will, we hope, carry us above all difficulties and discouragements, in the maintenance of that good cause, wherein we appeare, both for sacred and civill Liberties.

26 p. 166.
27 Markham, p. 148, states that Lendal Postern was used but gives no authority.
28 Slingsby, Douglas, Rushworth, Hildyard and Drake pass no judgement.
29 In a letter addressed to the Committee of Both Kingdoms eight days before the explosion, the Earl of Manchester had written — 'We are on all sides very near the town walls, and I hope within a few hours Sir James Lumsden [responsible for the mine under Walmgate Bar] and myself will have our mines ready, if not hindered by the tempestuous rainy weather.' (*CSP. Dom.*, p. 217, dated 8 June).
30 *Short Memorial*, p. 394.
31 Baillie, pp. 195–6. Dated 'End of June 1644.'
32 *CSP. Dom.*, 1644, pp. 241–2. Dated 16 June, York.
33 *CSP. Dom.*, 1644, p. 246. Dated 18 June, 'Leaguer before York.'
34 *CSP. Dom.*, 1644, p. 246. Dated 18 June. 'At 4 a.m. Leaguer before York.'
35 *CSP. Ven.*, p. 114. Dated 8 July 1644.
36 *CSP. Dom.*, p. 519. Dated 20 September 1644.
37 *Intelligence* No. 5.
38 Listed in R. Davies, *A Memoir of the York Press .... in the sixteenth, seventeenth, and eighteenth centuries.* Nichols & Sons, Westminster, 1868, p. 69. no. xxvii. Davies adds this note about it — 'This sermon was most probably the latest production of Stephen Bulkley's press during his then residence at York.'

39 *Musick's Monument,* pp. 18–20.
40 David Leslie. 'David Lesley' above is, of course, incorrect. The Earl of Leven was Alexander Lesley.
41 Bernard, p. 189a, and Drake, preface and p. 575, are the chief authorities.
42 *The life of that learned antiquary, Sir William Dugdale, Kt* .... *Published from an original manuscript* [written by (?) himself] 1719, p. 21. Bernard, p. 189a, says they were in *diversis cistulis* [=several chests].
43 For his life see DNB; Jos. Hunter, *Three Catalogues* .... *of the Dodsworth Manuscripts in the Bodleian Library* .... 1838, pp. 59–79; *Yorkshire Deeds* vii, ed C. T. Clay (YAS Record Series, lxxxiii, 1932), pp. x-xi.
44 *Op. cit.,* p. 73.
45 *The Life of that learned antiquary* . . ., 1719, p. 24.
46 Bernard, p. 190a.
47 *Monasticon Boreale* i ms. 7 (MS. in Bodleian Library, Oxford). Quoted in Bernard, p. 189a and Drake, p. 575, n(h). Cf. Anthony Wood, *Athenae Oxonienses* ii (1692), col. 696.
48 J. Hunter, *Three Catalogues* .... *of the Dodsworth Manuscripts in the Bodleian Library,* 1838, pp. 73–4.
49 Vol. xlii Pts. 166 (1968) and 167 (1969).
50 G. R. C. Davis, *Mediaeval Cartularies of Great Britain,* 1958, no. 1101.
51 Davis, *op. cit.,* no. 1103.
52 John Lewis (1675–1747) was an antiquarian and religious controversialist, who became vicar of the church of St. John the Baptist, Margate in 1705. His biography appears in DNB.
53 *Deeds of the Manor of Clifton.* Unpublished MS. in York Public Library. M. 31.

Chapter Six

THE FORTNIGHT BEFORE MARSTON MOOR

AFTER THE ASSAULT on the Manor there were no more major episodes connected with the siege until the arrival of Prince Rupert with his relieving force on 1 July. The besiegers were dispirited after their failure of 16 June and illness seems to have been rife among them, while the expectation of Rupert's coming caused a rise in confidence amongst those inside the city.[1] Baillie[2] sums up the situation thus :–

> . . . . the unhappiness of our countreymen, Major Crawford's precipitation, in springing a myne by himselfe, and assaulting his alone, and losse upon it, had so discouraged all the rest of the armie, that they could not be brought to storme any more. Very many of our Scotts sojours were fallen sick; and, to bring our dangers to the topp, Prince Rupert, above all men's expectations, had brought over the hills of Lancashire, a very strong armie, both in horse and foot, eight thousand horse at least, and ten [thousand] of foote; these were marching directlie to Yorke. Within it [the city of Yorke], it is thought, were six thousand good sojours, very many gentlemen and officers.

Lord Fairfax in the following extract from a letter[3] addressed to the Committee of Both Kingdoms and dated 18 June (at four in the morning!) draws attention to other difficulties facing the besieging armies.

> I must solicit you for a speedy supply of gunpowder, match, and bullet for my own and the Scotch armies in very large proportions, otherwise the service of these armies will be much retarded, contrary to our desires and your expectations. For my own particular I must intreat a supply of muskets, pistols, and carbines, concerning which I have often written. I am necessitated still to move you to acquaint the Parliament with my want of money, for my men are like to mutiny and many run away, who I cannot in justice punish having nothing to pay them withall, while Manchester's men are very well

paid, and a considerable supply furnished to the Scott's army. I beseech you to consider what it is to have [the command of] an army and nothing to give them, while joined with other armies that are well paid. The pay of my army comes to 15,000 *l.* a month, and I have received only 10,000 *l.* for these four months past at the least. I endeavour to struggle against all difficulties whatsoever to carry on this work, not doubting but that your Lordships and the two Houses will take the condition of my army into your speedy consideration.

It is ironical to find that only a fortnight earlier (on 2 June) Parliamentarian intelligence was informed by one of its 'scouts' outside York that 'The soldiers in the leaguer are in very good condition and wanting nothing' ![4]

Because of the relative inaction on both sides during this period it is not surprising that contemporary authorities have little or nothing to say about the siege. The Royalist Slingsby gives most details; five entries in his diary — quoted below — relate to this period. A few others occur, notably in the diary of Robert Douglas, the Scottish chaplain to the Earl of Leven. Slingsby wrote[5] :–

> .... sallyes we made few or none, having only middlegate [Micklegate] barr open, & a little sally port at Munk [Monk] barr, where we once made a sally out against Manchester's men.

From other sources[6] we learn that this sally took place on Monday 24 June at about four in the morning and that it consisted of what is described as 'a commanded party' of about 600 men which 'furiously assaulted' Manchester's leaguer. After a 'sharp conflict' it was driven back into the city after suffering at least 40 casualties (about 20 slain and the same number taken prisoner) and inflicting only two or three on the besiegers. On Plate XXIV is shown a plan of Monk Bar[7] before the barbican was removed, which shows a sally port on the west side, doubtless the one used on this occasion.

Douglas,[8] says that 26 June was kept as a fast day by the Parliamentarian armies. In his diary, against this date, he also made this entry — 'Wind miln, all the great shop assayed to be burnt but not effected,' the meaning of which is obscure.

Apparently anxiety was beginning to be felt by the Royalists concerning their stock of provisions in the city: Slingsby[9] commented :–

.... but our provisions still wast'd & would have an end without we had releife.

It was the hope of such relief from Prince Rupert that buoyed up the spirits of the garrison. It is clear, however, that the siege was maintained so tightly that little news of what was happening in the outside world got into the city. In order to obtain this the garrison sent out a band of men (apparently horsemen) to try and get through the encircling armies and take news to the Prince : Slingsby[10] is again our informant :–

.... therefore my L[or]d [Newcastle] would make tryall to send to ye prince to inform him of ye condition ye town was in; he chuseth out 8 undertakes to go to ye prince & either pass ye Scouts undescern'd, or else break thro' ym [them], but all or most of these were taken; we made fires upon ye minster w[hi]ch answer's us again from Pomphret [Pontefract], but a messanger could hardly pass. They kept so strict guards, as I could not get any either in ye night, or day, to go to Red House & bring me back word how my children did, but were taken either going or coming.

The first incident described here may have taken place earlier in the siege. Slingsby gives very few dates in his account and it is evident that the events he relates are not necessarily recorded in chronological order. Douglas[11] has an entry in his diary which almost certainly refers to the same episode which would put it earlier than anything described in this chapter :–

13th June.   9 horsemen break out betweene Akham [Acomb] and Dringhouses, 6 of them taken, 2 killed, 1 escapes.

The Earl of Manchester, writing to the Committee of Both Kingdoms, confirms the signalling system which Slingsby mentions :–

.... these last two nights they [the Royalists inside the city] made fires upon the top of the Minster, and have been answered with like signals from Pontefract.[12]

Slingsby's home was at the Red House at Nun Monkton only six miles north-west of York. The implication is that during the earlier part of the siege he had been able to keep in touch with his family there through messengers ; now the encirclement of the city was so tight that this was impossible.

It is now time to turn to Prince Rupert[13] and outline the decisive part which he and his army (estimated at about 8,000

77

foot and 6,500 cavalry at Marston Moor) was to play in the events in and around York during the next few days. After considerable hesitation the King ordered the Prince to move his army from the vicinity of Oxford and advance northwards. On 16 May Rupert left Shrewsbury and marched via the west side of the Pennines through Chester and Knutsford into Lancashire. Parliamentarian strongholds such as Stockport (25 May), Manchester, Bolton and Liverpool (11 June) were stormed and captured, Preston capitulated without a fight, Wigan and Lathom Hall, staunchly Royalist, gave enthusiastic welcomes to their deliverers.

The reasons for taking this route and for the comparative leisureliness of the campaign are varied. Rupert wanted to ensure that he had a conquered Lancashire behind him before he struck eastwards to York. He wanted a north-western port which could be a link with Ireland. He augmented his army with new recruits, especially cavalry, which before his arrival were scattered over a large area of the north. He concentrated, organised and trained his forces for the trial ahead. Finally, the timidity of the King was perhaps the dominant factor. He hesitated to throw against the numerically superior Parliamentarian armies around York the only really effective force which remained under his command. It was not until 18 June, when Rupert was resting at Lathom Hall that he decided that he had the King's mandate to march on York. The Prince advanced over the Pennines via Skipton which he reached on 26 June. On 29 June he slept in Denton Hall in Wharfedale, Sir Thomas Fairfax's own house! The next day he was at Knaresborough, only 14 miles west of his objective.[14] By sending forward some of his cavalry to Skip Bridge (over the River Nidd), four miles west of York (and less than a mile from the battlefield of Marston Moor) Rupert convinced the Parliamentarian commanders that he intended to make a direct assault on the city from that direction. To block his approach they raised the siege, concentrating their forces in, and around, the villages of Long Marston, Tockwith and Hessay. Manchester's army crossed the Ouse by the bridge of boats in the Poppleton/Clifton area (see p. 36) and Fairfax by that in the Fulford/Middlethorpe area (see pp. 34–5). By failing to destroy the former they made it

PLATE IX

St. Mary's Tower 1970. Following the explosion of 1644, the demolished walls were rebuilt slightly smaller.

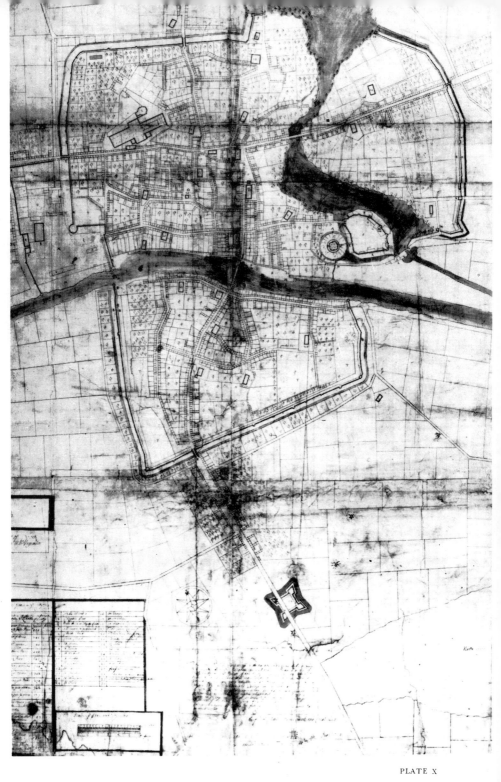

PLATE X

James Archer's Plan of York of *circa* 1682.
Note: The Mount Sconce is at the bottom centre.

possible for the Prince to use it to get his own army across the river on the morning of 2 July, the day of the battle of Marston Moor.

But Rupert did not advance directly to York. In fact, by a brilliantly executed manoeuvre, 'more daringly conceived even than the relief of Newark,'[15] he moved the rest of his army via Boroughbridge (to cross the Ure) and Thornton Bridge (to cross the Swale)[16] down the east (or left) bank of the Ouse, so that on the evening of 1 July it was somewhere in the Skelton/Rawcliffe/Clifton area, only a few miles north of York. Rupert is quite explicit about this :—[17]

> Julye 1.   Munday. quarter[e]d all night in Galres [Galtres] woode.
> York seige reysed [raised]: and theyr boate bridge gayned,
> over the Ouse.

If Slingsby[18] is to be trusted, the garrison was not aware of Prince Rupert's arrival in the immediate vicinity of the city until the dawn of Monday, 1 July, the day after the besiegers raised the siege,[19] and then only because the sentinels of the garrison, who had every night talked to those of the enemy, received no replies to their pleasantries ! Slingsby describes the incident :—

> . . . . but at last he whom we so long look'd for was heard of coming to our releif: not so beleiv'd but yt [that] we were still in some doubt, till we perceiv'd ye Scots had drawn off their guards, w[hi]ch our Centinells gave us notice of; mistrusting it by reason their Centinells had given over talking w[i]th ym [them] & would not answer wh[en] they call'd to ym [them] as usually they had done.

Slingsby[21] goes on to explain in some detail how Sir James Dudley, who was in command of the Walmgate Bar sector of the defences, sent a small body over the walls to investigate what had happened to the besiegers ; how more followed them ; how they found the besiegers' huts deserted ; how a body of Royalist horse under a Major Constable advanced down the York–Selby road until, near Fulford, they encountered a body of enemy cavalry apparently covering the passage of Fairfax's army across the Ouse ; how a skirmish ensued in which there were casualties on both sides including an unmarried Parliamentarian Cornet and a Royalist Captain named Squire. His actual words are these :—

S[i]r James Dudl[e]y yt [that] command'd at Waingate [Walmgate] barr, sends out over ye Wall 12 foot men & as many horsemen, w[hi]ch they might lead over an earth work att ye end of ye stone wall yt [that] is towards ye Castle Mills,[22] to discover w[ha]t became of ye enemy. W[he]n these went, there was no stay, but all ye Troop would go, & a great many more of ye foot: they find their Hutts empty, their horse command'd by Major Constable advanceth further towards fowlforth [Fulford]; about half ye way distance they perceiv'd some horse in ye Town, & presently ye trump[e]t sounds to charge. Our horse was forc'd to stand, yt [that] our foot might ye better retreat to ye walls, & stays so long till they were forc'd to charge, & presently mingl'd one w[it]h another; in this charge they took some of ours prisoners, & we kill'd a Cornett of theirs wh[i]ch they said should have marry'd S[i]r Tho[mas] Notclift [Norcliffe] his sister, & they shot Capt. Squire a Yorkman in ye back. Thus they part'd, we to our Gar[r]ison & they to their Randevous on Knapton Moor, where all of ym [them] meet, & for hast[e] had lost a boat load of shoes and other provisions w[hi]ch they could not carry away.[23]

Soon after his arrival in the vicinity of York the Prince received this effusive letter[24] from the Marquis of Newcastle :—

> You are welcome, Sir, so many several ways, as it is beyond my arithmetic to number, but this I know, you are the Redeemer of the North and the Saviour of the Crown. Your name, Sir, hath terrified three great Generals and they fly before it. It seems their design is not to meet Your Highness for I believe they have got a river between you and them but they are so newly gone as there is no certainty at all of them or their intentions, neither can I resolve since I am made of nothing but thankfulness and obedience to Your Highness's commands.

Writers on the siege differ as to whether Prince Rupert entered York in person on this evening or during the night[25] and also as to whether he actually passed through the city in his passage to Marston Moor on the morning of the battle (2 July). Terry[26] has summarised this evidence. It is now generally accepted that Rupert did not enter the city but — as he specifically states in his *Journal* in the passage quoted on p. 79 — spent the night somewhere in what is vaguely called the Forest of Galtres, sending on ahead his chief of cavalry, General George Goring, to present his compliments to the Marquis of Newcastle and to order the latter to be ready to march against the enemy at four o'clock the next morning. But at dawn the next day Newcastle and his troops did not appear and the Prince 'not wishing to lose the chance of attacking his opponents while they were still baffled by his movements'[27] took his army over the bridge of boats captured the previous evening and marched towards the enemies' rendezvous on Marston Moor. Cholmley[28] says that the Prince had got the whole of his army across the river by 4 a.m. Slingsby and Stockdale supply some details as to how this was done. The former wrote :—[29]

> The prince now [the evening of 1 July] was come w[i]thin 3 or 4 miles of York, upon ye forest side, & sends in to my L[or]d of Newcastle, to meet him w[i]th those forces he had in York; & it was upon ye 2d of July 1644 w[he]n my L[or]d march'd out w[i]th all those forces he had, leaving only in ye town Coll. Bellasyse Regiment. S[i]r Thos. Glemham's Regiment, & my own w[hi]ch was ye Citty Regiment. The prince pass'd over at Poppleton where ye Scots had made a bridge of boats. & follows ye Scots in ye rear, who were now upon their march towards Marston, & in so much hast[e] as if they meant to march clear away; ye prince follows on & makes an hault at Marston town.

Stockdale[30] said :—

> . . . . and in his march by Popleton hee there surprised a bridge made of botes by the Earle of Manchesters order, who had left a Regiment of dragooners to guard it, intending it for a pass for our [Parliamentarian] Armyes to the North side of Ouse, in case the enemy should come that way; but the enemy coming suddenly upon the guard beat them away & seized upon the bridge, and then quartered his army thereabouts, not suffering them to goe to Yorke, yet keeping it in his power to enter thither with his whole army when it should be to his advantage, and to give and receive supplyes from thence as there should bee cause.
> . . . . about 9 a clock in the morning [on 2 July, the day of the battle of Marston Moor] they discovered that the enemy [i.e. Royalists] had drawne over a great part of their army by the bridge they surprised the night before, and by a foord neare to it.

When Prince Rupert's advance troops reached Marston Moor and made contact with the enemy, the Parliamentarians were strung out from the Long Marston area to near Tadcaster. The events which followed relate more particularly to the story of the battle of Marston Moor than to the siege of York, and consequently, are not dealt with here. One point should, however, be noted as it has some bearing on the siege and its resumption after the battle. Rupert did not take all his artillery to the Moor on the morning of 2 July. Ogden[31] describes the cannon lost by the Prince after the battle 'which hee carryed into the field' as '4 or 5 midling brasse pieces' but adds that 'the great and the little pieces with the grosse of his carriage were left safe in Yorke.' Later, writing of the renewal of the siege after 4 July, he says that 'Yorke salutes them [the besieging armies] with 3 peeces of ordnance w[hi]ch they never heard before.'

While Rupert was massing his army on the battlefield events in York had taken an unhappy, and indeed an ugly, turn.

> Newcastle, on receiving Rupert's order, had — as always when he thought himself slighted — announced his intention of resigning. The Scots professional, Lord Eythin, had personal reasons for disliking Rupert. Six years before, when the Prince had been taken prisoner in a skirmish at Vlotho on the Weser, Eythin had been in command and had been criticised for abandoning Rupert to his fate. Over the years his resentment of this criticism had grown; he ministered to Newcastle's anger and with culpable irresponsibility stirred up the irritation of the soldiers in York which it should have been his business to allay. He said, in the hearing of many, that he did not think the men should be expected to march until they had at least received all their arrears of pay. The opinion soon became a general mutter in the camp; many of the men believed that Eythin had positively commanded them not to march. By two o'clock in the morning, there was a general mutiny; they would not move a step.[32]

Eventually the Royalist garrison — with the exception of the three regiments mentioned earlier[33] which were left behind to guard the city — was marched out to Marston Moor. But it was not until 4 o'clock in the afternoon that they and their commander, the Marquis of Newcastle, had been allocated their positions on the field of battle. By that time, the initiative, originally with Prince Rupert, had passed to the Parliamentarians with the disastrous and fatal results to the King's cause which the next few hours were to show. Many of the regiments comprising the original York garrison, especially the famous Whitecoats, were to be decimated.

---

[1] Against the date 28 June, Douglas, p. 60, mentions another episode which, while not directly relating to the siege of York, must have had a depressing effect on the besiegers when they heard of it:– 'Enemies horse from Pomfred [Pontefract] Castle, rescue 40 prisoners out of Carwood [Cawood], whereof 2 Colonells and one Lieutenant Colonel.' This incident is also mentioned in *Exact and Certaine News.*

2 p. 200.

3 *CSP. Dom.*, p. 246. Cf. *Parliaments of Scotland*, p. 99.

4 HMC Luke, p. 661 no. 144.

5 pp. 109–110.   [*News*.

6 Rushworth, p. 631; Drake, p. 166; *Intelligence* No. 5 and *Exact and Certaine*

7 After T. P. Cooper, *York — the Story of its Walls, Bars and Castles*, Elliott Stock, London, 1904, facing p. 282.

8 p. 60.

9 pp. 109–110.

10 p. 110.

11 p. 60. Wedgwood (p. 332) — presumably using this as her authority — embellishes it somewhat thus:– 'Nine volunteers had been separately despatched to slip through the enemy lines; *one only reached him* [Prince Rupert]' (my italics). I have been unable to find any evidence that the one surviving messenger actually reached the Prince.

12 *CSP. Dom.*, p. 246, dated 18 June.

13 For a detailed account of Prince Rupert's movements during the six weeks before his appearance before York see C. V. Wedgwood, 'Prince Rupert's Campaign of 1644' *Geographical Magazine*, July 1944, pp. 136–8.

14 See, *inter alia, Intelligence* No. 5; Cholmley, p. 347.

15 Wedgwood, p. 333.

16 Stockdale, p. 73.

17 *Journal*, p. 737.

18 pp. 110–1.

19 Cholmley implies that the besiegers quitted what he calls their 'trenches' early on 1 July but states that it was not 'till about noon that day Captain Leg brought news of the Prince's approach.'

20 pp. 110–1.

21 pp. 111–2.

22 At the present time there is a distance of some 30 yards between Fishergate Tower and the River Foss. If this gap existed in 1644 — and we do not know the river level as compared with today, though Gent (p. 224) says that the Spring tides at York were 'above Five Foot' in 1644 — it would have been necessary to block it up with some form of earthwork; it is probably this to which Slingsby refers. (Markham, p. 150 — quoting no authority — says that this squadron from the garrison went out through Fishergate Postern which conflicts with what Slingsby has to say).

23 Ogden, p. 71, is clearly referring to these self-same events in this passage:–

> Whyle the Prince [Rupert] was towards the Enemy [i.e., crossing the Ouse by the bridge of boats north of the city] the Marquesse went out to Fayrefax his tents, and there found foure thousand payre of boots and shoes, 3 morter pieces, some ammunition, and other carriage.

Perhaps the boots formed part of the cargo brought up to York by the *Deliverance* of London (see p. 22).

[24] *Pythouse Papers*, p. 19. Quoted in Wedgwood, p. 334.

[25] Warburton, p. 442, for instance says — 'Rupert at the head of two thousand cavalry, dashed into York.' Wedgwood, *Geographical Magazine*, July 1944, p. 138 accepted that version. Now (*The King's War*, 1958, p. 335) she has rejected it.

[26] p. 229, footnote.

[27] Wedgwood, p. 335.

[28] p. 347.

[29] p. 112. Cf. *Parliaments of Scotland*, p. 105.

[30] pp. 73–4.

[31] pp. 71–2.

[32] Wedgwood, pp. 336–7, where the authorities are quoted; Cholmley, p. 347, is the authority for the 'mutiny.'

[33] Slingsby, p. 112; see p. 81.

Chapter Seven

THE CAPITULATION

THE NIGHT THAT FOLLOWED the Royalist defeat at Marston Moor, that of 2/3 July, was one of horror and anxiety for the citizens of York. All night long the wounded and dispirited soldiers, who had managed to escape slaughter or capture on the battlefield and during the retreat, wended their way back to seek refuge and succour behind the city walls. *Full Relation* says that the 'fore troopes' of the victorious armies 'did execution to the very walls of Yorke,' while Stockdale,[1] a Parliamentarian, wrote :–

> And at this second charge our men performed their duty with such resolution and courage as they utterly routed the enemyes army, and chased them into the gates of Yorke as many as could escape; and all this performed before 12 a clock in the night, the moone with her light helping something the darknes of the season . . . After the battell our men pursued the enemy neare Yorke.

More Exact Relation expressed it thus — '[chased] them within a mile of Yorke, cutting them downe so that their dead bodies lay three miles in length.' According to Ogden :–[2]

> [Prince Rupert] came into Yorke alone about 11 o'clocke at night: glad were his friends to see him there: and his gentlemen came dropping in one by one, not knowing but marvelling, and doubting what fortune might befall one another.

Micklegate Bar was thronged with soldiers clamouring for admission, it being on the west side of the city and so nearest to the approach roads from Marston Moor, the present Rufforth/ Acomb/Holgate (the modern B 1224) and the Boroughbridge/ Skip Bridge/Holgate (the modern A 59) roads. According to Slingsby those inside the city tried ' discriminate between those

85

who had constituted part of the original garrison, and the new-comers who had arrived the previous day with Prince Rupert, allowing only the garrison to enter. He wrote :—[3]

> We came late to York, w[hi]ch made a great confusion: for at ye barr none was suffer'd to come in but such as were of ye town, so yt [that] ye whole street was throng'd up to ye barr with wound'd & lame people, w[hi]ch made a pitiful cry among ym [them].

However, it is clear that the remnants of Rupert's army were eventually admitted, for the following morning, after (according to Ashe[4]) 'warme words'[5] had passed between Rupert and the Marquis of Newcastle 'after their Rout; they charging each other, with the cause thereof.'

> The Prince ye next morning march'd out w[i]th ye remaining horse,[6] & as many of his footmen as he could force, leaving ye rest in York . . . .
>
> The prince marches out of Munck [Monk] barr, & so Northwards towards Richmond,[7] where he meets w[i]th Coll. Clavering [the Duke of Montrose], w[i]th some forces coming towards him.[8]

The Marquis of Newcastle, Lord Eythin, Lord Widdrington 'and twenty more of good ranke'[9] went to Scarborough, where they took ship for Hamburg. Newcastle did not return to England until after the Restoration. His authority was delegated to Sir Thomas Glemham who combined the commands of Colonel-General of the Northern Army with that of Governor of York (before Marston Moor Newcastle had held the former command and Glemham the latter). Glemham and his staff (of whom Sir Henry Slingsby, the author of the *Diary*, was one) made valiant efforts to restore some sort of order out of the chaos resulting from the disaster on the Moor. Those of Rupert's forces left behind in York were, according to Slingsby[10] 'entertain'd into several Regiments, as well to have them to do duty as to provide for them Quarter and billet.' Inevitably morale was low, and as the siege was not resumed immediately by the Parliamentarian armies, some people took advantage of the opportunity to leave the city.

> Thus we were left at York out of all hope of releif, ye town much distract'd, & everyone ready to abandon her: & to encourage ym [them] yt [that] were left in ye town, & to get ym [them] to stay, they were fain to give out false reports, yt [that] ye prince had fallen upon ye enemy suddenly &

86

rout'd ym [them], & yt [that] he was coming back again to ye Town; yet many left us, not liking to abide another siege.[11]

Those inside the walls had taken the opportunity provided by the raising of the siege to re-provision the city. *A Particular List* says that on, and after, 1 July 'the Citizens much rejoyced and sallyed forth and hunted about, and got in Provision; but many of the Countrey people tooke it very heavily' and on the day after the allied armies had renewed the siege some of the Parliamentarian soldiers 'drove away 60 Cattle close from under the walls.' Ogden[12] says that when the Prince retreated northwards he left 'Yorke well provided w[i]th men, victuals and ammunition.'

Of the wounded who came back into the city after the battle of Marston Moor only a few are known by name. One was Lord Grandison who was immediately put 'under the Surgeons hand in York.'[13] He died a few days later. Another was John Dolben who, forty years later, was to return to the city as Archbishop (1683–6). In 1643, as a student at Christ Church, Oxford, he joined the Royal army :—

.... he rapidly rose to the rank of Ensign, and accompanied the army in its march to join the forces of Prince Rupert and the Marquis of Newcastle in the North. In the rout of the Royalists at Marston Moor .... whilst carrying the colours he was dangerously wounded in the shoulder by a musket ball. But his youth and good constitution served him well, and he was soon able to take part with the Royalists in the defence of York. During the siege he received a severe wound in the thigh, which broke the bone, and confined him to his bed for a year. For his bravery on these two occasions he was promoted to be Captain and Major in succession; but he did not wear his military honours long, for in 1646 the King's cause was lost, his army disbanded, and Major Dolben, exchanging his helmet and cuirass for cap and gown, returned to his studies at Christ Church.[14]

On his death in 1686 he was buried in York Minster in the south choir aisle against one of the arches of the crypt, and a marble monument was erected to his memory by his widow. It is still there and shows his reclining figure, robed and mitred (Plate XXI). It has a long Latin inscription, of which the following three lines refer to his activities at Marston Moor and in the siege :—

.... exardente Bello Civili partes regias secutus est, in pugna Marstonensi vexilliarus in defensione Eboraci graviter vulneratus, effuso sanguine consecravit locum olim morti suae destinatum.

[When the Civil War broke out he followed the Royalists, carrying the colours at Marston Moor. Severely wounded in the defence of York, he consecrated the place with his blood, long before marked out for his death.]

His portrait hangs in Bishopthorpe Palace and is reproduced on Plate XX.

Some of the dead of Marston Moor escaped mass burial there. Slingsby[15] records that there

.... I lost a Nephew, Coll. John Fenwick, & a kinsman, S[i]r Chas. Slingsby, both of ym [them] slain in ye field; ye former could not be found to have his body brought off, ye latter was found & buri'd in York minster.[16]

It is impossible to imagine Royalists carrying a dead body off the battlefield with pursuers at their heels, and the presumption is that in the forty-eight hours after the battle some arrangements were made by which the bodies of 'gentle folk' could be identified, handed over to their relatives and given honourable burial.

The Parliamentarian armies resumed the siege on Thursday 4 July,[17] taking up their old quarters around the city. Slingsby[18] thought the delay was caused by

.... ye enemy taking a few days respite to bury their dead, to provide for ye wound'd, & to gather up such scatter'd troops of foot & horse as had left ye feild, (for by this time their Generals were return'd).

This is confirmed by Douglas[19] who records :–

That night [i.e., 2 July] we stayed on the fieldes all night; on the morrow I viewed the dead; we keeped the fields all that day.

During the battle on the Moor, according to Douglas,[20] Lord Leven had fled as far as 'Bredford' [Bradford] and Fairfax as far as 'Carwood' [Cawood]. Manchester also left the field of battle but if Ashe is to be trusted, was back again at his post by 11 p.m., i.e. within an hour of the victory being won.[21] In this tract Ashe goes on to say that 'very few of the Common Souldiers, did eat above the quantity of a penny loafe, from Tuesday till Saturday morning; and had no beere at all.' Drake[22] — Royalist in sympathy — considered the delay due to other factors :–

Dissensions amongst the northern generals of the parliament's side, were very considerable both before and after the battle.[23] The Scots, according to their custom, wanted to be marching home with their booty, and they had another reason, for the Marquis of Montross [Montrose] had

88

already lighted a flame in their country which the parliament at Edenborough [Edinburgh] could not extinguish. Then such quantities of provisions had been thrown into the town, that they had little stomach to the renewing of the siege, till the certain intelligence of the king's two generals [i.e., Newcastle and King] abrupt and final departure so far reconciled them, that where nothing else could, they, after two days, returned to their posts before the city.

On 4 July when the siege was resumed, the city was summoned to surrender 'about seven of the clocke [in the evening] . . . but the Governour, Sir Thomas Glenin [Glemham], answered, he could not render up on such absolute termes'[24] Ogden[25] says, 'They sum[m]oned the City to yeeld within 6 houres, but they set them at defyance and S[i]r Tho[mas] Glemham sent the Prince word that hee would keepe it to the last man.'[26] Warburton[27] prints this letter and incorrectly dates it to 4 *June* (my italics) and so ascribes it to an earlier phase in the siege when it makes no sense. The letter reads :–

> May it please Your Highness,
> This afternoon, about one of the clock, the enemy's van marched from their quarter at Long Marston to Middlethorp, the rest of their army follows. The three generals have sent a letter directed to me and my Lord Mayor to deliver them up the town in six hours, or else I must expect all extremities of war. I shall not obey their summons, but keep it for the King as long as I possibly can. I thought it my duty to acquaint your Highness with it, not doubting, but your Highness will take us into your consideration to hasten for the relief of
> Your Highness's most affectionate & humble servant
> Thomas Glemham
> York, the 4th of July, 1644,
> at five in the afternoon.

Douglas[28] records :–

> Batteries were made, cannons planted, ladders brought.[29] After all were in readiness, the battery on our quarter shot down a tour [tower]. After, one was yet sent in desyring them to render, then they desyred a parley.

The Scots 'quarter' stretched from Lendal to Baile Hill and the tower 'shot down' must have been somewhere in this sector. It is possible that it was the so-called Sadler Tower in the corner of the defences at Toft Green. In March 1645, eight months after the siege was over and when the Parliamentarian garrison under the command of Lord Fairfax was in possession of the city, many of the defences which had been damaged or destroyed during the siege were hastily repaired to withstand an anticipated Royalist attack. These included 'a platt forme for a peece of Ordnance and a Guard house on Toft Greene . . . neere the corner of the Tower att Toft Greene'[30]

Slingsby[31] gives a more detailed account of the preparations of the Parliamentarians for the renewal of the siege. He says that new batteries were erected

> One between Waingate [Walmgate] barr & Laterne [Layerthorpe] Posterne, & another upon ye hill in Bishops feilds; & had made a bridge to clap over ye Fosse and store of Hurdles for a storme, where by ye Laterne [Layerthorpe] Posterne it was most easy, having nothing but ye ditch, w[i]th drought[32] almost dry, for to hinder their entrance.

Once it was evident that no further relief could be expected from Prince Rupert the garrison had nothing to hope for but honourable surrender. Its greatest weakness was in man-power. *Full Relation* says that there were not '500 fighting men in the Towne, besides the Citizens' and alleges that the Royalists had 'quitted their great Fort[33] for want of men to maintaine it.' *True Relation* gives a somewhat higher figure — there were 'not one thousand mercinaries in the City besides the City Regiments.' Stockdale[34] says that 'S[i]r Thomas Glemham [was left] with some small force in the Citty.'

By Thursday 11 July the Parliamentarian armies were ready to storm the city 'having made near approaches to the Wals of York, and having raised batteries, whereby was made some execution, we were busie in preparing Ladders, and other instruments, for the storming of the Town.'[35] According to Douglas[36] a last appeal was made to the garrison, probably on that very day,[37] to surrender: the offer was accepted and 'they desyred a parley.' Ashe's statement[38] — 'Hereupon a treaty being desired by the enemy' — does not exclude the possibility that the parley was, in fact, initiated by the besiegers. As a result, on Saturday, 13 July, in the morning, Sir William Constable and Colonel Lambert were 'sent by the Lord Fairfax' into York after hostages had been sent out of the city for their 'securitie and safe return'[39]. After spending the whole day in discussion the two envoys returned with a request to the three generals that Commissioners be appointed and authorised 'to treat and conclude upon Articles for the peaceable surrender of the Citie.'[40]

> Our three Generalls having demanded the judgement of some Ministers, whether the work of Treaty, might be approved on the Lords day, and receiving incouragement[41] they appointed the Lord Humby, Sir William Constable and Colonell Mountague,[42] to go the next day into the Town, three Hostages being sent out of the Town for their securitie: They continued their debate till Munday,[43] about noon they returned; with the Articles to be subscribed by the Generals.[44]

An anonymous letter from 'a trustie Gentleman' in the Scottish army besieging York to 'another Noble and Honourable Lord, in the Kingdom of Scotland'[45] gives further details of this incident :—

> My Lord,
>   At our coming before Yorke yesterday, the towne was summoned to render to our Generall by a trumpeter. We had this day a fair answere from Sir Thomas Glenning [Glemham] and the Mair [Mayor] of the citie Master Cowper [Cooper], which was neither a grant nor a refusall. But we hope since the Prince hath left them with a small bodie of horse, and our whole cavaliers is in pursuit of him, and that the Marquess of Newcastle, with our country-man King, and all their good officers are gone, they will shortly accept of quarters; for as we understand and by certaine intelligencers from the town, this day they have not five hundred souldiers[46] in the town, beside the traine bands and the burgars [burghers]: so if they render not upon our quarter, which we heartily wish, to prevent more blood, we intend, by Gods assistance, to take it by storme. Wee were certainly informed from one which came out of the town today, that the Prince brought scarce in with him to the toune of his foot (confessed by Sir Charles Lewcas [Lucas] to be twelve thousand) not five hundreth, but were either killed or run away. The Papists and Bishops, and their [ac]complices, have all left the town bag and baggadge.

The statement quoted earlier from *Intelligence* No. 6 to the effect that Sir William Constable and Colonel Lambert were sent into the city '*by the Lord Fairfax*' (my italics) to parley over the surrender is worthy of comment. In writing his report of what was happening before York, Ashe is clearly drawing particular attention to this fact, otherwise he would not have troubled to mention it as the reader would naturally assume that the two envoys had gone into the city on the authority of either the three generals acting in concert or on that of Leven as the senior commander present. Two unpublished entries in the York

'Corporation Housebooks'[47] seem to afford an explanation. The first of these mentions 'The former Letter of summons sent by the three Generals Leven, Fairfax and Manchester' and either relates to the letter sent into the City on 4 July or to the later one received on either 12 July or the day before. This seems to have been followed by a private letter from Fairfax, presumably with the connivance and approval of the other two generals. Fairfax's letter — as much as the summons — seems to have been the reason for calling together a meeting of the Common Council and 'the best Cittyzens.' The fact that it was 'well liked' suggests that it was moderate in tone. Presumably Fairfax was acting as an intermediary between the generals on the one hand and the Lord Mayor and Citizens, Governor and Garrison on the other. The citizens in particular were doubtless anxious and fearful of the fate likely to befall them if the garrison capitulated. It was here that Fairfax, who knew the city and its leading citizens so well, could do much to allay the anxieties and pave the way for a sympathetic solution. That the city realised what they owed to Fairfax for their lenient treatment and safe delivery is made clear in the second of the 'Housebook' extracts referred to. The reference to Fairfax's 'great love and affection' rings out as a heartfelt tribute from the city to one who had steered it safely through a situation fraught with many and great dangers. Fairfax was nominated as Governor of the city after the capitulation and here again the citizens owed much to his moderation, sympathy and understanding, because as far as can be ascertained, no violent reprisals were taken against the defeated Royalists there. The presentation of the sack and French wine took place nine days after the city surrendered; the Articles of Surrender as entered in the 'Housebook' are dated 15 July, but as they follow on naturally and in the same handwriting as the entry dated 25 July recording the presentation, they were obviously entered up at that time.

York owes a great debt of gratitude to the Fairfax family in connection with the siege: to Sir Thomas for ensuring that Roger Dodsworth was able to make transcripts of most of the monastic records stored in St. Mary's Tower before they were destroyed or damaged when the tower was blown up (pp. 70–2);

to Sir Thomas and Lord Fairfax for preserving the Minster from damage (p. 118): to Lord Fairfax for the clemency he showed at the surrender (pp. 91–2), for the understanding and moderation with which he brought both sides together when the final capitulation was negotiated, and for the tact and sympathy with which he governed the city after its surrender until his death in 1646. This gratitude to Lord Fairfax has never been better expressed than by James Torre who, in 1719, addressed this dedication in his *Antiquities of York City* . . . to 'Robert Fairfax; Alderman of the City of York.' The significance of what he says will be better appreciated when it is remembered that Torre was himself a Royalist.

> To publish the Antiquities of the City of York, without some Acknowledgement how Propitious Your Name and Family has been to this Ancient City, would be injurious and ungrateful to its Benefactors: That generous and tender regard of the then Lord Fairfax (altho' at that time in a detestable Rebellion against his Sovereign) to the Preservation of that Ancient and most Magnificent Structure the Cathedral of this City, when he Commanded the Parliament Army at the Seige of it, by making it Death to level a Gun against it, notwithstanding it was then a Refuge and Shelter to the Loyal Citizens who defended it against Him, and his saving the City, as well as its Cathedral, from being made a Heap of Rubbish, ought always to be remembered with due Respect.

Writing nineteen years earlier Samuel Gale[48] had this to say :–

> S[i]r Thomas Fairfax (then Generall of the Rebells) after he had beseidged and taken the Cittie (which had been valiantly defended three weeks (*sic*) by S[i]r Thomas Glemham) Strictly and Rigorously forbad the Souldiers to lay hands upon any thing in the Church though they did steal Brass from several of the Gravestones, and also Defac'd some Images, particularly one of the Virgin Mary between the Chapter House Doors. This was an Honourable and Noble Act in the General.

In 1932 the twelfth Lord Fairfax commemorated his ancestors' services to the city by erecting a tablet in the Chapter House of the Minster: it is reproduced on Plate XXII.

The following are the terms on which the city was surrendered.

> *Articles agreed upon between Alexander Earle of Leven, Generall of the Scottish Forces, Ferdinando Lord Fairfax, and the Earle of Manchester, Generalls of the English Forces about Yorke on the one part, and Sir Thomas Glenham [Glemham] Knight, Governour of the City of Yorke and Collonell*

Generall of the Northerne Army, of the other part Anent the surrender, and delivery of the said City, with the Forts, Townes (sic)[50] *Cannon, Ammunition, and furniture of Warre belonging thereto, in manner after specified to the said Generalls, for the use of King and Parliament, the* 15 *day of July,* 1644.

1. The said Sir Thomas, as Governour of the said Citie, shall surrender and deliver up the same, with the Forts, Tower, Cannon, Ammunition, and furniture of Warre[51] belonging thereunto, betweene this and the sixteenth of July instant, at our [or] about the 11 houre thereof in the forenoone, to the said Generals or any in their names for the use aforesaid, in manner, and upon the condition after written.

2. That the Governour, and all Officers and Souldiers, both Horse and Foot, the Governours, Officers and Souldiers of Cliffords-Tower, the Officers and Souldiers of the Sconce, the Officers and Souldiers belonging to the traine and outworkes, shall march out of the City on Horse-back & with their Armes, flying Colours, Drums, (comma *sic*) beating Matches lighted on both ends, Bullets in their mouths, and withall their bag and baggage, that every souldier shall have 12 charges of Powder.

3. That the Officers and Souldiers shall not march above ten miles a day, that they have accommodation of Quarter and convenience of carriages that a Troop of Horse out of every of the three Armies, shall attend upon them for their convoy in their march, that no injurie or affront be offered them to Skipton, or the next Garrison Towne within sixteene miles of the Princes Army.

4. That such Officers and Souldiers as are sicke and hurt and cannot march out of the Towne, shall have liberty to stay within untill they be recovered, and then shall have passage given them to goe into the Princes Army, where ever it shall be, or to their owne houses and estates, where they may rest quiet, or whither else they shall please. That it may be recommended to my Lord Fairfax for their subsistence during their cure or being ill.

5. All Officers and Souldiers wives, children and servants, now in Towne, may have libertie to goe along with their husbands, or to them, or if they please to returne to their owne houses and estates, to enjoy them under such contributions as the rest of the Country payes, that they may have libertie to carrie with them their goods, and have a convenient time and carriages allowed to carrie them away.

6. That no Officer or Souldier shall be stopt or plundered upon his march.

7. That no man shall intice any Officer or Soldior as he marches out of the Towne with any promises of preferment or reward, or any other grounds whatsoever.

8. That the Citizens and Inhabitants may enjoy all their priviledges which formerly they did at the beginning of these troubles, and may have freedom of trade both by Land and Sea, paying such duties and customes as all other Cities and Towns under the obedience of King and Parliament.

PLATE XI

Clifford's Tower, 1970.

PLATE XII

Clifford's Tower, as it was before 1684.   Engraved by William H. Toms after a drawing by Francis Place.

9. That the Garrison that shall be placed here, shall be two parts of three at the least of Yorkshire men, and no free quarter shall be put upon any without his owne consent, and that the Armies shall not enter the City.

10. That in all charges, the Citizens resident and inhabitants shall bear such part with the Country at large as was formerly used in all other Assesements.

11. That all Citizens, Gentlemen, and Residents, Sojourners, and every other person within the City, shall at any time when they please have free liberty to move themselves, their families and goods, and to dispose thereof, and of their Estate at their pleasure, according to the Law of the Land, either to live at their owne houses or elsewhere, and to enjoy their Goods and Estates without molestation, and to have protection and safeguard for that purpose, so that they may rest quietly at their aboad [abode], and to travell freely and safely about their occasions, and for their better removall, they shall be furnished with carriages, paying for their carriages reasonable rates.

12. That all those Gentlemen and others whatsoever that have Goods within the Citie, and are absent themselves, may have free liberty to take, carry away, and dispose of those Goods, as in the last Article.

13. That no building be defaced, nor any plundering, nor taking of any mans person, or of any part of his Estate, and that Justice, according to Law, within the Citie shall be administred in all cases by the Magistrates, and be assisted there if need be by the Garrison.

14. That all persons whose dwellings are in the City, though now absent, may have the benefit of these Articles, as if they were present in the City.

By the Articles of Agreement touching the Rendition of the City of Yorke.
    The Generals of the Armies have treated as Generals in reference onely to themselves and their Souldiers, and it was not intended to intrench upon any Ordinances of Parliament, but all such persons and estates as were subject to Sequestrations, might still be liable and subject thereto, notwithstanding any generall words in the Articles.
    And thus these Generals doe declare under their hands, and the Commissioners of the Treaty doe declare, That they did severall times during the Treaty expresse to the other Commissioners, that they had no order to meddle with any Ordinance of Parliament, or to goe further then [than] the bounds of the Army. Subscribed by

The Lord Fairfax	Sir Adam Hepborne [Hepburn]
The Earle of Manchester	Lord Humby
	Sir William Constable

The three generals informed the Committee of Both Kingdoms of their success in these words :—

This is to acquaint you that the city of York is now reduced to the obedience of the King and Parliament, and was upon the 16th instant surrendered to us by treaty; a copy of the conditions you shall herewith receive, into which we were moved to condescend, not out of any diffidence of our own power through God's assistance by storm to have gained it, but out of our earnest care to preserve a city so considerable and to avoid the effusion of Christian blood, forseeing that the effects of a forcible assault could be no other than the destruction of the City of York and the ruin of the innocent with the guilty in it. The Marquis of Newcastle's army being now reduced to nothing and Prince Rupert's forces being much weakened.[52]

Ashe[53] comments in a similar strain upon the leniency of the terms :—

> If any upon the perusall of those Articles, do imagine that too much favour was granted to the enemy, we desire that this may be considered for their satisfaction. That the benefit which could be expected for our Armies, or the Kingdom, by taking the Town by storm, could not possibly in any measure counterveil the miserable consequences thereof, to many thousands. Who knows how much precious blood might have been spilt upon so hot a service? How few in the Town could have preserved their houses and shops from spoyl, if more than 20 thousand Souldiers had broken in upon them with heat and violence? How much would this County have suffered in the ruines of this Citie? And how many of our good friends in other places who drive Trades with Citizens here, would have been pintched [pinched] in their estates, by the impoverishing of their Debtors?

On 16 July the garrison marched out of the city. To Slingsby,[54] one of those who departed, it was an humiliating occasion :—

> Thus disconsolate we march, forc'd to leave our Country, unless we would apostate, not daring to see mine own house, nor take a farewell of my Children, altho' we lay the first night at Hessey [Hessay] within 2 miles of my home.

Ashe[55] records the event thus :—

> Upon Tuesday the enemy went out of the Town, according to Articles, our Souldiers were set on both sides the way, where they were to passe, for the space of a mile from Micklegate: and the Officers according to command, went from place to place, to prevent the doing of any wrong to the enemies, as they marched a way. That morning very early, as I should have told you before, all the Souldiers in the Royall Fort, which is a curious and strong work, possessed with needlesse fear, did run away, and left their arms behinde them.
>
> The fourth part of them, at least, who marched out of the Town were women, many very poor in their apparell, and others in better fashion. Most of the men had filled, and distempered themselves with drink; the number of the Souldiers, as we conjectured, was not above a thousand, besides the sick and wounded persons.

No other account of the curious episode connected with the so-called 'Royall Fort' has come down to us. This fort was clearly the sconce built about 500 yards out of Micklegate Bar on the highest part of The Mount, roughly at the junction of what is now Dalton Terrace and The Mount (see further pp. 144–5). This fort, built by the garrison as one of the outworks in its defences, remained in Royalist hands throughout the siege. According to the *Articles of Surrender*, it was to be handed over to the besiegers on 16 July. The garrison seems to have panicked before this was formally effected; perhaps because the terms of surrender had not been made clear to them and they thought they were going to be left behind as prisoners.

> When the enemies were departed, our three Generalls went together into the Citie,[56] attended with many of their Officers. The first house they entered was the Minster-Church, where a Psalm was sung and thanks given unto God by Master Robert Duglas [Douglas], Chaplain to the Lord Leven, for the giving of that Citie into our hands, upon such easie terms; at which time notice was given, that Thursday after should be kept by the whole Army, as a day of thanksgiving for that great mercy, which accordingly was observed,[57]

Douglas[58] in his diary describes his part in the day's events thus :–

> They rendred the city about 12 a clock, they were marching till 6 a clock; at that time the 3 Generalls marched with a great traine to the minster; they desyred me to pray, and intimat the thanksgiving for the great victorie to be upon the 18 day [i.e., 18th July]. I went to the pulpit, and first exhorted out of the 60 Psalm, 9 verse[59]; then, 1. A Question, 2. An answer, urged upon God by the people. 3. An earnest prayer for help. 4. A declaration of confidence in tyme coming; after that a prayer; after the prayer a psalme. Then an exhortation to the souldiers to abstain from sin and injuring the inhabitants; after all the blessing.

Douglas[60] then refers to the services held on the Thanksgiving Day fixed for 18 July. He himself preached in the morning to the text Psalm 12, verse 8,[61] while in the afternoon he says that 'Mr. Someone, Manchers [Manchester's] minister' preached to the text Psalm 68, verse 20.[62] The 'Mr. Someone' was either Simeon Ashe or William Goode.

Ashe[63] gives this short description of the city at the time of its surrender :–

I might here take occasion to tell you the ruines which our eyes saw in al suburbs of the Cittie, all the houses in some streets being burnt and broken downe to the ground by the enemies, whereof heretofore I gave some intelligence. It is judged that an hundred thousand pounds will not re-edifie and repaire the buildings demolished by them, who as Lords possessed the Towne, and opposed our entrance, besides the breaches made in the walls, and elsewhere by our Cannons.

Through the long siege the Town was unhealthfull, we found and left many sick of the spotted Fever.

Another near-contemporary who mentions the decayed state of the city is Sir Thomas Widdrington in his *Analecta Eboracensia*. This was written *c.* 1660.[64] Sir Thomas was Recorder of York during the reign of Charles I and the Commonwealth, and M.P. for the City in the Parliaments of 1654, 1656 and 1660. He had this to say :–

There were also several streets, and many good houses without the other three gates of the city, that is to say, Monkgate, Walmgate, and Micklegate, but these all being of late years destroyed by fire, in time of war, there is hardly left any footsteps of them.

The city corporation replied to Sir Thomas's request that they should publish his work at their cost in a remarkable letter which Caine prints in the introduction to the *Analecta*.[65] While many of the reasons for the decay in York were due to long term factors which had nothing directly to do with the siege, the effects of the latter — particularly the destruction of the suburbs — are referred to in this extract :–

Trade is decayed, the river become unnavigable by reason of shelves . . . . the subburbs, which were the legs of the city, are cut off . . . . As for our wealth, it is reduced to a narrow scantling; if we look upon the fabric and materials of the city, we have lost the suburbs which were our skirts, our whole body is in weakness and distemper, our merchandise and trade, our nerves and sinews, are weakened and become very mean and inconsiderable.

One matter connected with the surrender remains to be considered. Articles 3 and 6 of the terms of surrender guaranteed the garrison against 'injurie or affront' during their journey to Skipton 'or the next Garrison Towne within sixteene miles of the Princes Army.' 'Upon these Articles' says Slingsby[66] 'we march out, but find a failing in ye performance at ye very first, for ye soulgier was pilleg'd, our Wagons plunder'd, mine ye first day, and others ye next.' Douglas[67] refers briefly to the incident, saying that Manchester's and Fairfax's cavalry were involved but 'no Scotsman.'[68] Ashe [69] had a great deal to say on the matter, so that, to quote his own words, 'the truth of that business may be rightly understood.' 'The Horse-quarters of my Lord of Manchester' which he mentions in the first paragraph stretched, as far as can be ascertained, from about Wetherby to Pontefract and/or Wakefield.

In their march through the Horse-quarters of my Lord of Manchester, the day after they went from Yorke, some of the Troopers rememb[e]ring how they had been pillaged at Newark of all they had, contrary to agreement, fell upon their Carts and Waggons, and pillaged them very deeply, taking away both cloathes, plate, and some moneys, which when some of our Officers had notice of, they presently rode from their quarters and restrained them.

This miscarriage which casts dishonour upon us, and hath been an occasion of much griefe to my noble Lord, and to many others, was occasioned through negligence of the officers, who were appointed to publish the agreement through the army, that the enemies goods should be protected from violence, but had not done it. And one reason of that omission may be in regard of the shortnesse of time from the sealing of the Articles by the Generalls, and the marching out of the enemy: the one being about Munday noon, and the other to be eleven a clock next day, and our horse quarters lying dispersedly many miles distant. Upon examination of the businesse, the Troopers do all plead ignorance of the agreement, which (if true) may in some measure lessen the offence. These things comming the next day after to the knowledge of the three Generalls, they were all filled with indignation against such unworthy carriages, abominating and being ashamed of breach of faith (even with enemies) though formerly and false and unfaithfull in their covenants. Hereupon my noble Lord (whose soule abhorred the thoughts of this wickednesse, being contrary to his profession and disposition), sent commands to Lieutenant generall Cromwell, and some other officers of horse, presently to sit and make diligent enquiries who were the actors and confederates in so horrid a crime, to the end that not only restitution might be made of the goods so plundered, but also that the offenders might be punished according to their deserts. These Gentlemen sate divers days in the pursuance of his Lordships commands; and upon examination they found divers Troopers deeply guilty, some whereof they committed to the Provost Marshall, others (upon their Captains engagements for their forth-coming) enjoyed libertie for the present; they causing to be delivered in to them all the goods they had so taken. A perfect return of which proceedings being made to my Lord, his Honour resolved for better finding out of the rest of the goods unjustly taken, & that full restitution of them (if possible) might be made, was

99

pleased to command this ensuing Declaration to be published in the head of everie Troop of Horse under his command.

The Declaration Iuly 25. 1644.

Being informed that divers Souldiers and Troopers under my command, did plunder divers Waggons and Carriages belonging to the enemy when they came out of Yorke, and were by the Generalls articuled with to have safe conduct for their Persons, Arms and Baggage. And forasmuch as endeavours having been used to discover in whose hands the goods so plundered are, the successe is without any considerable effect hitherto. I doe hereby declare, that if any person who hath a hand in this action, so much to be abhorred by all honest men, (being a breach of faith, which being once given, ought by all professing Christianitie inviolably to be observed) and shall, out of a true remorse for their offence, within two dayes after publication hereof, bring into the hands of the severall Captaines respectively of his or their said Troops, to which he or they belongs, all such money, plate, Horse, Armes, or other goodes so taken as aforesaid, they shall be freed from punishment for such his or their offence. But if any Trooper or other Souldier shall through obstinacie wickedly detain any of the things before mentioned, beyond the time hereby limited for the same to be brought in, or shall not at least acquaint his Captain, Lieutenant, or other Officer, with his resolution, so to do (in case the said goods be not now in his or their hands, and by reason thereof cannot be restored within the time appointed,) The said person or persons so offending, shall expect no favour or mercy at all, but the uttermost severitie, being death by the Articles of Warre, published by his Excellencie the Earle of Essex in that behalfe.

Given under my hand the 25 of July, 1644.

Manchester.

This being duly executed, his Lordship was pleased on Thursday the 25. of July to appoint a councell of war of select field Officers, and some others, for making further inquiry into the matter, as well for finding out who were further faulty herein; as for proceeding against them with greatest severity, according to the rules of war;

The names of the Officers appointed for this purpose

Lieutenant Generall Cromwell President	Major John Alford
Generall Major Crawford	Major Gabriel Holmes
Col. Vermndon (*sic*) Quarter-Mr Generall	Major Henry Ireton
	Major William Hamilton
Col. John Pickering	Major George Mountgomery
Lieutenant Col. Nathaniel Rich	Major John Jubbs
Lieutenant Col. John Dayns	Captain James Burye, and
Lieutenant Col. Edward Whalley	Mr. John Weaver Advocate
Lieutenant Col. Henry Warner	

All whom they find guilty in having a hand in the crime, do confidently profess they never heard that it was part of the agreement with the enemy, that they should march away with their baggage, or be protected through our Army, which had they known, they would not have committed this violence for the greatest advantage. And divers of these Troopers are known to be so honest and conscionable, as their Captains do affirm (who are men likewise of unquestionable integrity) that they believe they would not have touched one peniworth of goods in that kind, had they known the same to have been prohibited.

And they further say, in their own defence (which also is seconded by the report of standers by) that many of the enemies souldiers themselves set them on to plunder, discovering to them which were Papists waggons and Carts, and incouraged them to pillage them, in which they assisted them, and got their share.

And in further defence of those their actions, they say (and it doth appeare by the testimony of divers honest men) that the Enemy, contrary to the agreement, did carry out in their Waggons, sundry sorts of Armes, which should have been left in the Garrison; and under one Coach was bound (*sic*)[70] five muskets, which the Scots took from them, as they passed through them; if this proove true, the enemy by first violating the agreement, had forfeited their protection. This business is still in agitation, and the result will discover (as is hoped) the conscienciousness and faithfulness of our Officers. This by (*sic*), bad business having occasioned this digression, I return to tell you our removalls from York where we left Generall Leven, who since is marched Southward with his Army, to Wakefield and Leeds, and other Townes adjacent.

On Saturday the 20. of July, my Lord of Manchester advanced Southward to get fresh quarters for his Army, that his souldiers, who had done & indured much in various places and imployments, might receive some rest and refreshings. That night and the Sabbath day, our foot quartered in Tadcaster, and towns thereabouts, and our horse before us toward Pomfret [Pontefract] Castle, a strong Garrison of the enemies.

On 20 July the three Parliamentarian armies 'upon Consultation between the Generals and Parliamentary Commissioners,'[71] 'being heartily tired of one another's company'[72] left York and went their several ways.

Lord Fairfax remained in York but detached a 'thousand Horse into Lancashire, to joyn with the Forces of that County, and of Cheshire and Derbyshire, to attend the motions of Prince Rupert, who was marched that way, and endeavouring to secure the County of York.'[73] As the passage from *Intelligence* No. 6[74] quoted above makes clear, Manchester's and Leven's armies marched out of the city towards Tadcaster where they parted. The foot of the Eastern Association spent that night and the following day — the Sabbath — at Tadcaster 'and towns thereabouts, and our horse [went] before us towards Pomfret [Pontefract] Castle, a strong Garrison of the enemies.' On 23 July they reached Doncaster. The Earl of Leven himself 'stayed the Lords day [21 July] in York.'[75]

Writing to the Committee of Both Kingdoms in London from Ferrybridge the day before he reached Doncaster, the Earl of Manchester painted a dismal picture of the condition of his own and the Scottish armies.[76]

> The great necessities that the Scotch army and mine were in hath caused us to divide our armies and to march into fresh quarters . . .
> My men through want of clothes and other necessities fall sick daily. I hope the Lord will preserve us from any pestilential disease, yet the Scotch army and mine is very much weakened through sickness.

The Scottish army moved first to Leeds and Wakefield and 'other Townes adjacent' and then marched northwards to besiege Newcastle.[77]

Two letters[78] written to the Committee of Estates in Edinburgh (the Scottish equivalent of Parliament) underlines the weakness of the Scottish army when they moved from York. In the first, dated 'York, July 18, 1644,' Leven writes of 'the weakness of the severall regiments of this army, occasioned by much service and very hard usage, since our coming from Scotland,' asks for reinforcements and also 'for seasing and apprehending of all such, as are run away of late, that condigne punishment may be inflicted upon some, and the rest sent to there cullors.'

Lindsay, in a letter[79] dated the following day, touches on yet another problem besetting the army :—

> . . . . absent officers, who contrary to their duety so long desert their charges, that we have thought it absolutely necessary for the good of the service and standing of the army, to desire your lordships to mak proclamation at the mercat croce [market cross] of Edinburgh and all other places needfull, commanding all officers, of what quality soever, to repare into thair severall charges at or before the fifteint day of August next.

Before they separated after the siege the three Parliamentarian generals received requests from numerous individuals for safe conducts. It is clear that many women of all classes had come into York to join their husbands who constituted part of the garrison. They — and in some cases their husbands as well — wanted to return to their homes now the Royalist cause in the north was lost. Although they were guaranteed safe conduct under Article 5 of the terms of surrender, they had no illusions about the dangers that might threaten them on a journey through hostile territory. A safe conduct signed by one, two or three of the Parliamentarian generals might afford them a little protection at least from the troops of the general(s) who had signed it. Here are three examples of such documents :–

(i)[80]

Protection to the Lady Margaret Monckton.

We the Generalls of the Scottish and English Armies for the King and Parliament in Accomplishing of certaine articles concerning the rendition of the Citty of Yorke doe hereby give protection to the Lady Margarett Mounckton of the Citty of Yorke, of freedome from all trouble and damage to her person, estate familie and goods. And therefore wee require and Command all Commanders, Captaines and Souldiers under the Command of Us or any of Us, to forbear to molest or trouble either the person, house, familie, or goods of the said Lady Margarett Mounckton as they will answer the contrary att there perril — And that she, her familie, and goods may passe in safety from place to place according to there occasions without Interruption. Given under our hand att Yorke the fifteenth day of July 1644—
(Signed) Leven

(ii)[81]

Wee the generalls of the Scottish & English armyes for ye Kinge & Parliament in accomplishment of certaine artickles concerninge the rendition of the Citty of York doe hereby give protection to the right worshipfull Mrs Ann Kaye of Denbigh Grainge in the West Riddy [Riding] of the county of York widow, off freedome from all trouble and dainger to her person, family, estate and goods; & therefore wee require and camaund [command] all comaudrs [commanders], captains, officers and souldiers under ye comaund [command] of any of us, to forbeare to molest or trouble the person, family, house or goods of the said Mrs Ann Kaye, as they will answere the contrary at their utmost perills; And herself, family and goods may pass in safetye from place to place accordinge to their occasions without interuption; Given under o[u]r hands and seales at Yorke the nineteeth day of July anno d[o]mi[ni] 1644.
Leven, Fer[dinando] Fairfax, Manchester.

103

Alexander Earle of Leven, Lord Balgorie, Lord Generall of the Scottish Forces &c.

Whereas the bearer Mr. Allane Lawmonth is to repaire to his studies in the University of St. Andrewes in Scotland. These are to will and require all Officers and Souldiers or others whome it may Concerne to suffer him with his servant horse and baggage to pass freely and quietly without trouble or molestation. Given at Middlethorpe the 15th of July 164[4].

Leven

[1] pp. 75–6.

[2] p. 71.

[3] p. 114.

[4] *Intelligence* No. 5.

[5] 'Warmer,' it may be supposed, than the innocuous exchanges reported by Margaret, Duchess of Newcastle (Newcastle, p. 80):–

My lord . . . . went towards York late at night, accompanied only with his brother and one or two of his servants; and coming near the town, met his Highness Prince Rupert, with the Lt.-Gen. of the Army, the Lord Ethyn [Eythin]. His Highness asked my Lord how the business went? To whom he answered, that all was lost and gone on their side.

That night my Lord remained in York.

[6] *True Relation* puts this figure at about 2,000.

[7] *Intelligence* No. 5:– 'Prince Rupert is marched into the Dales, the Mountainous parts of Yorke, to Recru[i]te his broken Armie.'

Full Relation:– 'his Rendezvous was twelve miles on the North side of York, where appeared about fifteene or sixteene hundred horse, and eight hundred foot. Upon Thursday at night he was at Richmond.' Ogden, p. 72,:– 'hee marcht and came the second night being Thursday to Richmond.' Cf. also *CSP. Dom.*, p. 311 (5 July).

[8] Slingsby, p. 114.

[9] *Intelligence* No. 5. Cf. Slingsby, p. 114; *Full Relation; Manifest Truths* and Newcastle, p. 80.

[10] p. 114.

[11] Slingsby, pp. 114–5.

[12] p. 72.

[13] *Intelligence* No. 5 and No. 6; Ogden, p. 71.

[14] Paul Dolben, *John Dolben, Dean of Westminster, Bishop of Rochester, and Archbishop of York. In the Time of Charles the Second. His Life and Character.* E. J. and F. Blackwood, London Street, Reading, 1884. Cf. DNB.

[15] p. 114.

[16] Confirmed in *Register of Burials in York Minster*, p. 236 (see p. 133).

17 Douglas, p. 65; Ogden, p. 72.
18 p. 115.
19 p. 65.
20 *Ibid.*
21 *Intelligence* No. 5.
22 p. 169.
23 But see p. 106 n.[72] further on this.
24 Douglas, p. 65.
25 p. 72.
26 *Full Relation* says that the answer was returned under 'Sir Thomas Glenhams [Glemham's] and the Major [Mayor] of the Townes hands.'
27 p. 433.
28 p. 65.
29 *Full Relation* says that the intention was to 'storme it [the city] once this weeke following' [i.e. on 11 July].
30 YCHB. For the full entries see Appendix II A. Nos. 54 and 58, pp. 169 & 170.
31 p. 115.
32 It is apparent that up to the arrival of Manchester's army before the city (3 June) the late spring of 1644 had been very wet (see p. 32); the reference here to 'drought' suggests that from mid-June the weather changed and dry conditions prevailed.
33 This was the sconce on The Mount. This seems to be a mistake, however, as it was held after this date, see p. 96.
34 p. 76.
35 *Intelligence* No. 6.
36 p. 65.
37 This date seems likely in view of the YCHB entry dated 12 July (see Appendix II A, no. 32, p. 164).
38 *Intelligence* No. 6.
39 *Ibid.*
40 *Intelligence* No. 6.
41 An interesting example of the influence wielded by the preachers in the Parliamentarian armies, comparable to that of political commissars in some modern armies!
42 Douglas, p. 66, has 'My Lord Hum[bie] and Sir Wm——, with Colonell Monticue.'
43 Douglas, p. 66, also comments on the long time taken to draw up the Articles — 'they dealt so near a length of time.'
44 *Intelligence* No. 6.
45 *Historical Fragments relative to Scottish Affairs from 1635 to 1644.* Edinburgh 1833, pp. 45-7.
46 Cf. this figure with that of 'not above a thousand' (p. 96).
47 Cf. Appendix II A, p. 164 nos. 32 and 33.

48 *A breif historicall view of the severall foundations and buildings of the Cathedrall Church of York*, 1700, (York Minster Library, MS Add. 43), pp. 47–8.

49 The text given here is that of the tract *Articles of the Surrender* (Plate XIX). With small grammatical differences the same text is printed in *Intelligence* No 6 and Rushworth, pp. 638–40. The Articles are also entered in the YCHB xxxvi (1638–50) fos. 102b–103 under 25 July 1644.

50 'Towers' is obviously intended.

51 Hildyard, p. 59 (cf. Drake, p. 170) says that 'five and thirty Pieces of Ordnance, three thousand Arms, five Barrels of Powder, and other Ammunition, was yeilded up to the Enemy by the Governour Sir Thomas Glemham, with the Consent of the Lord Mayor and Magistrates.'

52 *CSP. Dom.*, 1644, p. 359. Dated 18 July.

53 *Intelligence* No. 6.

54 p. 116.

55 *Intelligence* No. 6.

56 To the accompaniment of a peal of bells from at least one York Church — that of St. Martin-cum-Gregory in Micklegate. Geo. Benson, 'Churchwardens Accounts of St. Martin-cum-Gregory, York,' vol. i 1560–1670. *Associated Architectural Societies' Reports and Papers*, xxx (1908), pp. 6–7.

57 *Intelligence* No. 6.

58 p. 66.

59 Psalm 60, v. 9 reads — 'Who will bring me into the strong city? who will lead me into Edom?'

60 pp. 66–7.

61 Psalm 12, v. 8 reads — 'The wicked walk on every side, when the vilest men are exalted.'

62 Psalm 68, v. 20 reads — 'He that is our God is the God of Salvation; and unto God the Lord belongs the issues from death.'

63 *Intelligence* No. 6.

64 It was not published until 1897, being edited by Caesar Caine. The passage quoted is on p. 128.

65 pp. x–xi.

66 p. 116.

67 p. 66.

68 The incident is also mentioned in *CSP. Ven.*, p. 123, dated 5 August.

69 *Intelligence* No. 6.

70 While this may be a misprint for 'found', the muskets could, of course, have been tied (bound) underneath the coach.

71 Rushworth, p. 641.

72 Drake, p. 171. Clarendon, *History of the Great Rebellion* viii, p. 73, speaks of the 'irreconcilable differences between the officers and indeed the nations' at this time. Nevertheless, on 10 September 1644, less than two months later, the Committee of Both Kingdoms was quoting the 'example of the three Generals before York' as one to be copied by other Parliamentarian commanders *CSP*

Dom., p. 488) while *Manifest Truths* said 'the siege was carried on with very commendable unanimity, and correspondency of Counsels on all sides, each acting their part.'

73 Rushworth, p. 741.
74 Confirmed by Douglas, p. 67.
75 Douglas, p. 67.
76 *CSP. Dom.*, 1644, p. 366 (22 July).
77 *Intelligence* No. 6; Douglas, p. 67; Rushworth, p. 641; *CSP. Dom.*, 1644, p. 366 (22 July).
78 Thurloe, pp. 39–40. Printed in full in Terry, p. 289. Cf. *Parliaments of Scotland*, p. 99.
79 Thurloe, pp. 39–40. Cf. *Parliaments of Scotland*, p. 145.
80 Monckton Papers, pp. 47–8.
81 *Collectanea Hunteriana*. Extracts from the Collections of John Wilson, Esq., of Bromhead. ii, p. 121. (MS in York Minster Library).
82 YRCP, i, pp. 22–3.

Chapter Eight

MISCELLANEOUS REFERENCES TO THE SIEGE

I. DAMAGE TO THE CITY.

An unpublished history of York written c 1680 and now in the library of Trinity College, Cambridge[1] gives this list of damage done to the city during the siege.

p. 107. 'For the suburb of this city they are neither large, fair nor beautiful, for the most part hurt and distroyed in the late unnaturall warr by the rebells, so that now of three or four fine streets wee have onely some few straggling houses here and there built of late to let us see that in time there may be hopes that she may againe recover her self.'

p. 138. St. Deny's Church. 'It hath a lofty spire in the tower w[hi]ch in the late warr was shot thro' and thro' but received no further damage.'

p. 140. St. George's Church. 'But being ruined in the late warrs it hath never bene rebuilt since.'

p. 146. St. Lawrence's Church. 'This church stands in the suburb without Walmegate barr and was much ruined in the seige here, 1644, and had not bene able to hold up its head untill the year 1669.'

p. 158. St. Nicholas' Church. 'This church situate in the suburb without Walmegate barr was disroffed by those enimies to churches and church government in 1644 at the time of the seige and hath not bene repaired since so that now you have nothing but the walls or outward shape of a curious pyle, as by what remains thereof seems to bespeak of.'

p. 162. St. Sampson's Church. 'It seems the Rebells who layd seige to this city in 1644 mightily stomacked these steeple houses (as they then scornfully termed the most solemne structures set apart for the service of God & his divine worship) by their continuall shooting against them and endeavouring to distroy them. For this church among others was shot thro' and thro' and participated of their impietys as well in as after the seige where they have left us not so much as one tomb, monument, or gravestone.'

The latter incident may be linked with further nearby damage — in Thursday Market, only 50 yds. from St. Sampson's Church. Hildyard[2] has this to say. The inference is that the damage so described was effected by the Parliamentarian battery on Lamel Hill though he does not specifically say so.

> During the Leiguer, the Enemy shot well-nigh forty hot Fiery Bullets out of their Morter-pieces, which Providence so directed, as that most of them were quenched in the River Fosse; onely one, slew a maide in Thursday Market, and a shell of that fell into Master Clerkes the Writing-masters Chamber there, which brake down a Sparr of the House, and cast down a Couple of Ling upon old Mistris Clarke, which knocked her under the Table, being almost fourscore years of age, so that the Table did preserve her from hurt, save onely that there was a Scarr without a Wound.

I. P. Pressley[3] commenting upon this passage says — 'The upper part of the curious structure that used to stand in St. Sampson's Square, was used as a school, sometimes as a theatre, and sometimes as 'Assembly Rooms.' The lower part with its pillars, formed a 'stance' for market women on Thursdays. The ling were the large dried fish used more commonly long ago when fresh fish were more difficult to obtain.'

Keep's information can be expanded and added to from other sources. A number of references, especially in the *Relations* and *Intelligences*, have been noted of the destruction of buildings in the suburbs and elsewhere. Further, the City of York 'House-books' and 'Chamberlain's Accounts'[4] give some indication of the extensive repairs which had to be carried out to the Bars and City Walls during the years immediately following the siege. The barbican of Walmgate Bar, for instance, had to be rebuilt; it bears the date 1648 when this was done. Raine[5] and Markham[6] refer to damage done to St. Deny's Church while the former[7] says that all the mediaeval houses in Lawrence Street were destroyed in the siege. St. Lawrence's Church, mentioned above by Keep, was eventually patched up and remained in use until 1881 when the present church replaced it.[8] Only the tower now remains of the 1644 building. The mediaeval hospital and church of St. Nicholas also in the Walmgate suburb had survived the Reformation and its chapel was later used as a parish church. As Keep says[9] it was so badly damaged as never to be used again. Sir Thomas Fairfax preserved the porch[10] which was afterwards removed to St. Margaret's Church in Walmgate where it still is. Its peal of bells was eventually taken to St. John's Church, Ousebridge. This recital of damage to buildings in the suburb outside Walmgate Bar shows how widespread the destruction was there and how few of the pre-1644 buildings survived the siege. The suburbs outside the other three bars suffered also though not quite so badly. Individual buildings there which are known to have been damaged are considered below.

Ingram's Hospital[11] was so badly damaged that it required extensive rebuilding in 1649.[21] This building also has another connection with the siege as one of its inmates — Jane Hoopes — was made homeless as a result of it.

Under the regulations of the Ingram Charity ten widows were allowed to live in the hospital and were given pensions of £5 a year, paid quarterly. On receiving their pensions they had to sign a receipt, or append their marks if they could not write. One of these receipts is extant, for 25 April 1644 — a day or two after the siege started but before the city was closely beleagured on the Bootham side — and two more for 1645 and 1646 respectively. Whether the widows were actually living in the ruined hospital at these later dates is not clear.

Among the Temple Newsam papers is another[13] which reads :–

To the Right Worshipfull Sir Arthur Ingram Knight.

The humble petition of Jane Hoopes widow humbly sheweth that your peticioner was late wife to Edward Hoopes a Clarke in the Courte before the Counsell at York who dyeing left her very poore but she hath maynteyned her self hitherto by her Hand Labour but being now stricken in yeares is not now able to worke but is like to perish if she be not some wayes provided for for the time to come.

She humbly prayeth your good worship to admitt her to the next place that shall happen in the hospitall and the allowance which your father charitably erected and bestowed to the reliefe of poore aged widdowes.

And your peticioner shall daily pray for your worship.

Your peticioner also doth intreat your worship to take into Consideracon that her estate without the Barr was pulled downe and burnt in the siege time.

Her 'estate' may, of course, have been outside any one of the four

THE
NON-PAREIL,
OR, THE
VERTUOUS DAUGHTER,
SURMOUNTING
ALL HER SISTERS:
Described,
In a Funerall Sermon upon the Death of that
vertuous Lady, ELIZABETH HOYLE, late wife of
the Worshipfull Thomas Hoyle, Alderman of the
City of Yorke.

By that godly and Reverend Divine,
Mr. JOHN BIRCHALL,
late Pastor of the Church of St. Martins in Micklegate.

*The righteous shall be had in everlasting remem-
brance, but the memoriall of the wicked shall
rot.*

YORK:
Printed by Tho: Broad dwelling in Stone-gate over
against the Starre. 1644.

A
SERMON
PREACHED IN THE
Metropoliticall Church of York, up-
on the 19. Day of May, being the fourth
Sunday after Easter last,

BY
WILLIAM RANSON, Vicar
of Barton upon Humber,

BEFORE
HIS EXCELLENCIE
The MARQVES of Newcastle,
Lord Generall, &c.

And Published by his Speciall Command.

Printed at York by Stephen Bulkley,
1 6 4 4:

PLATE XIII

Title pages of two sermons printed in York in 1644.

General Leslie.

PLATE XIV

Alexander Leslie, 1st Earl of Leven,   Artist unknown.

PLATE XV

1. Damage caused during the siege to the Roman Wall near the Multangular Tower.

2. South-East Prospect of York from close to the site of the battery on Lamel Hill.
Artists Samuel and Nathaniel Buck.

PLATE XVI

Wooden settle in the Star Inn, Harome, near Helmsley. Dated 1651.

bars. Her name does not appear in the receipts for 1645 and 1646 but it does appear on one dated 11 October 1653 when she signs by a mark. As she is not named in the next one dated 6 April 1655 the presumption is that she was then dead.

The Grammar School of St. Peter. At the Reformation this school was housed in what remained of St. Mary's Hospital in the Horsefair off Gillygate. This was burned in the siege though part of it remained standing till 1667 when Archbishop Neale instructed the Dean and Chapter 'that the school house in the Horse Fair demolished in the late warre be re-edifyed and the fine taken for a lease of the same.'[14]

The church of St. Maurice just outside Monk Bar was badly damaged and the houses near it burned down.[15] Agar's Hospital which was in the same suburb was also burned down.[16] Layerthorpe Bridge was broken down and remained impassable until April 1646 when the corporation ordered that planks should be laid across the broken part 'for foote passengers to passe that way.'[17]

St. Catherine's Almshouse which stood on the Mount, opposite what is now the end of Scarcroft Road, was rebuilt in 1652. This was probably necessitated by damage during the siege.[18]

St. Olave's Church. The pamphlet guide[19] to this church asserts that the tower was damaged by the bursting of a Parliamentarian (sic) gun mounted on it. No authority is quoted though Drake[20] was probably intended; he says that the roof of the church was damaged through supporting a platform of guns during the siege. According to Caesar Caine[21] this was a Parliamentarian battery and he quotes as his source a letter[22] dated 12 June 1644, from Sir Henry Vane the elder. The relevant passage reads :—

> The three generals before Yorke have possessed themselves of thrice of the gatis [gates] of the cittie the mannor and abbey church uppon the topp of which they planted a batterie, they have also taken all the hills round about the toune that are within cannon shott and have made batteries, so as it is considered the toune wilbee taken this weeke, if itt bee not all reatie.

It is quite impossible to believe that a Parliamentarian battery could have been mounted on St. Olave's as this church actually constituted a short sector in the perimeter of the Royalist defences and was less than 100 yds from St. Mary's Tower. A *Royalist* battery on this church would however have been both logical and useful. The information as handed on by Caine must be inaccurate. A possible explanation is as follows. The letter noted above was probably written by Sir Henry Vane in London who was passing on, in garbled form, news he had received from York. This news could have come from his son and namesake who was a regular and copious correspondent. The younger man is known to have visited the Parliamentarian armies outside York on 9 June. He might have written to his father the following day about a battery on, or near, some other church (? St. Lawrence's). Equally, the father might have obtained the information from a pamphlet. *Exact Relation* mentions in its title 'the taking of the King's Mannor house' and refers to a battery at St. Lawrence's Church. This was published on 12 June and the elder Vane could have written the letter from which this extract is taken after superficially scanning it.

Breach in wall near Multangular Tower.

In a paper published in the *Philosophical Transactions* of the Royal Society of London[23] Martin Lister, who practised medicine in York 1670 – 1683 established the fact that the Multangular Tower and the adjacent wall were Roman. In it he included a drawing with this caption — 'Mediaeval Wall on Roman Wall and Angle Tower shewing breach during the Siege.' Benson[24] reproduces this: it is included in this present work as Plate XV. No other contemporary or near-contemporary documents have been found which mention any incident in the siege which can be linked with this particular 'breach.' A battery mounted on Holgate Hill, 1,300 yds. distant, would seem the most likely one to effect such damage.

Heworth Hall.

Mary Ward (1585–1645) was a Roman Catholic and the founder of the teaching order of nuns called the Institute of the Blessed Virgin Mary.[25] This order still flourishes and now has 57 houses in various parts of the world including the Bar Convent in York. Mary Ward spent most of her life on the Continent but returned to England in 1642 and, in the next year, moved into Heworth Hall two miles east of York with her followers. On her death (30 January, 1645) one of these wrote an account of her life entitled 'Brief Relation.' This was circulated among her followers on the Continent and, in addition to a 17th century English version, others in French and Italian have survived. The English 'Brief Relation' has never been published. It contains interesting references to the siege of York.

When York was invested by the Parliamentarian armies Mary Ward and her ladies moved inside the city walls for protection, and after the garrison surrendered they moved back to Heworth Hall. Mary Ward died there six months later. The passages in the 'Brief Relation' relating to these episodes are printed below :—[26]

.... When York came to be besieged .... it could not resist, seeing the apprehension and fears of those about her, she said 'Fear not! we will have our recourse to God and His Angels and Saints, They will help us, we will place St. Michael at one end of the village [of Heworth] and St. Joseph at the other, and put the power of the great cannons and pieces on the Sacred Name of Jesus which will keep them from hurting.' The effects of these her devotions were apparent by the protection of herself and hers with all belonging to them as also in the village that with the shot of five hundred cannons bullets that were found besides those that were lost in the water and other hidden places, and thirty grenades only two men were killed.

Her inclination was far more to have remained at Heworth than to go into York, and did not stir till the enemy was camped before the town, when the persuasion of friends was so strong as she not to seem particular or temerarious left herself and followed the common opinion. When being to remove must pass the enemies' scouts and troops who pillaged all they laid hands on. While they were robbing of others, and searching them to the very skin, her servants passed by with pots and beds on their backs and heads (for men or horses durst not venture) without a word or whatsoever the least interruption. The like blessing she found during her stay in the town, and in her return back to Hewarth [Heworth] when York was taken by the Parliamentaries. One may conceive part of her sufferance in that siege, when but briefly is considered her so great infirmity as to be either in bed, on bed, or in a little chair rocked so as to get some little rest and ease of the great pains of the stone that she suffered deprived of all kind of fresh or free air which of the human was her chiefest livelihood. Yet she, as it were, so much lady and mistress of herself and sufferance, as to give life and courage not only to her own family but to all sorts of persons that came to visit her. Many would say 'they came to her as dead and lost, with her revived, and went away with courage.' Nor did she this in a severe saintly way, but with such a human manner, as made each one not only capable to do it, but ashamed to do other.

When the town was already rendered, and all that could, as the greatest happiness, prepared and hastened to go with the King his army to their garisons, (which was one of the conditions agreed upon at the yielding up of the town), our dearest mother not only for her infirmity which she suffered was made incapable to do the same but forth of a great feeling that she had that so was the best, resolved to stay and therefore persuaded other friends to do the same. Which was so far from human conceit as none could believe it, but to their cost afterwards proved, and by word and letter expressed with sad repentance. When one of her own said 'What will become of us?' 'Well, I warrant you' said she 'I am assured God will help me and mine, wherever we are' and in another occasion, saying 'We must be content' she replied 'Nay, we will be content.' Notwithstanding all these feelings of her own, and her great desire to return to Hewarth, did so far condescend to others as to inform herself of all the garrisons what convenience and security there was for herself and family but found there was none, and that her first inclination carried to what was best, and so returned to her former habitation of Hewarth which was in an ill condition to receive her, all the lead off the house all the iron from the windows and doors, full of stink and vermin, four hundred soldiers besides the sick having lodged therein. But what was very remarkable was that God should please to put as it were, a defence so powerful that the rooms that had been employed for the Chapel and our dear mother her chamber, were both left neat and clean, not so much as the mats on the floor hurt. In the garden they had buried diverse of their soldiers, the whole air so infected as in the whole village there were not three well, all that was delightful taken away, the lovely trees cut down, the garden unpaled and wholly ruinated. In this manner the blessed servant of God returned joyful, content and satisfied . . . .

'Chimney . . . beaten down'

In his book *Memorials of the Civil War*[27] R. Bell quotes Dr. P. du Moulin, Rector of Wheldrake, whose MS formed part of his source material — 'To pay my vow I first made this book which was begun at York during the siege in a room whose chimney was beaten down by the canon while I was at work.'

(2) WINDOW IN THE GUILDHALL

In 1942 the 15th century Guildhall of York was badly damaged in a German air-raid. It was rebuilt in 1960. The east window was reglazed by Mr John Harvey, a local craftsman, to designs prepared by the late Dean of York (Eric Milner-White).

These designs depict some of the outstanding personalities and events connected with the history of York. One of the figures is that of Sir Thomas Fairfax and one of the scenes is representative of the siege of 1644.

(3) MAYOR OF BEVERLEY

In 1644 Robert Manbie, the Royalist Mayor of Beverley, seized the town's mace, the regalia and 'diverse soomes of moonie out of the publique treasurie' and fled with them to York. After the capture of York Manbie was dismissed from his office and the regalia returned to Beverley.[28]

(4) THE OLD STARRE INNE, STONEGATE

T. P. Cooper[29] wrote :–

> The name of the first host of the Star Inn, Stonegate, we have observed is that of William Foster, who was in possession during the Siege of York 1644. He favoured the Royal cause and in a despondent mood saw his house invaded by Roundhead troopers flushed with victory at the capitulation of the city. The scene has been thus described in verse:
>
>> A bande of soldiers, with boisterous dinne
>> Filled ye large kitchen of ye olde Starre Inne,
>> Some rounde ye spacious chimney, smoking, satt,
>> And whiled ye time in battle-talk and chatt,
>> Some at ye brown oake table gamed and swore,
>> While pikes and matchlocks strewed ye sanded floore.
>> Will Foster ye hoste, 'mid ye group was seene,
>> With full redd face, bright eye and honest miene;
>> He smoked in silence in his olde arm chaire,
>> No joke nor jeste disturbed his sadden'd air.

Cooper quotes no authority. *Register of the Freemen of the City of York*[30] has this entry under the date 1649 :–

> 'Thomas Foster, sadler, fil[ii], Willemi Foster, inholder.'

(5) ROYALIST BADGES AND SIEGE MONEY

Benson,[31] writing in 1925, recorded :–

> Of Royalist badges, looped for wearing around the neck, there is in the [Yorkshire] Museum an oval one with [the] bust of the King stamped 'Carolus D.G., Mag. Br. Fra. et H. Rex,' and on the reverse a shield within the crowned garter, 'Florebunt' above, and beneath T.R. (T. Rawlins). Although a number of Siege money pieces of Scarborough and Pontefract are known, there appears to be only one of York.; it is a half crown struck on a

square piece of metal, and was in the Maxwell (*sic*) Collection till in November, 1888 it was sold for £25. Half crowns bearing C.R. under a crown and in the reverse IIs. VId. were issued.

It has proved impossible to discover anything more of the badge. Dr. J. P. C. Kent of the Department of Coins and Medals, British Museum, has kindly written this note about the 'half-crown' :—

> The reference is to the Marsham, not Maxwell, Collection. The piece was sold 23 November 1888, lot 625 and last went through the sale room on 17 October 1956, lot 2363. It is now in a private collection. It is certainly not a siege piece any more than are the other coins minted in York in 1644. I suppose one should call it a 'proof,' since it is a strike from ordinary dies on an extraordinary blank of metal.

(6) BULLETS AND CANNON BALLS

Benson[32] says that — 'Now and again relics of the Siege are met with. Bullets and cannon balls have been found, chiefly in the Moats, on Scarcroft and, in 1880, on Clementhorpe Hill, near Nun Windmill.' The last reference is considered further in connection with the gun emplacement on that site (see p. 144). *The Yorkshire Gazette*[33] reported that :—

> A cannon ball was found last week embedded in the city walls, near Micklegate Bar, by workmen engaged in repairing them. This was doubtless a relic of the war of the great rebellion.

(7) LADY ALICE WANDESFORD

Two side-lights on the siege are supplied by *The Autobiography of Mrs. Alice Thornton*.[34] In 1643 — before she was married — Alice Wandesford was living with her mother, Lady Alice Wandesford, and her two younger brothers Christopher and John at Snape, near Bedale in North Yorkshire. Late in 1643, or early in 1644, Christopher, who was 'exceedingly tormented with the fitts of the spleene,' was sent to school in York so as to be near to Dr. John Bathurst who eventually cured him. Early in 1644 Lady Wandesford decided to take the whole of her family to live in York so as to be near Christopher and to allow John to join his brother at school there. The party had got about half way to York when they were warned by a kinsman who had ridden post haste from the city 'that as she loved her life not to goe to York, for the parliament forces had mett with the king's, and they were all betrayed . . . and that towne [York] would be besieged.' The incident referred to is doubtless the storming of Selby which took place on 11 April. Lady Wandesford and her children beat a precipitate retreat to the family residence at Kirklington.

On the evening of 2 July Christopher Wandesford apparently played truant from school in York and rode 'towards the [Marston] moore with other boys, which was goeing in their simplicity to see the bataile.' A little way out of Micklegate Bar Christopher encountered — by a thousand to one chance — his eldest brother George who 'was newly come out of France' where, with a tutor, he had been doing 'the grand tour.' According to Mrs Thornton's account, George knew nothing of the impending battle. When it was clear that the Royalists had been defeated George took his brother up behind him and rode, 'pursued by a party of horrse of Scotts,' until both reached Kirklington safely between eleven and twelve at night.

(8) ELIZABETH THURCROSS

In Torre's *Antiquities Ecclesiastical of the City of York* 1691[35] is the incomplete transcription of a floor slab formerly in the church of St. Michael-le-Belfrey.[36] Its present whereabouts are unknown. Torre read it as :–

> Bonae Famae clarissimae
> Elizabetha . . . .
> quae superstes emicuit propria pietate & virtute,
> nunc cupit splendere Radijs mariti D. Timothei
> Thruscross Exuvias mortalitatis hic deposuit
> A°. ultimae patientiae sanctorum
> 1644
> circa difficillimum illud Tempus obsidionis
> & Redditionis hujus
> Urbis:
> Quam qui non praecesserit sequetur.

A free translation would read something like this :–

> To the Good Name of the dearest Elizabeth
> [Thurcross] whose piety and virtue, displayed by
> herself during her lifetime, are now reflected in

her husband Timothy Thruscross. Her mortal remains
he laid here in the year 1644 at that difficult
time of the siege and surrender of this city. Your
time too will come!

St. Michael-le-Belfrey parish register under 'Burials 1644'
has the entry 'The wife of Timothy Thriscrosse, buried the
29th July'[37] The following entry under 'Burials' in this same
register shows that she was buried in the chancel.

8th November 1658.   Mr. John Brieires of bishopthorpe, bur[i]ed in ye
Chancell under Mis[tress] Thriscroses Stone ye
8 day of November.

Timothy Thurcross (as the name is usually spelt) was
Prebendary of Langtoft in York Minster 1622–71 and Arch-
deacon of Cleveland 1635–8, and died in London in 1671; his
will is in the Prerogative Court of Canterbury.[38]

(9) HORN OF ULPH

Samuel Gale, writing in 1779, said :—[39]

Thomas Lord Fairfax the General . . . . , being himself a lover of
antiquities, took care to preserve it [the horn of Ulph] during the confusions
of the civil war, and his memory is still deservedly honoured for other generous
acts of this nature; such as his allowing Mr. Dodsworth the antiquary a yearly
salary to preserve the inscriptions in churches, his giving his valuable MSS to
the university of Oxford, and preserving the public library there, as he did
the Cathedral at York, from being spoiled and defaced after the surrender of
that city.

(10) CAPTAIN EDWARD PLACE

Among the archives of the Place family at Skelton Grange
near York is a piece of paper dated 23 November 1665 written
by Captain Edward Place, a copy of which (printed by kind
permission of Captain A. J. Place) is given below.

At Ṣṭriknam [?Strickland] House. At Leeds. At Adderton [Adwalton]
Moor. At Bradford. At Selby skirmish. At Hull on desperate service for 20
days together. At Gainsborough for 14 days together, taken prisoner there.
At Newark for 11 days together, taken prisoner there. At storming of Selby.
At York siege. At Marston Moor battle. At West Chester. At Scarboro
Castle. At Sherburn battle. At Sandall Castle many days. In Scotland at
several places nigh three quarters of the year. At Warrington Bridge twice
in one day. At Upton Bridge. At Worcester battle. This paper shows the

several places where I have been engaged in battles, sieges and skirmishes to mind me of the great mercies of God in my deliverance.

[Signed] Edward Place.

Other records in the Skelton archives show that before Marston Moor Place fought in Darcy's Regiment in the army of Ferdinando Fairfax. After that he presumably fought as a reformando or gentleman volunteer in the Parliamentarian armies.[40]

Place has got the order of events wrong in the above account; an amended version follows.

1642

Strickland House.

1643

23rd January	Leeds captured by Fairfax.
30th June	Battle of Adwalton Moor.
1st July	Bradford occupied
	Skirmish at Selby.
September— October	Siege of Hull.
October	Attack on Gainsborough. (Taken Prisoner of War).

1644.

March	Siege of Newark. (Taken prisoner of War).
11th April	Storming of Selby.
22nd April— 16th July	Siege of York.
2nd July	Battle of Marston Moor.
c. 25th July	West Chester. (Prince Rupert arrived there then).

1645.

25th July	Scarborough Castle surrendered by Sir Hugh Cholmley to Sir Matthew Boynton.
2nd October	Sandal Castle, near Wakefield, surrendered.
15th October	Battle at Sherburn in Yorkshire (when the Royalist Generals Langdale and Digby were routed and Sir Richard Hutton killed.)

1650.

Campaigning in Scotland.

1651.

Late August— early September	Skirmish at Upton Bridge near Worcester.

119

1651 [*continued*].

3rd September   Battle of Worcester.
                 ?1658.
                 Warrington Bridge. (This was a skirmish in Booth's
                 rising).

(11)   AN ECHO OF THE SIEGE

The memory of the siege doubtless lingered long in York. The following entry[41] in a lease dated 1659 by a Thomas Robinson of a messuage in St. Saviourgate only makes sense if it is read in the context of the siege. The lessee was to perform all necessary repairs to the property 'excepting casualties by fyre, by grenadoes or cannon bullets.'

(12)   PROCEEDINGS OF THE COMMITTEE FOR COMPOUNDING

One of the devices used by Parliament to meet its expenses in the Civil War — particularly the maintenance of its own armies and that of the Scots — was to make the Royalists (or 'delinquents' as they were called), in districts captured by their troops, compound for their estates. The body responsible for this was called the Committee for Compounding and it sat at Goldsmith's Hall in London. As its work increased sub-committees were set up in the provinces, one being at York. The national committee began its operations in 1644, the York Committee two years later. Abstracts of the findings of the former were published in 1889 in five monumental volumes — *Calendar of the Proceedings of the Committee for Compounding*. Fuller accounts of these proceedings relating to the Yorkshire folk involved have been published by the Yorkshire Archaeological Society — *The Yorkshire Royalist Composition Papers*.[42] Many of the records of the York Committee have also been published — *Proceedings of the Commonwealth Committee of York*.[43]

The following table contains extracts from these works. In a few cases it is not clear whether the persons named were in the city during the siege: the names of these and of some others of general interest, are enclosed in square brackets [ ]. Apart from such exceptions the extracts refer to people who were actually in York at the time of the siege.

Name	Residence, etc.	Calendar of Compounding Reference	YRCP Reference	Fine	Other references and notes.
Aldburgh, Arthur	Ellenthorpe Hall	III, 1986–7	ii, 217	£400	
Bowes, Richard	Babthorpe	II, 1414	ii, 171	£510 (reduced to £289)	Owned a tenement in York.
	"... sent in a man and a horse to the enemy.... Being disquieted by the Parliament soldiers went to York, where he remained till its delivery. He is a very aged man and not able to travel".				
Brooke, James	York	III, 1831	iii, 109	No order	See further p. 48
[Bubwith Richard]	Yeoman, Rothwell	II, 1350	ii, 26–7	£60	
	"Was compelled by Sir Wm. Savile Knt, then Colonel of the Trained Bands in the Co. of York to send a pick [pike] & coslet [corselet] with other arms belonging for the use of the King's army".				
Caley, Arthur	Brompton	II, 953	i, 42–5	£150	
	"... being young and unexperienced he was persuaded and drawne in to be a Captaine of horse of ye king's partie.... his laying downe of Arms.... caused 300 men at least to lay downe Armes with him...."				
Carr, John	Lesbury and West Ditchburne, Northumberland.	III, 1715	—	£80	
[Cartwright, Robert]	Draper, Hedon and Kingston-upon-Hull	II, 928	ii, 5	£47	

Name	Residence, etc.	Calendar of Compounding Reference.	YRCP Reference	Fine	Other references and notes.
Collinson, Anthony	Wistow.	II, 805	ii, 62-3.		
Copley, Edward	Batley	II, 1001-2	i, 182-7	£320	
	"....was a capt[ain] of a troupe of horse under the Earle of Newcastle from the first of January 1643 untill the 27 of July 1644."				
Cripling, Edward	Wilberfoss and York	II, 974	ii, 86	£53. 10s. (reduced to £37.)	Owned property in York.
Danby, Francis	South Cave.	II, 1235-6	ii, 160-1	£320	YAJ xxiii, p. 358.
	"....was Major of a troop of horse under the Earl of Newcastle."				
Edmunds, Thomas	Worsborough	II, 1003	ii, 19-21	£350	
Elmhurst, Richard	Houndhill	II, 987	i, 224-8	£566	
	"......he fortified his howse against the Kinge and Parliam[en]ts fforces, and afterwards"				

"That he being put out of the town of Kingston-upon-Hull, where his place of habitation then was by Sir John Hotham, then governor thereof did go into the enemies' quarters and there lived; that he was a captain in the Earl of Newcastle's army and had a commission from the Earl to raise a foot company which he endeavoured to raise, that he was in arms in the late leaguer against Hull and did ordinarily ride in the Earl of Newcastle's army being armed with sword and pistols; that he being beyond the seas in Holland out of the enemy's power came from thence voluntarily into the enemy's quarters, viz. to Newcastle then held for the King and brought thither by shipping carbines, trumpets and 'sacke' therewith furnished the enemy and did usually trade in the enemy's quarters.... Is now [1645] a prisoner [for debt] upon the bridge [at York]."

Name	Place				Notes
[Goodrick, Sir John, Bart.]	Hunsingo [Hunsingore]	II, 1059-60			He commanded a troop of horse under Newcastle.

"went and resided in Yorke whiles it was kept a garrison for the Kinge.... he haveing another house in the City of Yorke."

"A howse with thapportenances lying within the walls of the City of Yorke now defaced & ruinated not worth anything at p[re]sent, w[hi]ch Howse is in the possession of the Lady Goodrick his Mother for her life formerly worth p[er] ann[um] 10 li. 000. 0d."

Name	Place				Notes
Graham, Sir Richard, Bart.	Norton Conyers	II, 1018	i, 128–134	£2,384. 17. 4.	YAJ xxiii, p. 361

".... at the battell of Edgehill, and there hurt."

Greene, Robert	Ecclesfield	II, 1018	ii, 23–4	£100	
[Grey, George]	Co. Durham	III, 1919	—		
Grice, Henry	Sandal	IV, 1747	ii, 187	£75	
Hall, Lodowick	Great Chilton Co. Durham.	II, 1238	—	£1,025 (reduced to £419, 11s.)	
Harland, Richard senior	Sutton-on-the-Forest	II, 974–5	ii, 100–2		YAJ xxiii, p. 362

".... upon the rendition of York deserted that service."

| Hawkesworth, Walter | Heworth, York | III, 1827–8 | ii, 185 | £240 | |

".... That his habitation being within half a mile of York to secure his person from the violence of soldiers deserted the same and repaired to the city."

| Headlam, John | Kexby | II, 1142 | i, 172–4 | £340 | YAJ xxiii, p. 362. Son of Leonard Headlam, Town Clerk of York. |

Name	Residence, etc.	Calendar of Compounding Reference	YRCP reference	Fine	Other refences and notes.
Hildyard, Christopher	Lissett in Holderness & Winestead, E.R.	II, 891	i, 19–21	£109	
Hillyard, Christopher	Routh "....he was an officer upon the surrender [of York]".	II, 1283	ii, 11–12	£130	
Hodgson, John	Beeston "....that he did absent himselfe from his usual place of abode and fled into the enemies garrisons and lived there duringe the seidges of Yorke and Pomfret [Pontefract], and before that sent a man and horse into the King's Armye."	II, 597	i, 174–7	£590	
Holme, Christopher (father) and Holme, Henry (son)	Holm-in-Holderness	II, 1022	ii, 139–40	£350	YAJ xxiii, p. 363.
Horner, John	Kingston-upon-Hull "... before these troubles, being apprentice of Mr. Matthew Toppin late of Kingston upon Hull, merchant, and his friends being bound in 300 li. for his true service, the said Mr. Toppin about 3 years since [1642] was by S[i]r John Hotham turned out of Hull and after resided at Yorke and your petitioner did perform his duties as an apprentice to him there, and when Yorke was besieged he did, being constrained, bear arms for the defence of the City but immediately after that place was taken he went beyond seas and returned not till 8 Nov. last [1645] and came to London, he prays to be discharged of his delinquency being but a common soldier and not worth in lands and goods 200 li."	II, 1049	iii, 92–3	No order	
Jackson, Thomas	Clothier, Leeds	II, 975–6	i, 47–51	£345	
Jacques, Sir Roger	York	II, 882	i, 195–200	£896. 8s.	Lord Mayor of York

Name	Place / Note		1639. Owned property in York. (reduced to £800)
[Jennings, Jonathon]	Councillor-at-Law, Ripon	II, 1159	ii, 58-9 £156. 12s.
[Lawe, Tobias]	Leventhorpe "....he deserted his dwelling and went and lived in the enemies' quarters at York, but left the same before the surrender, and repaired to his own house."	II, 1542	ii, 121 £350
Lewins, Lewis	Heslington "....served as a Maior under S[i]r Thomas Glemham In Yorke duringe the tyme that the City was in the enemies' hands".	II, 1040	i, 126-8 £316. 13. 4.
[Lilburne, George]	Co. Durham "....though 60 years old in York gaol for refusing to join Earl of Newcastle."	III, 1921	—
Lukeupp, Bryan	Middleton "Hath sett forth.... a Dragoon under the Commande of Sir Thomas Remington, one of the com[mande]rs at Yorke."	II, 1272	i, 223-4 No order
Marshall, Robert	Selby "....living near York being an old man, went from his dwelling at Selby for his quiet to live at York when it was held as a garrison."	II, 1193	ii, 16-17 £116
Martin, William	Attorney, York	IV, 2565	iii, 37 £83
[Mason, Symon, D.D.]	Naburn "....Half her [Mason's widow's] estate consists of houses in York, which are irreparably consumed with fire, so that she and her three small children are exposed to great want and misery".	II, 1454	ii, 193-4 £48
May, Charles	The Strand, Middlesex	II, 1587	
Middleton, John	Stockeld	III, 1834-5	iii, 110 —
Monckton, Sir Francis	Howden "....deserted his dwelling and went into York whilst it was a garrison for the King."	II, 805	ii, 62-3

Name	Residence, etc.	Calendar of Compounding Reference	YRCP reference	Fine	Other references and notes.
[Munks (or Muncks) Richard]	Gisborne [?Gisburn]	II, 1609	ii, 220		
	".... has been in prison in York Castle"				
Nevile, Francis	Chevet	II, 842–3	ii, 3–5	£2,000	YAJ xxiii, p. 369.
Otby, Tristram	Loft-Marish, Pickering Lyth	III, 2008	ii, 203	£50	YAJ xxiii, p. 370.
Palmer, Sir George	Naburn	IV, 2580–1			
Reynolds, Thomas	Postmaster of York	V, 3303	(iii, 193)		
	".... begs to compound for an estate worth but 4 l a year."				
Robinson, Sir Wm., Knight	Newby	II, 977	ii, 115–6	£1,377	Son of Wm. Robinson, Lord Mayor of York, 1619.
[Savile, Sir Wm.]		IV, 2917	iii, 164		YAJ xxiii, p. 373 Died at York 24th January, 1644.
	".... Late Governor of the City of York when it was a garrison for the King against Parliament"				
Shipman, Thomas	Hanthwaite	II, 1448	iii, 97		
Shirtcliffe, William	Ecclesfield	II, 1032	ii, 24–5	£108	
Slingsby, Thomas	York	II, 1154	i, 123–6	£340	YAJ xxiii, p. 374. Was a younger brother of Sir Henry Slingsby whose Diary covers the siege.
	".... was a Collonell in the king's Army."				

PLATE XVII

Details from the Harome settle. Busts of four Parliamentarian Generals.

Fleetwood   Lambert

Skippon   Manchester

PLATE XVIII

Edward Montagu, 2nd Earl of Manchester.   Artist Peter Lely.

RELATION

Of the most

Remarkable Occurrences

From the Vnited Forces in the North, under the Command of those three approved and Faithfull Friends both unto the Church and Common-wealth. Generall *Lesly*, the Lord *Fairefax* and the Earle of *Manchester*.

From Saturday the 1. untill Munday the 10th, of this instant *June*.

Sent from the Leagure before *Yorke*,
By *Sim. Ash*, } Chaplaines to the Earle of
Will. Goode, } *Manchester*.

TOGETHER

With a true and most credible Relation of Prince *Ruperts* inhumane carriage at his raising of *Boulton*, in a Letter from M. *Herrick* of *Manchester*, to the Lady *Herrick* in *London*.

View'd and Order'd to be Printed according to Order.

LONDON,
Printed for *Thomas Vnderhill* at the Bible in *Wood-street*, M.DC.XLIIII.

ARTICLES

Of The

SVRRENDER

Of The

City of YORKE

To the Earle of L E V E N, Lord *Fairefax*, and Earle of *Manchester*, on Tuesday *July* 16. 1644.

Together with an explanation of some part of the ARTICLES.

LONDON,
Printed for *Mathew Walbancke*,
July 23. 1644.

PLATE XIX Contemporary tracts relating to the Siege.

1. *The Articles of Surrender of the City of York 1644.*
2. *A Particular Relation No. 3.*

PLATE XX

John Dolben, Archbishop of York, 1683–1686.   Artist Unknown.

Name	Place / Details			Amount	Notes
Sothaby, Robert	Pocklington	III, 2054	iii, 14–15	£726. 17. 6. (reduced to £426. 17. 6.)	His son fought for Parliament.
Story, John, senior	Wakefield "…. he was an aged man 80 years old or thereabouts and not able to travill."	II, 1124	i, 82–4	£50	
Swinburne, Tobias	York "…. tooke upp armes when his Ma[jes]ty [Charles I] was last in Yorke agenst the Parl[i]ament and was one of the Princes Rupert [Troope] and was at Edg[e]hill Bat[t]le where hee was dangrusly hurt and thereupon returned home and was in this Cittie of Yorke in the Leager tyme."	II, 977	i, 149–2	£170	Owned property in York.
Tempest, Sir Thomas	"the Isle, co. Durham."	III, 1999	—	£134	YAJ xxiii, p. 377.
Tomson, William	Hemingbrough	II, 1464	ii, 81	£60	
Topham, Matthew	Merchant, Kingston-upon-Hull "[After the siege of York]…. went from Holland where he hath lived for a longe tyme…. being now [1645] in Rotterdam beyond the seas where the River being ffrozen…. [he] cannot come to Tender himselfe."	II, 1037	i, 143–5	£90	
Vavasour, Sir Walter, Bart.	Hazlewood "[After the siege]…. took a pass from my Lord fferdinando ffairfax to go by Hull to Holland and accordingly went with the first ship from Hull to Rotterdam."	III, 2228–30	iii, 116–7		YAJ xxiii, p. 378. Colonel of a regiment of horse under Newcastle.
Vavasour, William	Weston "…. he supplied the forces raised against Parliament with two men, and horses, and after went and lived in York."	II, 1037	ii, 29–31	£447	

Name	Residence, etc.	Calendar of Compounding Reference.	YRCP reference	Fine	Other references and notes.
Waller, Edward	Sikehouse [Sykehouse] "Compounds for delinquency in going, on his own private occasions, to York, and other King's garrisons, when the Earl of Newcastle prevailed in the North"	II, 1272	i, 207–11	£164	YAJ xxiii, p. 378.
Watkinson, James	Kingston-upon-Hull Merchant, ".... That he was the keeper of or an Assistant in the Maggazine at Yorke while that citty was held a Garrison for the Kinge.... and duringe that tyme constantly and from tyme to tyme issued out of the said Maggazine to the Earle of Newcastle and his Army divers Armes, Ordinance, Musketts, Carbines, Pistolls, powder, Shott, and other Ammunc̄on"	II, 930–1	i, 109–123	£400	
Wilson, Marmaduke	Monk Fryston and Dighton [?Deighton] ".... before these troubles was a major of the trained bands, and when the Earl of Newcastle's army came down into these parts he was commanded to join with those forces, and did accordingly adhere to them, and went with Coll. S[i]r John Ramsden to Leeds, and was also in York when it surrendered."	II, 1219	ii, 51–2	£320	

(13) PAYNE FISHER 1616–1693

The career of this extraordinary man is given in DNB. After spending four years (1634–1638) at the universities of Oxford and Cambridge, he saw military service in the Netherlands, returning to England in 1639 to enlist as an ensign in King Charles I's army in the Scottish wars. After further service in Ireland he returned to England in 1644 and was made sergeant-major of a foot regiment in Prince Rupert's army. With this he marched to the relief of York and fought at the battle of Marston Moor. Finding himself on the losing side, he deserted and went to London where he lived as best he could by his pen, writing Latin verse. One of his poems, published in 1650, celebrating the Parliamentarian victory at Marston Moor, was entitled *Marston Moor: sive de obsidione praelioque Eboracensi carmen*[44] (the title page of which is shown on Plate XXIII) and was printed over the name of 'Paganus Piscator.' Fisher invariably used this sobriquet or that of 'Fitzpaganus Fisher.' He became one of the fashionable poets of his day, and, to use his own word, was appointed 'scribbler' to Oliver Cromwell. At the Restoration he changed sides once again and, to ingratiate himself with the new masters of England, wrote scurrilous verses about Cromwell and other Parliamentarian dead. But his character was too notorious and his flattery too palpable to attract any attention in court circles. He spent several years in the Fleet prison and died in poverty in 1693.

Fisher's Marston Moor poem consists of 1288 lines and is divided into five parts, the second and third of which relate more particularly to the siege of York and the fourth and fifth to the battle. By no stretch of imagination can the work be considered as serious history. It is rhetorical, imaginative, fanciful and vague, being profusely interlarded with classical references and allusions. Rarely does it mention a particular locality or describe a specific event. In sweeping, general terms it refers to attacks by the besiegers, repulses by the garrison and the privations suffered by the citizens. Here are some typical extracts translated from the original Latin :–

p. 18,   l. 3–14. Not far from the walls there rose high into the sky a mound of earth from which could be viewed the whole city and the towers of York.

Approving the situation and satisfied that his lines of retreat were safe, the general (*Ductor*) placed his standards there, measured out his camp and strengthened it with ramparts crowned with turves. On this he placed a battery (*crebra*)[45] and ordered cannon balls to be fired against the walls so that he might break through the lofty chains of the gates and smash the obstinate defences. Immediately the walls shook with the hellish onslaught, flames and fires belched forth as the hoarse cannon roared, hurling smoking shot against the defences.

p. 26,   l. 3–9. In another sector (for the walls encompass a wide circuit) the soldiery crossed the river, fearlessly entering the rushing waters. The offended Ouse was amazed at such daring and was aflame with the flashing of their weapons. You would have marvelled at the energy and determination of the besiegers as they mingled their blood with the waves and laid down their lives in the foaming waters.

Even incidents as noteworthy as the explosion under St. Mary's Tower and the attack on the Manor on 16 June are described in vague and rhetorical terms. The account of the latter is, however, of more than passing interest as it does name Samuel Brearey (*Brierus* in the poem)[46] and underlines his bravery, already vouched for from other, more reliable, sources (see p. 6of.) It reads :–

p. 25,   l. 9–

p. 26,   l. 2. Soon a breach was effected and the Scots[47] quickly broke through the core of the gaping wall to enter *Domum celsisque Palatia tectis*.[48] But scarcely had they entered than they were put to flight by the courageous *Brierus* who, with avenging hand captured their weapons. At this time he performed many amazing feats as he charged all alone into their midst plunging his sword hilt-deep into their bodies. But at last, alas! while fearlessly attacking his adversaries who so greatly outnumbered him, he fell mortally wounded. The citizens of York felt his death and mourned his loss more than the deaths of all the other slain. They esteemed him as much more than Leslie and the whole Scottish army as gold compared with lead.

All such passages naming particular individuals are reproduced here in translation :–

p. 19,   l. 18–

p. 20,   l. 13. That valiant warrior *Ballantinus*[49] was brought to the ground, the reins snatched from his hands. (Scotland never produced a man of greater courage and daring. His death showed how laughable is destiny and what small reliance is to be placed on the things of this world.) Unhappy man! while he was recklessly charging the enemy, flushed with warlike ardour and rampaging here and there inspiring terror into all he encountered, he, a warrior fully armed, was brought down by a small piece of lead [i.e. a bullet].

The sure aim of your right hand *Donnelle*[50] laid low so great an adversary in close combat. *Donnel* (a man of obscure origin but a gentleman in all he did) thus enhanced his proven reputation for valour. But the warlike Scots were not dispirited by the loss of this their leader. No, they set about avenging his death by fighting even more ferociously and carrying out his orders even more valiantly.

p. 21,   l. 7–

p. 22,   l. 2. Manchester, that wisest of noblemen, kept his troops safe behind defence works . . . . That watchful general displayed not only courage but stratagems and subtle tricks of various kinds. On one occasion, so as to cause the maximum of loss to the enemy and the least to his own forces, he pretended that his men were running away so as to draw on the foe with false hopes.

p. 27,   l. 17–

p. 28,   l. 11. How should I speak of the memorable *Widdringtonus*[51] and the other renowned commanders (*Dynastas*) thanks to whose commands the towers of York stood more securely and the defences took on new strength? How should I mention your great and unforgettable name, *Huddlestonus*,[52] who gave your life for king and country?

Am I to remain silent about *Dakerus*[53] who, lacerated with wounds, after slow torment yielded up his sick and struggling soul? You, famed *Cobbus*,[54] are still alive and bid fair to outlast the peaceful years of Nestor. Under your command Clifford's Tower (*Cliffordia Turris*) thundered against the foe and rained flying cannon balls on the enemy's entrenchments.

But your glory, *Glennhammus* [Glemham] will survive through far distant ages: time will never wipe it out . . . . Then [after death] what city's government shall rest on your shoulders, what rewards shall equal your good deeds? . . . . When shot rained over the city, you did not flinch in your duty, but stood up all the more stoutly against fate.

It is just possible that this poem must bear some of the responsibility for two of the most widespread 'heresies' concerning the siege, 'heresies' which have crept into many subsequent general histories of York. The first is that Prince Rupert entered the city in person[55] on the evening (1 July) preceding the battle of Marston Moor and the second that when the city was relieved on that occasion the inhabitants were on the brink of starvation. The relevant passage reads :–

p. 34, l. 8–

p. 38. l. 16. Suddenly Prince Rupert appeared to help the besieged, to speak comforting words to them and to renew their flagging spirits. Great was the people's joy when this renowned general appeared, filling the surrounding plains with his troops . . . . Neither did his men come empty handed. With them came heaped baskets of fresh grain and flour . . . . How the crowds poured into the streets to meet them. The towers were seen to be swaying with the weight of the people who climbed on them. There was one building — the Minster (*Monasterium*)[56] — scarcely equalled for beauty by any other in Britain — whose lofty pinnacles soared over everything. Now the people struggled with each other to climb its lofty towers; the roar of their shouts filled the roofs as they clung to the tops of the walls. Now they mingled with their comrades, told yet again the tearful tale of the great siege, recounted their losses and embraced each other with joy . . . .

Then the King's Manor (*Regia*)[57] resounded to the hub-hub as servants hastened to prepare the banqueting couches gleaming with gold and to hang out the huge tapestries. Others adorned the ceilings with hanging lamps . . . . So, most worthy Prince, the city sparkled to delight your eyes. . . . O long to be remembered day!

But the Prince, his mind filled with many anxieties, experienced both joy and apprehension. As he wandered through the city accompanied by a number of his men, he strode here and there, inquiring into serious matters — 'What supplies are there for the troops? How many men are under arms? How strong are the walls?'

(14) PARISH REGISTERS

Below are extracted all references in the Parish Registers of York churches to 'soldiers,' 'strangers' and others of more than merely parochial interest who can reasonably be assumed to have come into the city as a result of the siege or with the events immediately preceding or following it. The period covered is that from 1 January to 31 December 1644 (modern reckoning).[58] Full titles of the registers consulted are given in the bibliography on pp. 226–7. All entries marked with an asterisk (*) date to the actual period of the siege i.e. between 22 April and 16 July: those marked with a dagger (†) refer to persons known to have been slain at Marston Moor. Notes followed by the entry (PY) indicate that the additional information was kindly supplied by Brigadier Peter Young.

(i) *Published*

(a)[59] *The Minster*

Burials

1644

*26th April	S[i]r[60] William Howard
*10th June	Major Clarke
*12th June	S[i]r Francis Armitage
*16th June	The Lady Preston
*17th June	Colonel Biron[61]
*17th June	Major Huddleston[61]
*2nd July	Colonel Steward
*3rd July	Captaine Stanhope
*7th July	†Colonel William Evers
*7th July	†Colonel Charles Slingsbye
*9th July	Bishop of Glosco [Glasgow][62]

(b) *All Saints, Pavement.*

Burials

1644

18th March	George Smeton, of Dunnington
*23rd May	Robert Foster, a lewetenant
*19th June	Christopher Tillson, a souldger died at Gregerie Empsons
*3rd July	Francis Weste of Ottley
11th December	Thomas Triggett, militar. paup. sepult .... [in] cem[itorio]

Baptism

1644

*6th May	Shyrlott Carye, fillia S[i]r Edward Carye.

(c) *St. Crux.*

Burials

1644

*22nd May	John Tompsonn, soulger.
*28th May	Willm. Tinesdaill, soulger.
*2nd June	John Slee, soulger.
*8th June	Thomas [–blank–], soulger
*13th June	Adam Ward, soulger.
*17th June	Nicholas Ranold, soulger.
*20th June	Willm Watsonn, soulger.
*3rd July	Leonard Tompson & John Knese, soulgers.
18th July	Francis Loge, soulger
26th July	A Soulger from John Bellaie house.
8th August	John [–blank–], soulger.
21st September	Mrs. Elizabeth, the wife of Captaine Markinfeld.

133

Burials

1644	*27th April	Luke Kirbey, a Soldger.
	*7th May	Le[o]nard Tomson, Servant to S[i]r Thomas Cleman [?Glemham].
	*15th May	Henry Burbecke, Captaine under ye L[or]d Widdrington.
	*17th May	Samuel Sparrow, souldier to Captaine Bramhall.
	*17th June	John Swanne, Quartermaster.
	*21st June	Rob[er]te ferreman, a Soldger.
	*22nd June	John Craw, a souldjer.
	*23rd June	M[ist]ris Mary Ransome, ye wife of Captaine Jane (*sic*) Ransomme.
	*28th June	John King, souldjer under Captaine Owsman.
	*5th July	William Pigg, souldjer under Colonell Goring.
	*11th July	John Hill, servant to S[i]r ffrancis Mackw[i]ths Secretary.
	18th July	S[i]r Richard Dakers, Collonel.[63]

Marriages

| 1644 | 6th August | Edmond Peacocke and Prudence Arthur, Country people. |

The published volume only covers the years 1716–1812 transcribed from the actual registers and the years 1631–1715 from the archbishop's transcripts. The latter are clearly incomplete and there are no entries whatever between 1640 and 1663. The earliest original register covering the years 1616–1716 has now come to light and is in the Borthwick Institute of Historical Research, York. The following entries relating to the year 1644 have been transcribed from this register.

Burials

| 1644 | *26th June | Thomas Fisher Soldier under Captaine [–blank–]. |
| | *26th June | Gabriell Winn soldier under Captaine [–blank–]. |

Marriages

1644 *9th July

Raiph Addison of the p[ar]ish of Lytham in the Countie of Cumberlande Jane Wilin [Wilkinson] of All S[ain]ts upon the Pavement.

(f) *Holy Trinity, Micklegate.*

Burials

1644 14th March

Thomas Craven which was slaine by Lieuetenant Godfray.

*2nd July   Captaine Hougton
*9th July   †Major Sprat.[64]

(g) *St. Lawrence, Walmgate.*
No siege references.

(h) *St. Martin, Coney Street.*

Burials

1644 *7th June

Thomas Tompson, Souldier under [Colonel] S[i]r Jo[hn] Girlin[g]ton.

*8th July

The Lady Vaveso[u]r had a son and named John, and Robt. Taylor the post m[aste]r sone of Tadcaster was buried both together.

4th August   The Ladey Cunstable.
7th August   Richard Tooley, sarvant unto the Lord Morley.
8th August   Robt. the sone of Capt. Vaine

(i) *St. Martin-cum-Gregory, Ousebridge.*

Burials

1644 *22nd April

Capton Britton was buryed in Side queare.

*22nd June

Mr. Samuel Breareay[65] was buryed att Sa[i]nt John['s Church, Ousebridge].

*8th July

[Captain] Sir Richard Gleden [Gledhill].

*16th July   Capton Drimdrig.

Baptisms

1644 *19th June

Thomas fflood, son of Coranal [?Colonel] fflood.

29th December

Anna Gill, doughtar to magar [?Major] Gill.

(j) *St. Mary Bishophill, Junior.*
No siege references.

135

Burials

1644	26th January	John, the sonne of mr. Willm. Lodg, a stranger.
	30th January	Walter Kaine, a stranger.
	11th February	Joseph Jefferson, a stranger.
	16th February	Capt. Francis Ward.
	4th March	Cornet John Usher.
	*22nd April	A sonne of S[i]r John Middleton, kt.
	*5th May	Thomas, sonne of Thomas Richardson, a soldier.
	*10th May	Michaell Chappell, a stranger.
	*12th May	Daniell Tayler, serv[an]t to S[i]r Willm. Carnaby.
	*15th May	George, sonne of Jonas Binns, soldier.
	*19th May	Sandy Gibbins, soldier.
	*7th June	Mr. Willm. Willyscott, a stranger.
	*9th July (*sic*)	Isabell Richardson, a stranger.
	*13th June	Mr. Tho. Romsey, Quarterm[aste]r.
	*15th June	Willm. Sidday, a stranger.
	*16th June	Willm. Dalby, a soldier.
	*22nd June	John Jefferson, stranger.
	*25th June	Katheryne, wife of Capt. Abraham Bell.
	*27th June	Nicholas, sonne of [Colonel] Sir John Girdleington.
	9th August	Eliz[abeth] daughter of Robert Owston[66]
	20th August (*sic*)	Eliz[abeth] daughter of Robert Owston[66]
	20th August	Mr. Willm. Belt, a stranger.
	20th August	Mr. Humphry Mascall of wortley.
	20th July (*sic*)	Mr. Henry Wolstenholme, a stranger.
	29th July (*sic*)	the wife of Timothy Thriscrosse.[67]
	29th July (*sic*)	Mr. Barker, serv[an]t to Lord Fairefax.

Baptisms

1644	27th March	Sarah, daughter of Rich. Goodwin, a stranger.
	5th April	Thomas, Sonne of L[i]eut[enant] Willm. Shaw.
	9th April	Elizabeth, dau[ghter] of Robt. Owston, a stranger.
	11th April	Mary, dau[ghter] of [Major] S[i]r Richard Tankard [Tancred], knight[68]

*30th April	Thomas, soone of Thomas Richardson, a soldier.
*8th June	Grace, daughter of Lt. Coll. Robt. Portington[69]
*4th July	Roger, sonn of Sariant [Sergeant] major Nicholas Burnet.
*6th July	Alice, the daughter of Tho. Parr, a stranger.
*6th July	Thomas, sonn of Edward Mathewes, stranger.
12th September	Thomas, sonn of Tho. Lund, stranger.
13th September	Thomas, sonn of Capt. Thomas Stockdale.
26th September	Ellen, daughter of Sariant [Sergeant] Maior Andrew Grey.[70]

(l) *St. Olave; Marygate.*

Burials[71]

1644	20th April	Mary the daughter of John Croft . . . a stranger.
	*27th April	Richard Wright a soldier
	*11th May	Henry Kenywell a soldier.
	*15th May	Richard Parkin a soldier
	*20th May	Edward Troquere a soldier of Maior Hudleston Companie.
	*20th May	Sem Askcum a soldier.
	*21st May	Steven Magson a soldier under Captaine Mozin.
	*26th May	Thomas Pople a soldier under Captaine Rutter.
	*28th May	Thomas Paxton yeoman of Littlethorpe in Bishoppricke of Durham.
	*2nd June	Christopher Lofthouse under Captaine Rutter.
	*4th June	William Parker a soldier under Sir Richard Huttons Regiement.
	*6th June	John Emson a soldier
	*9th June	William Meke a soldier.
	*10th June	Robert Cave a soldier.
	*10th June	William Wright a soldier.
	*11th June	Walter Menell a soldier.
	*12th June	William Clifton a soldier.
	*12th June	Captaine L[i]eutenant [--blank--] Peytifer.

137

*13th June	John Waynwright a soldier.
*16th June	John Leadbetter a soldier.
*17th June	John Winter a soldier.
*20th June	John Hobson a soldier.
*27th June	Robert turpin a soldier .... sergant to Cononell [Colonel] Hiltons Reigiment.
*1st July	William Robinson a soldier of Sedgfield in Bishopprick of Durham .... Cononel [Colonel] hiltō [Hilton].[72]

(ii) *Unpublished*

The following are entries in original unpublished registers in the Borthwick Institute of Historical Research, York.

St. Cuthbert.

Burials
1644	*2nd May	Young Mr. Pudsaye.
	*23rd May	A souldyer Buried that died at William Harrisons house the 23 of May 1644.
	*29th June	Lieutenant Skadlocke.
	*4th July	Captain Menell.
	17th ?July	A souldier buried from Thomas Carters house (?) xvii of July.[73]

St. Deny's

Burials
1644	*9th June	John Beronye, Lieutenant.
	*10th June	Thomas Gotherwicke, Miles [= soldier].

St. John's

Burials
1644	2nd September	Liet. William Grundell.[73]

St. Margaret's

Burials
1644	*21st May	John Hilton, soldier.

St. Mary's, Castlegate[74]

Burials
1644	29th March	Richard Ellikir, soldier.
	*24th June	Richard Dickenson, soldier.
	*28th June	William Plowman, soldier.
	27th July	William Smethman, soldier[73]
	12th November	Thomas Vickers, soldier[73]

Burials

1644   *23rd April   Henry Ubancke, Lieutenant.

       *2nd June   John Parker, Ensigne.

       *2nd June   Mr. Rudd, Drum Major.

       *2nd June   John Baits, Captain.

       *18th June   George Nelson, Lieutenant.

       *19th June   Daniel Purvey, Major.

St. Sampson's

Burials

1644   *16th June   Roger Rawe, Leuietent.

       31st July   Captain Henry Chomalley [Cholmley].

1   Keep. The page references from the MS are given against the items listed.

2   p. 57.

3   *A York Miscellany*, p. 38.

4   Appendix IIA and B, pp. 159-177

5   p. 103.

6   p. 147.

7   p. 290.

8   Raine, p. 294.

9   See also Raine, p. 292.

10   Markham, p. 147.

11   For an account of its foundation see E. Brunskill, 'Some York Almhouses' (York Georgian Society Occasional Papers No. 7) 1960, p. 16.

12   Leeds Public Library. Temple Newsam Collection MS:. York II. Building Accounts of Bootham Hospital 1649.

13   York II. Bootham Hospital iv (two copies).

14   Raine, p. 273.

15   Raine, p. 278 and 'Housebook' Appendix IIA, p. 166 no. 40.

16   Benson III, p. 35.

17   Raine, p. 287 and cf. Hildyard p. 63.

18   E. Brunskill, 'Some York Almhouses' (York Georgian Society Occasional Papers No. 7) 1960, p. 9.

19   'A walk round St. Olave's Church, York' by H.E.C.S 1963. (No page

20   p. 259.   [numbers)

21   *Martial Annals of the City of York*, 1893, p. 160.

22   BM. Add. MS 33, 084 f. 86. Actually it is on f. 46–7.

23   xiv (1683), p. 238.

24   Opposite p. 32.

25 Numerous accounts of her life have been written, the most definitive being that of Mary Chambers, *The Life of Mary Ward*, London 1885 The writer has a particular interest in Mary Ward. In 1965 he supervised an excavation (report impending) in the churchyard of Osbaldwick near Heworth which resulted in the discovery of what was almost certainly her coffin and skeleton.

26 By kind permission of Reverend Mother Ancilla, Superior of the Bar Convent, York.

27 i (1849) p. 123.

28 Details of the incident are to be found in J. Dennett, *Beverley Borough Records 1575–1821* (YAS Record Series lxxxiv, 1933), pp. 48–49; G. Poulson, *Beverlac; or the Antiquities and History of the Town of Beverley* 1829, p. 366.

29 'Some old York Inns....' *Associated Architectural and Archaeological Societies' Reports and Papers*, xxxix Pt. 2, pp. 273–318.

30 Vol. ii *Sur Soc.* cii (1899), p. 109.

31 pp. 37–8.

32 p. 38.

33 9 July, 1831.

34 Ed Charles Jackson. *Sur. Soc.* lxii (1875), pp. 40–43.

35 p. 70. Unpublished MS in York Minster Library.

36 Quoted in Drake, p. 342 (with minor variations).

37 Listed on p. 136.

38 See Venn, *Alumni Cantabrigienses*, iv. p. 239. For references to Thurcross see Ridsdill Smith, *passim*.

39 'An historical dissertion upon the antient Danish horn, kept in the Cathedral Church of York.' *Archaeologia* i (1779), 2nd ed., pp. 181–2.

40 I am indebted to Brigadier Peter Young for this suggestion and also for help with the reconstructed career of Place as given later.

41 York Public Library. M 31:64. Clifton Deeds.

42 Vol. i (1893), vol. ii (1895) and vol. iii (1896).

43 See under *Miscellanea*, p. 224 of this work.

44 In the Minster Library in York there are two copies of this work. On the fly leaf of one is a note in Latin in Fisher's handwriting to the effect that it was presented by the author (who signs himself 'Fitz-Paganus Piscator') to Mynheer Gerard Schaeph, Commissioner from Holland to the English Parliament. Schaeph arrived in London in May 1650 and remained there until September of the following year (*CSP. Dom.*, 1650, p. 169 and 1651, p. 484).

45 A marginal note reads:– 'Anglicè – A Battery.' In very general terms the situation of this battery would fit the Parliamentarian one known to have been erected on Lamel Hill.

46 He was buried in St. John's Church on 22 June (see p. 135).

47 *Sic* ('*Scoti*' in the original). Manchester's men, not the Scots, were, of course, responsible for the attack on the Manor.

48 A marginal note reads:– '*Quae vulgo dicitur* — The Mannor.'

49 A marginal note reads:– 'A most experienced cavalry officer who excelled all others in strength and courage alike.' That he was highly esteemed by the Scots is known from other sources (see p. 25).

50 A marginal note reads:– 'An officer of distinction (*Dux strenuus*) under the command of the Marquis of Newcastle.' *Donnelle* or *Donnel* (or perhaps Donnelly) is not known from any other source as having been responsible for Ballantyne's death.

51 A marginal note reads:– 'Lord Widdrington, Baron.'

52 A marginal note reads:–'Major Huddleston, sprung from the ancient Cumberland family of that name.' He took part with Brearey in the defence of the Manor, being killed. He was buried in the Minster the following day, 17 June (see pp. 6of. and 133).

53 A marginal note reads:– 'Sir Richard Dakers, knight.' He was buried in the church of Holy Trinity, Goodramgate, on 18 July (see p.134).

54 A marginal note reads:– 'Sir Francis Cobb, knight.' Drake, p. 289, says that at the beginning of the siege when Cobb was made Governor of Clifford's Tower — 'The tower being repaired and strengthened with fortifications, a draw-bridge, deep moat, and pallisadoes; on the top of it was made a platform, on which some pieces of cannon were mounted; two demy culverins and a saker, with a garrison appointed to defend it.'

55 George Benson, *York* . . . ., Pt. III p. 35. Cf. p. 80.

56 A marginal note reads:– '*Quod vulgo dicitur* — The Minster'

57 A marginal note reads:– 'The Mannour-house.'

58 The article, 'Burials of soldiers at York during the Civil War' by C. B. N[orcliffe] (*Genealogist* iii (1879), pp. 322–6) is incomplete and inaccurate in many instances. The seven unpublished registers (see pp. 138–9) listed in it have been checked against the originals.

59 These letters refer to the Bibliography, pp. 226–7.

60 Short biographical notes on some of the people named appear in the published register.

61 They were both killed when repulsing the Parliamentarian attack on King's Manor on Trinity Sunday, 16 June (see p. 60).

62 For a curious note on this burial, see Baillie, p. 213.

63 The following entry in the Holy Trinity (or Christ Church), King's Square register (published) doubtless refers to him and his daughter:–
    Christening 20 December, 1643. Marie Daughter of Mr. (*sic*)
    Richard Dakers, Colonell.
    This must be the Richard Dakers mentioned in *Carmen*, see p. 131.

64 Presumably Edward Sprot. Adjutant General of Horse to Prince Rupert. Mortally wounded or killed at Marston Moor (PY).

65 Undoubtedly Lieutenant Colonel Samuel Brearey killed during the attack on the Manor, 16 June (see p. 6of.).

66 See entry below under 'Baptisms,' dated 9 April.

67 For a further reference to her see pp. 117–8.

68 Lt. Colonel of Horse. Sir William Savile's Regiment (PY).
69 Tankard was Major to Sir Richard Hutton's foot (PY).
70 Possibly Major Grey of Sir Henry Slingsby's regiment (PY).
71 All these entries, except the first, are prefixed with the word 'Manner' or 'Mannier.' St. Olave's parish is subdivided in the registers into various wards one of which was the King's Manor, variously spelt 'Manner,' 'Mannier.'
72 John Hilton. Colonel of Foot. His regiment may have been billeted in the Manor parish and guarded this sector of the Royalist defences. Most of his officers came from County Durham (PY).
73 In view of the dates these are likely to be Parliamentarian rather than Royalist soldiers.
74 R. H. Skaife's, 'Extracts from the Registers of the Church of St. Mary, Castlegate, York' printed in YAJ xv (1900), pp. 142–198 is incomplete and does not include all the entries quoted here.

PLATE XXI

Tomb of Archbishop Dolben in York Minster.

IN MEMORY OF FERDINANDO
FAIRFAX 1584-1647 AND THOMAS
FAIRFAX 1612-1671 SECOND AND
THIRD LORDS FAIRFAX OF CAM-
ERON AND GENERALS OF THE
PARLIAMENTARY FORCES WHO
DURING THE CIVIL WAR 1642-
1646 PRESERVED FROM DESTRUC-
TION THE TREASURES OF GLASS
OF YORK MINSTER. THIS WIN-
DOW RESTORED BY MEMBERS
OF THE FAIRFAX FAMILY WAS
UNVEILED BY ALBERT TWELFTH
LORD FAIRFAX OF CAMERON
SEPTEMBER 14TH 1932

PLATE XXII
Fairfax Memorial tablet in the Chapter House, York Minster.

Chapter Nine

FORTS AND EARTHWORKS

DANIEL DEFOE[1] toured England during the years 1724–6. He visited York and had this to say about what were clearly the ruined remains of earthworks thrown up around the city as a result of the Civil Wars :–

> York is indeed a pleasant and beautiful city and not at all the less beautiful for the works and lines about it being demolished, and the city, as it may be said, being laid open, for the beauty of peace is seen in the rubbish; the lines and bastions and demolished fortifications have a reserved secret pleasantness in them from the contemplation of the publick tranquility that outshines all the beauty of advanced bastions, batteries, cavaliers, and all the hard named works of the engineers about a city . . . .
>
> The old walls are standing, and the gates and posterns; but the old additional works which were cast up in the late rebellion, are slighted; so that York is not now defensible as it was then. But things be so too, that a little time, and many hands, would put those works in their former condition and make the city able to stand out a small siege.

These 'lines and bastions and demolished fortifications' are considered here in some detail.

(a) WEST OF THE CITY

To the west of the City the defences had been strengthened by three sconces built by the Royalists before the siege began. Although the contemporary authorities[2] do not give their precise location, topographical considerations and archaeological discoveries make it possible to site them with some degree of certainty. They are considered separately here.

*No. 1.[3] *On the site of Southlands Chapel, Bishopthorpe Road.* (NG. 60135042)

This is described[4] as the sconce or emplacement 'nearest to the Towne' and as being surrounded by a double ditch; it housed 120 soldiers. It was captured by the Scots on 7 June and then used by them against the city. (see p.40f). Southlands Chapel — built in 1887 on what is variously called Nunmill Hill and Clementhorpe Hill — is some 50 ft. above the Ouse at Skeldergate Bridge and was the site of an earlier windmill. The site commands the approach to the city from Bishopthorpe; would be useful against an enemy using the river and, if held in conjunction with another such fort (as indeed it was) on The Mount (No. 2 below), would command the whole of the ridge of higher ground to the west of the city. It is 520 yds. distant from the tower in the city walls at the junction of Price's Lane and Bishopthorpe Road, 900 yds. from Clifford's Tower, 460 yds. from the Ouse at Skeldergate Bridge and 880 yds. from the nearby Mount emplacement.

Exhibited in the Yorkshire Museum in 1891 (they cannot be traced there now) were what were described[5] as 'Cannon balls of various sizes, and musket bullets of lead, found on the site of one of the Parliamentary batteries, during the siege of York, on Clementhorpe Hill, near the Windmill, in 1880.' This sconce was slightly smaller than its neighbour on The Mount but in plan and elevation it was similar.

*No. 2. *On the highest part of The Mount.* (NG. 59235105)
On 7 June this sconce was captured for a short time by the Scots. It was recaptured by the Royalists almost immediately by means of 'a strong party both of Horse and Foot . . . out of the Towne'[6] which advanced through Micklegate Bar. The sconce was then held by the Royalists throughout the rest of the siege The curious circumstances of its 'capitulation' have already been described (pp. 96-7).

More is known of this sconce than of any around York. It is dealt with in considerable detail in Appendix VIII. Defoe almost certainly saw some ruined remains of it in 1724–6. Most of it was removed in 1742. The last vestiges of it disappeared in 1953.

Early in the present century in what was then a market garden and is now part of the playing fields of the Mount School lead musket balls were found which could well have been fired from this emplacement.[7] Two of these are now in the Department of History of St. John's College of Education in Gray's Court, York. Their diameters and weights are as follows :—

	Diameter (mm) (least and greatest)	Weight (gms)
No. 1	16.8 – 17.0	27.8
No. 2	15.5 – 16.0	24.0

*No. 3 (?) *On Holgate Hill* (*modern Wilton Rise*) (NG. 58955151)

It apparently had 'only 50 men to maintaine it'.[8] All that can be gleaned with certainty from contemporary sources about its location[9] is that it was to the north-west of The Mount sconce. Many of these sources refer to a 'strouse' (battery) at Acomb. Whether this Acomb emplacement is to be equated with the Holgate one is unresolved. Holgate Hill, however, seems a most natural and suitable site and, in view of what follows, there can be little doubt that an emplacement of some sort was built on it before or during the siege. The hill is 50 ft. above the level of the Ouse at Lendal Bridge and commands the approaches to York from the Acomb and Poppleton directions where these roads join near the crossing of Holgate Beck. In 1644 the hill would have had an uninterrupted view of the city walls west of Micklegate Bar ; it is 350 yds. from the tower in the city walls at the corner of Toft Green, 750 yds. from the Multangular Tower and 660 yds. from The Mount sconce.

Until 1930, when destroyed by modern building, an earthwork was visible on the top of the hill. This was excavated by the late Philip Corder in 1936[10] who described it as a 'rectangular earthwork, with rounded corners, measuring 148 ft . . . [by] 160 ft.'[11] The rampart was made of soil thrown up from an inner ditch or hollow. There was archaeological evidence for the occupation of the summit of the hill 'during the first half of the 14th Century.' Of the dating of the earthwork Corder had this to say — 'The only clue to the date of the rampart was a small group of two mediaeval sherds and a few scraps of broken tile found in the body of the bank . . . [which] points to the rampart having been made at the same period as the occupation of the summit of the hill.' This interpretation is incorrect. These finds suggest an occupation on the hill top in the 14th century and *prove* a later one. Corder considered the possibility that the hill was used to take one of the 1644 batteries and concluded that 'Though it is extremely likely that Holgate Hill was so used, no single relic was found during the excavations to give support to this.' It might be added that Corder's ex-cavation — of three small trenches — uncovered only a small part of the whole site. Further, if, as seems likely, an entry in the 'York Corporation Housebook'[12] concerning the demolition of 'works in Houlgate' relates to this site, very little of it would, in any case, have survived after 1645.

Since Corder's time evidence has come to light which indicates that this Holgate earthwork is typical of the kind of military works — 'redoubts' — which the Scots, in particular, were wont to throw up in the Civil War. In particular Newark has produced what look like very close parallels to the Holgate earthwork.[13]

No. 4 *'Works' near the Clifton/Poppleton bridge of boats* (NG. 588528)

When the Earl of Manchester raised the siege on 30 June he left behind a 'regiment of dragooners' to guard the bridge of boats over the Ouse in the Clifton/Poppleton area (see p. 36). They failed in their task and, of course, Prince Rupert made use of the bridge to get his army across to Marston Moor on the morning of 2 July. It is reasonable to assume that the bridge was covered — at least on the south-west, the Poppleton/Holgate side — by some sort of defence work. This is certainly implied by what follows.

'York Corporation Housebook'[14] records that in May 1645 orders were given by the Corporation to demolish 'the worke att the Brick Killnes in or neare Holegate feilds.' Brick Kiln Bridge is the name of the bridge which carries the modern Salisbury Road over Holgate Beck near Acomb Landing.[15] On his map of mediaeval York Raine[16] calls this bridge 'Fleet Bridge' and prints across the area east of it in the loop formed by the river Ouse the words 'Tile Pits.'[17] It seems likely that the 1644 'worke' was somewhere in this vicinity which would mean that the bridge of boats was probably either at Acomb Landing or at Clifton Ings near where the new (1963) bridge has been erected — probably the latter for the Water End crossing at Clifton appears to date from time immemorial.

'Lines' 'Breastworks'

On the analogy of 17th century military practice in general and of the Newark defences in particular there can be little doubt that in this western sector of the original city outworks the various sconces, batteries, emplacements &c. were linked together by a series of trenches or similar defensive works. We have hints of these in contemporary or near-contemporary sources. Defoe's 'the lines and bastions and demolished fortifications' and 'old additional works' may conceal references to these while the 'Housebook' entry — 'the worke in Houlgate and the brest-worke in Bishopfeilds' — implies more than just the redoubt on Holgate Hill.

(b) SOUTH OF THE CITY

No. 6   *Lamel Hill* (NG. 61455097)

Drake[18] is the earliest writer to call this site Lamel Hill. Rushworth[19] calls it 'a hill near Walmgate Bar;' Slingsby[20] 'ye Windmill hill, as ye way lyes to Heslington;' Hildyard[21] 'the mill hill above St. Laurence Leyes, without Walmgate Bar' and, in another place[22] 'Heslington Hill.' It is now in the garden of The Retreat and has a summer house built on top of it. The summit of the hill is 73ft. above the ground level at Walmgate Bar and 90 ft. above the summer level of the Ouse; this dominating position *vis-à-vis* the city defences is obscured nowadays by intervening modern buildings. Dr. John Thurnam excavated this hill top in 1849 — the first scientific excavation to be conducted in York.[23] He concluded that the topmost 10–12 ft. of the hill — which contained a considerable quantity of disturbed human bones — had been thrown up to support a Parliamentarian battery in 1644. Underneath this, to a depth of some 4 ft. below the pre-1644 ground level, he found undisturbed skeletons indicating a cemetery of considerable extent which he considered 'had afforded interment to from two to three hundred bodies :'

he actually uncovered 20–30 complete skeletons together with 'detached bones of at least as many more:' After weighing up carefully the evidence for a Romano-British, as against an Anglo-Saxon, date for this cemetery he decided on the latter, concluding it was Christian and was 'to be attributed to . . . the seventh or eighth century.' Here is what he has to say about the finds relating more specifically to 1644:—[24]

p. 31.   The only probable relics of the occupation of Lamel-hill by the troops of Fairfax and Lesley, consist of a few coins, and a piece of cast-iron which weighs nearly two pounds, and seems to have formed part of the bottom of a large pot or boiler. A well-known iron founder of York informs me that he has little doubt that this had formed part of a camp-kettle, of a form different from those which are made at the present day. It was found at the foot of the hill, on the south side, within about two feet of the surface. The coins found at or near the surface of the hill, and to be attributed to this period, are chiefly of the reign of Charles the First, and consist of a silver penny well preserved, and two or three farthings of the Scotch coinage of that reign. There is likewise a small copper coin of the contemporary Louis the Thirteenth of France. I am informed, by a former occupier, that, forty or fifty years ago, as many as thirty or forty silver coins were found in the garden at the foot of the hill, but of what description I am unable to learn . . .

p. 35.   A few coins and counters were found at depths varying from six to ten feet [on the top of the hill]. Some of these are very much worn and not to be deciphered. Two of them, however, are Nuremburg counters, of the sixteenth or seventeenth century; one of which bears the name of Hans Schultz. One of the coins is that of a Ferdinand; and there is a second brass Roman coin, perhaps of Trajan. The most interesting object found at the same level is, however the brass seal of the keeper of a chapel dedicated to the blessed Mary at Morton Folliott [in Worcestershire]. This seal is probably of the fourteenth or fifteenth century . . . .[25]

p. 35–6.   The discovery of this seal and of the counters, at the depth at which they were found, seems to afford proof that the upper part of this mound has been disturbed within the last three hundred years. I incline, indeed, to a conjecture that the hill was turned over and raised to a greater height by Fairfax's army in 1644, for the purpose of obtaining a more commodious site for their battery. Another indication of such a change in the upper part of the mound is, perhaps, found in the circumstance of some of the bones having been curiously cut and bored, as if merely for amusement. This is the case with one of the metatarsal bones of *Bos longifrons*. The burr of the deer's antler had been cut into a kind of ring . . .

In 1966 the writer was given an iron cannon ball, weighing 9 lbs. with a diameter of 4¾ ins., which was apparently found in

1939 or 1940 with two similar ones at the foot of Lamel Hill during gardening operations. All three were found close together. It was found after the demolition of some pre-fabricated houses in the vicinity, where, for many years, it had been used as a doorstop. Shot of this size and weight were normally fired during the Civil War by culverins.[26] It has already been established (see p. 37f) that three of the four guns mounted on Lamel Hill by Lord Fairfax were, in fact, culverins.

(c)   EAST OF THE CITY

*No. 7 *Emplacement on Baile Hill* (NG. 62005124)

In *Intelligence* No. 3[27] Ashe speaks of 'another [Royalist] Fort Eastward in the City [which] played frequently upon our men.' This is the only reference to a 'fort' on this side of York. Taken literally the words 'in the City' mean that it was within the city walls, a description which fits Baile Hill exactly. Baile Hill represents all that remains of the motte of one of the two Norman castles (the other one is that under Clifford's Tower) which were built by William I in 1068 to control passage up the rivers Ouse and Foss.

Excavations on Baile Hill in the summers of 1968 and 1969, conducted by Mr Peter V. Addyman of the University of Southampton, revealed evidence of this 1644 occupation. At the time of writing no detailed report on the excavation has been published.

(d)   NORTH OF THE CITY

*No. 5.   (?) *Near St. Peter's School, Clifton* (NG.596526)

According to Slingsby[28] the Earl of Manchester 'rais'd a battery against ye mannor Wall.' A cannonade from this battery preceded the blowing up of St. Mary's Tower and the attack on the King's Manor (see further pp. 59f). The site of this battery is not known but the area immediately around St. Peter's School would suggest itself. This occupies a slightly elevated position and is some 500 yds. from St. Mary's Tower and the adjoining Abbey Walls.

It is possible that Manchester took over a Royalist earthwork already on the site: hence the asterisk (*) above. The evidence for this is discussed below in section (f).

(e) OTHER EARTHWORKS

The outworks listed above (including those numbered 1 – 6) relate more particularly to the period up to the time of the battle of Marston Moor (2 July).[29] The guns on the various Parliamentarian emplacements were removed and then brought back when the siege was resumed two days later. All the old emplacements were not necessarily re-used. Lamel Hill may have been one of those abandoned. Slingsby[30] speaks of a new battery 'between Waingate [Walmgate] barr & Laterne [presumably Layerthorpe] Posterne.' Hildyard,[31] presumably referring to the same one says it was on 'Garrow Hill.' This is about half a mile east of Lamel Hill (NG. 619512) — no. 6 on front end paper. It seems that this Layerthorpe area had been selected by the besiegers for a major assault. Raine[32] writes of the 'drying fishpond' at this time but quotes no authority. Slingsby[33] refers to a bridge made 'to clap over ye Foss' and a 'store of Hurdles for a storme' assembled there. He also mentions another battery 'upon ye hill in Bishops fields.' Whether this was on one of the old sites or on a new one it is impossible to tell; it would certainly fit admirably the Holgate Hill site (no. 3 above).

(f) DISCUSSION

There is a distinct possibility that some or all of the emplacements marked above with an asterisk had been constructed some time — even as much as four years — before the siege of 1644. This would imply that the work done in 1643 on the sconce on 'St. James's Hill' (The Mount) — no. 2 on front end paper — consisted of nothing more than repairs to an already existing structure. This would make sense of the comparatively few men and tools then used and the short time taken over the task. Such a possibility would also explain another enigma concerning the 1643 preparations — why there is no mention in the 'Chamberlains' Rolls' of similar work being done on the other emplacements, one of which we know existed at Nunmills (the modern Southlands Chapel) and another somewhere in the Holgate/

Acomb area (?Holgate Hill). If these had been already constructed before 1643 this silence becomes understandable: they were presumably still available in that year.

There is evidence to support this conjecture. In 1640 York expected an attack from the Scots and preparations were made to meet a possible siege. Hildyard,[34] writing 24 years after the event, gives the most detailed account :-

1640   This year on the 22th of August, the King came to York, in His expedition against the Scots; and on the 24th Dyned at the Lord Mayors, and Knighted him. And on the 29th day rode to Northallerton where Notice was given Him, That the Scots had taken Newcastle, and that they intended to be at York, againe within a Weeke. His Majesty returned for York againe, and sent to Hull for Ammunition, and within three Dayes came thirty great Brasse Pieces of Ordnance, with all such things fitting for Warr, which were drawn into Clifton Inggs, and Fields, and Bishop Fields; in all which places Tents were pitched, Ordnance placed, and many Bulwarks raised; and a Bridge of Boats was made over the River Owse. And the King's Army consisting of neer 12000. Foot, and 3000 Horse, kept Leaguer almost to Allhallontide;[35] and the cold weather approaching, the Souldier were disposed into Quarters in the Country.

Drake[36] almost certainly based his account of this episode on Hildyard though he embellishes it — the thirty cannon have become 'fifty odd pieces of ordnance great and small.' He also mentions 'six score and twelve waggons loaden with powder, match and shot, with several other carriages full of pickaxes, spades and shovels, all [brought] from the king's magazine at Hull. Many of the cannon were planted before the camp, where several ramparts and bulwarks were thrown up.' Earlier Drake,[37] quoting 'Ex. MS' as his authority, states that 'On the 31st of August, the king, for his greater security at York, rode about the city accompanied with the marquis of Hamilton, several general officers, some aldermen and citizens, and with pickaxes, spades and shovels marked out several intrenchments and fortifications.'

Further information about this 'leaguer' comes from an unexpected source. *The Parish Register of St. Olave, York*[38] has a number of entries — under Burials, Baptisms and Marriages — relating to soldiers, covering the period October to November 1640.[39] The 'leaguer' is mentioned a number of times, the most significant for our present purpose being these :-

p. 79.   'In the leager in the fields in Layre Close . . . .'
p. 97.   '1640 in the Leaguer time . . . .'
p. 98.   'Leager. George Channer was buried the xixth [October] under the
Captaine James Benton a Darbyshire gent. in the Regyment of S[i]r Jacob
Ashlay Sgte maior generall of his maties. forces 1640.'

Hildyard's 'ordnance placed and many Bulwarks raised,'
Drake's 'several ramparts and bulwarks' and 'several intrenchments and fortifications' may well be the precursors of the 1644
siege outworks. Their siting — Hildyard's 'Clifton Inggs, and
Fields, and Bishop Fields' and Drake's 'before the camp [at
Clifton]' and 'about the city' could certainly be equated with
those of the 1644 siege outworks attested on the west and north
of the city.

Dr. R. M. Butler of the Royal Commission on Historical
Monuments (England) has drawn my attention to the fact that a
field in Clifton, now around NG. 59055315 and occupied by
Ouse Lea and two plots of land to the west, was called 'Legar' in
1836 on a catalogue of sale of land in Clifton.

[1] Defoe. The first paragraph quoted is on p. 228, the second on p. 232.
[2] *Intelligence* No. 3. *inter alia.*
[3] These numbers relate to front end paper. Throughout this chapter an asterisk
(*) before an emplacement indicates that it was certainly or probably built
originally by the Royalists: emplacements not so marked are assumed to have
been erected by the Parliamentarians.
[4] *Intelligence* No. 3.
[5] YPS *Handbook* (1891), p. 221b.
[6] *Intelligence* No. 3.
[7] YAJ. xxix, Pt. 154 (1957), p. 299.
[8] *Intelligence* No. 3.
[9] See *inter alia* p. 150.
[10] YAYAS Report for 1951–2, pp. 31–5.
[11] Corder's plan and section of the earthwork is reproduced on p. 154 of this
work.
[12] For the full entry see Appendix IIA, p. 169 no. 55.
[13] Newark, pp. 40–44. Note especially the redoubt at Crankley Point (Pl. 5).
[14] Reproduced in Appendix IIA, p. 170 no. 56.
[15] O.S. 6 in. Yorkshire Sheet clxxiv, 6 (ed. 1937).
[16] Folder map at the back. On p. 311 he refers to 'Fletebrig' (Fleet Bridge).
[17] On p. 312 he quotes documentary evidence for the existence of the tileries here

as early as 1374/5. He writes — 'The part of the Bishopfields that received most frequent mention was the 'Tile House' which was on the ground in the bend of the river at Clifton Scope. Reminders of it in the shape of ponds where clay had been extracted existed until recently . . . The besiegers of York in 1644 had a battery there.' The hollows from which clay was removed are still to be seen in this area.

18 p. 262.
19 p. 622.
20 p. 108.
21 p. 56.
22 p. 60.
23 *Arch. Journal* vi (1849), pp. 27–39 and pp. 123–136; for a shorter version see *Proc. Yorks. Phil. Soc.* i (1847–54), pp. 98–105.
24 As given in the *Arch. Journal* account. The page references from this are given against the text above.
25 A description and drawing of the seal follows in this account. Thurnam was puzzled as to how it could have found its way to Lamel Hill. Perhaps it represented loot picked up by one of the soldiers responsible for the 1644 battery during his previous campaigning in the west country.
26 See, *inter alia*, Newark, p. 51.
27 See further p. 35.
28 p. 108.
29 The Royalist battery on The Mount remained in Royalist hands before and after Marston Moor (see pp. 90 and 96).
30 p. 115.
31 p. 57.
32 p. 15.
33 p. 115.
34 pp. 51–2. Brief references to it occur in *CSP. Dom.* 1640–1, p. 62: G. Hadley, *A New and Complete History of . . . . Kingston-upon-Hull* 1788, p. 143 and VCH York 1961, p. 187.
35 1 November.
36 p. 139.
37 p. 138.
38 Pt. I, 1538–1644.
39 *The Registers of St. Michael le Belfrey, York* (Pt. I 1565–1653) also have entries relating to this same incident though the word 'leaguer' as such does not occur. On 8 October 1640 'a Soldyer' married a widow of Clifton (p. 201); on 11 September 1640 'a Soldier, (slaine at Clifton)' is buried; six days later 'a Solder (dying at Clifton)' is buried (p. 202). Other military burials are listed, not mentioning Clifton (pp. 203–4) while on 30 July 1641 'a Soldyer, and Jane Poppleton of Clifton, maryed' (p. 205).

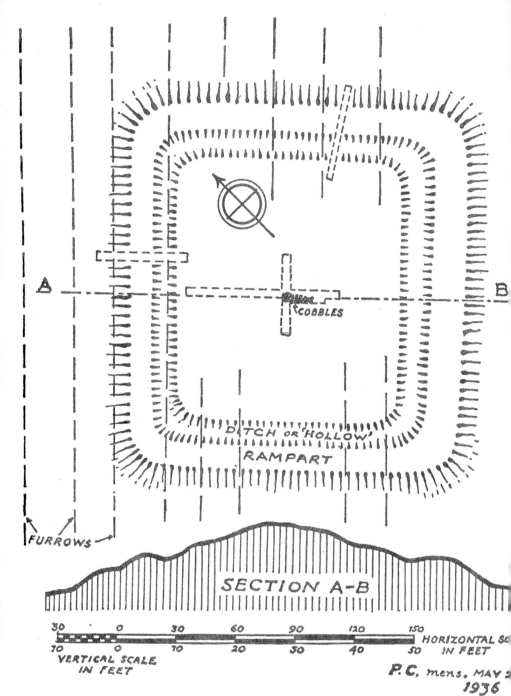

A   B

COBBLES

DITCH OR 'HOLLOW'

RAMPART

FURROWS

SECTION A-B

30   0   30   60   90   120   150
10   0   10   20   30   40   50

VERTICAL SCALE
IN FEET

HORIZONTAL SC
IN FEET

P.C. mens. MAY
1936

Plan and section of the excavation on Holgate Hill, 1936

154

Appendices

APPENDIX I

LETTER[1] FROM FERDINANDO, Lord Fairfax, concerning the Battle of Selby, 11 April, 1644.

My Lords:

According to the Orders sent to mee and my son from your Lordships, wee have now joyned our Forces together; and though the Enemy held all the passes from the East-riding to the West, and by that means intercepted divers of our Letters, and thereby became acquainted with our appointments, and so indeavoured to prevent them; which forced mee to decline Selby, and make a passage over the River, ten miles below it in Marshland, where my Men and Carriages being passed with some difficulty, on Sonday and Monday last, I instantly marched with the whole Army consisting of Two thousand Horse and Dragoons, and Two thousand Foot or thereabouts, to Ferry-bridge, and so to Selby, where Colonell John Belasyse (commanding in chief in Yorkshire) then lay with an Army of Fifteen hundred Horse, and Eighteen hundred Foot, as themselves confesse, though Reports made it much more numerous.

Upon Wednesday, our Forlorn-Hope of Horse beat in a partee of the Enemies Horse, and followed them into the Town, taking divers of them prisoners, and the day being far spent, I quartered the Army within a mile of Selby that night, and drew them out again early the next morning, and then with the Foot in three divisions, one led up by my self, a seconde by Sir John Meldrum, and a third by Lieutenant Colonell Needham, fell upon the Town, to storm it in three places altogether, where the Enemy received us with much courage, and made strong resistance for two hours or thereabouts; but in conclusion, my own Foot Regiment forced a passage by the River side, and my son with his Regiment of Horse rushed into the Town, where hee was incountred by Colonell Belasyse, and the Enemies Horse, but they being beaten back, and Master Belasyse himself wounded, and taken prisoner, and our Foot entred on all sides the Town, the Enemy was wholly routed, and as many as could saved themselves by flight, some towards Cawood, some towards Pontefract, and the rest towards York, over the River by a Bridge of Boats laid by themselves; We pursued them every way, and took in the Town

156

and chase, the Prisoners, Ordnance, Arms, Ammunitions, and Colours mentioned in the List inclosed.

Of my own Men, I lost in the fight divers gallant Commanders and Souldiers, and very many sore wounded; And indeed, all my Army, both Commanders and common Souldiers behaved themselves with as much courage as ever I observed in Men.

All which wee must acknowledge to God alone, who both infuseth courage, and gives Victory where hee pleaseth: I shall now, I hope, be able to raise more Forces in the country, and improve this Victory that God hath bestowed on us, to the best advantage. This being all for the present, untill further occasion, I rest

Your Lordships

Selby, 12 April   Most affectionate and humble Servant

1644.   Fer[dinando] Fairfax.

A List of the Officers taken Prisoners, the 11. of April, 1644.

Colonell John Belasyse
Colonell Sir John Ramsden
Sir Thomas Strickland
Lieut. Colonell Tyndall
Lieut. Colonell Forbes
Major Heskit

Commanders of Horse
3 Majors, 5 Captains [all named]

Captains of Foot
12 Captains and 2 Captain-Lieutenants [named]

Lieutenants of Horse
4 [named]

Lieutenants of Foot
20 [named]

Cornets
6 [named]

Ensigns
11 [named]

Quartermasters
9 [named]

Elias Walker, Master of the Magazine. Richard Ludlow, Provost Marshall; And divers Sergeants, Trumpets, Corporalls, Drums, and other Officers.

Divers slain, and lyes strewed in the way to York for four miles together; others that fled to Pontefract, were pursued as far as Ferry-Bridge.

157

Four Brasse pieces of Ordnance.
Seven Barrels of Powder. Sixteen Bundles of Match.
Two thousand Armes or above.

Many Horse and Foot Colours taken, but as yet sixteen or seventeen come in. And Sixteen hundred common Soldiers. Above Five hundred Horse. The Pinnace taken at Gainsbrough; All their Bag and Baggage, and many Ships and Boats upon the River.

SIVE DE
OBSIDIONE PRÆLIOque
EBORACENSI
CARMEN;
Cum Quibusdam
MISCELLANEIS

Operâ Studióque *PAGANI PISCATORIS*
ELUCUBRATIS.

LONDINI,
Typis *Thomæ Newcomb*, M.DC.L.

AND
Private Cabinet rifled.
AND
A DISCOVERY
OF
A Pack of his JEWELS.
By way of
DIALOGUE

Between, } Mercurius *Britannicus* and Mercurius *Aulicus.*

London, Printed by J. C's, Anno Dom. MDC XLIV.

PLATE XXIII   Contemporary tracts relating to the Battle of Marston Moor.

1. Payne Fisher's *Marston Moor* . . . *Carmen* 1650.
2. Prince Rupert hiding in a beanfield after the battle 1644.

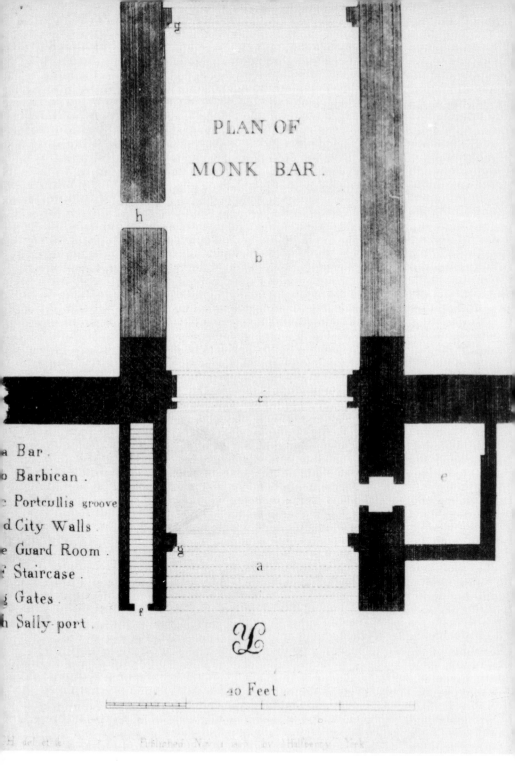

PLAN OF
MONK BAR.

h

b

c

a Bar.
b Barbican.
c Portcullis groove
d City Walls.
e Guard Room.
f Staircase.
g Gates.
h Sally-port.

e

g

a

g

f

𝒴

40 Feet.

PLATE XXIV

Plan of Monk Bar, showing the Sally-port, 1807.

Delineator Joseph Halfpenny.

APPENDIX II

A. *City of York House Books*, B.36 (1637–1650) and B.37 (1651 – 1663). MS. in York Public Library.

Below are extracted all the references which have any bearing on the events connected with the siege — either preceding it, during it or following it — from 31 January 1641/2 onwards. Entries within square brackets [ ] are abstracts: spelling and capitals are as in the original.

B. 36

fo. 65   (1)[2] 31st January 1641/2.

Ordered that the Magazeene of this Cittie be watched by such of the Trayned Bandes as my Lord Maior shall appoint, two on the daie and fower on the night.

Ordered that a reviewe be taken of the Armes for the Aynstie.[3]

fo. 65b–66   (2) 3rd February 1641/2.

[In addition to the Corporation Plate the new Lord Mayor (Edmund Cooper) had the following handed over to him:–][4]

.... 41 Barrils of good powder whereof three Barrils double are accompted for six. And two Barrils of bad powder, 200 waight of good ould match and [   ] of new, 4100 of bulletes and the keyes of the store house where the same lyeth.

fo. 67   (3) 11th February 1641/2.

Ordered that answere be given to Mr. High Sherriffe and the Gentlemen of the Countrie that they cann conceive no place fitting for the Magazeene of the Countie within this Cittie unless it be at Trinities in Micklegate which is Sir John Goodricks and if the[y] cann procure his consent they will willingly agree to it so that it be no charge to the Cittie.

fo. 67   (4)   14th February 1641/2.

Agreed. . . . that the Magazeene of the Countie according to an order in the house of Commons in Parliament shall be laid upp in the Merchants hall.

fo. 74b   (5)   30th August 1642.

Sir Edward Osburne, Sir Jo. Ramsden, Sir Henry Slingsbie, Sir Marmaduke Langdale and Sir Henry Griffith came into this Courte and offerred in theire names and the rest of the gent[lemen] of the Countie to advise in any thinge for the safetie of this Cittie and to ioyne with them therein if they thought good and desired an answere from this Courte therein.

fo. 75   (6)   2nd September 1642.

[The above offer was refused] the [City] Commons . . . . conceived the Cittie to be in noe danger.

fo. 75b   (7)   6th September 1642.

Ordered that there be a watch sett in this Cittie, viz. twentie on the daytime and fower score on the night and that they be taken by house Rowe and fortie of the fower score to be musqueteers and to be furnished with fortie musketts viz. ten out of each warde of the Common musquetts such as my Lord Maior shall appointe and the rest to be furnished with halberts, swords, and such other weapons as they cann provide . . . . And that the posternes be forborne to be blocked upp but that they be open on the day and lockt upp on the night and the keys brought to some warden of the warde. And that the Ferry boate at the Lendinge to be used on the day and lockt upp on the night and that one of my Lord Maior's officers see the same done.

fo. 76   (8)   21st September 1642.

Ordered that the King's Gunners shall have 55 *li* of powder lent them.

And nowe my Lord Maior moved that the watch att Magazin might be respited untill the Gent[lemen] of the Countie meete.

fo. 77   (9)   23rd October 1642.

And nowe [it is ordered] that my Lord Maior, by what good advise he may, take the best course they shall thinke fitt to secure the Cittizes plate in this time of danger. And that if the same notwithstandinge shall be taken that my Lord Maior and his suerties be discharged thereof and the losse thereof to be sustained by the Common Chamber.

160

fo. 77b   (10)   8th November 1642.

[Ordered that 4 Aldermen] goe to my Lord Generall to shew unto him that in respect what danger this Cittie now standeth wheither it be fittinge to move a treaty with my Lord Faireffax and the rest.

fo. 78b   (11)   26th November 1642.

Whereas all the souldiers now resident in the Cittie have paie after viiid. *per diem* except the Trained [Bands] of the Cittie it is desired therefore that they may have the like paye as well as the rest seinge that the cittizens contribute theire moneyes towards the charge.

[Fires were to be supplied for the sentinels on the walls].

fo. 78b   (12)   [If the Lord General and other gentlemen made further assessments, they should maintain the trained bands they had brought from the country. The City and Ainsty should maintain only their own trained bands because of the great charge to the City in] watching, fiers and candles and makeinge trenches.

[Those who were not charged with private arms and were able to bear them should be charged for the present].

[The trained bands of the Ainsty were to bear their own charges as did those of the City].

fo. 79   (13)   28th November 1642.

[The Lord Mayor and 2 Aldermen were to desire of the Lord General] that some course may be taken that the souldiers and others doe not fell and cutt upp anie timber trees, quickwood, fruite trees or hedgrowes aboute the Cittie as they now have begun to do.

fo. 79b   (14)   2nd December 1642.

[A formal greeting was to be given to the Earl of Newcastle by the Corporation when he entered the City with his army].

Ordered that notice be given to the Inholders that the[y] sell theire oates by Markett measure and Haye & other victualls at reasonable rates.

fo. 80   (15)   9th December 1642.

[Arrangements were to be made for sick and wounded soldiers to be housed in the Merchant Taylors' Hall and at the house of Alderman Vaux and for dead soldiers to be buried in a Christian manner].

fo. 81–82b   (16)   13th January 1642/3.

[Describes at length the circumstances surrounding the election of Sir Edmund Cooper as Lord Mayor for a second successive time. This was done forcibly on orders from the Marquis of Newcastle[5]].

fo. 84   (17)   23rd February 1642/3.

.... and it is thought fitt that the wood cominge from Sir John Bourch[i]er wood to the Citty be sold, the kid wood at six shillings a lode and nickt [notched] wood and lock wood at eight shillings a lode.

fo. 84b   (18)   27th September 1642/3.

[The four collectors of an assessment of 40s. were each to pay in £40 so that the men of the trained bands might all be paid 20d. per week for a month and the cost of bread and cheese for the army defrayed].

[Two Aldermen were to desire the Governor to ensure that no further damage was done to Alderman Vaux's house, so that Francis Jackson or any other person on behalf of Alderman Vaux might take care of the two soldiers remaining there].

fo. 85   (19)   3rd March 1642/3.

Ordered that out of the forty shillings for Armes for this month that the bread and cheese be paid for, viz. 45 and 41 *li* and that the 110 *li* dew to the Citty for 2s 8d per weeke for there trained band shalbe paid within a fortnight or 3 weekes, which Mr. Nevile[6] and Captaine Cocke have undertaken.

fo. 86b   (20)   20th March 1643.

Ordered that there be no more pouder and ma[t]ch yssued out of the Magazene till further order.

.... That the Committe[e] be moved to pay the £110 which Mr. Nevile and Captaine Cocke undertooke to pay for 20d. weekly to every soldyer of the trained bands of the Citty for a month.

And now that the Citty may have satisfaction or the 24 barrels of pouder and ma[t]ch and bullets dispended restored.

And now that the markett folkes be not hindered and robbed as they are in reparinge to the Citty.

And now to lett them know the great lose the Citty hath by pulling downe all the fences about it as also the Citty's houses.

fo. 87   (21)   28th March 1643.

Ordered that my Lord Generall be moved to write or send to those Aldermen and Cittyzens that are out of the Citty to come in and reside in the Citty.

fo. 87b	(22)	24th March 1643.

The Aldermen and 24 shall draw up a petic[i]on to the Lord Generall or the Quene's Majestie as they shalbe advised to be freed from the fre billitinge soldiers any longer.

fo. 88	(23)	3rd May 1643.

[Agreed with the Marquis of Newcastle that £3,000 shall be assessed on the City and Ainsty for the maintenance of His Majesty's army].

fo. 90b	(24)	19th July 1643.

And that my Lord Maior and Aldermen doe move the Lord Generall for his warrant to comaund the Aldermen that are absent to cominge and reside in the A[i]nsty as also to speake with the Committe about the assessment of 3000 *li* again required.

fo. 91	(25)	6th September 1643.

[Account to be taken of the £12 which Mr. David Pryrole received weekly from the various parishes in the City for making bulwarks].

fo. 94	(26)	15th January 1643/4.

[Letter from the Marquis of Newcastle insisting that Cowper remain as Lord Mayor for the following year. City acquiesced].

fo. 95b	(27)	29th January 1643/4.

And now my Lord Maior made knowne unto this Courte that Collonell John Bellassis being now Governor of this Citty doth desire that provision be made for 200 soldiers to keepe Clifford's Towre for thre months whereof he hath delivered a particular amounting to 549*l*. 19s. 4d. whereupon it is ordered by this Courte that looke how much cannot be gotten of the provider the rest shalbe undertaken by this Citty which my Lord Maior promised it shalbe paid out of the first moneyes that shalbe receaved of the assessments.

fo. 96	(28)	30th January 1643/4.

Ordered that looke what money so ever any of this Courte disburseth in makin provision for 200 soldiers in the Towre [Clifford's Tower] for three months shalbe paid by this Chamber if it can be noe othewaies gotten.

fo. 96b	(29)	31st January 1643/4.

Ordered that 100 *li* be borrowed at use for the necessary occasions of this Citty especially for making provisions for the Towre [Clifford's Tower] and that Sir Roger Jaques, Robert Hemsworth, Henry Thompson Aldermen and Mr. Paule

Beale shall be coum [become] bound for the same and that
they shalbe saved harmelese by this Corporacion.

fo. 98–98b   (30)   7th and 16th February 1643/4.

[Ordered that the City's plate was to be pawned to pay
£100 of the debt of £500 and that it] shalbe bought again
and restored as soone as money can conveniently be raised.

fo. 101   (31)[7]   29th April 1644.

Ordered that there shalbe 4000 soldiers that shall have 4d.
a day payed them for theire diet, the gent[lemen] already
named [no mention of them occurs in the book] excepted, to
have any of them and looke in what houses any officers are
bilited or lodged the allowance or proportion of victuals
allotted him or them shalbe delivered to the house keper
where he is bilited and the names of soe many soldiers as are
allotted to every house shalbe delivered to the householder
that he may pay them accordingly.

fo. 102   (32)   12th July 1644.

And now these presents with the Comon Councell
assembled and about a hundreth of the best Cittyzens, when
and where the Letter of summons sent by the three Generals
Leven, Fairfax and Manchester, as also certaine Artickles
wherein there opinion being taken the well liked of if soe be
my Lord Maior and Governor assented thereunto which they
wholy refered to them.

fo. 102b   (33)   25th July 1644.

Ordered that a butt of sack and a tunn of French wine
be presented to the Lord Fairfax, Generall of the North, in
regard the great love and affection he hath shewed to the
Citty.

And now my Lord Maior and Governor having had a
parley it is ordered and thought fitt that the City be delivered
up upon these Artickles following — Artickles agreed upon
betwene Alexander Earle of Leven, Generall of the Scottish
Forces, Ferdinando Lord Fairfax and the Earle of Manchester, Generals of the Einglish Forces about Yorke of
thone partie and Sir Thomas Glemham, knight, Governor
of the Citty of Yorke and Collonell Generall of the Northeren
Army on other party anent the surrender and delivery of the
said Citty with the Fortes, Towres, Cannons, Amunicion and
Furniture of warr belonging thereunto in manor after
specified to the said Generals for thuse [the use] of the King
and Parliament the 15th day of July 1644. [Then follow the
Articles of Surrender].

(34)   2nd August 1644.

And now the Comon Councell assembled with these presents and where it is ordered that there is a very great necessety of some present money for the repairing of bridges and highwaies and clearing of the gates and clensing of the streets in and about the Citty and for fortifiing of the same as also for releife of sick and lame soldiers: It is there for ordered that there be an assessment made of £300 throughout the Citty and that paid to Mr. Alderman Thompson for uses aforesaid.

(35)   13th August 1644.

And now the Comon Councell, Chamberlaines and most of the best Cittyzens when my Lord Maior made knowne unto them that my Lord Generall sent for him and the Aldermen yesterday and moved that the Citty would lay of 2000 groates a day to 2000 soldiers for one month and that it should be repayed them assuredly out of the assessments, wher upon it was agreed by all these presents that the same shalbe performed accordingly.

(36)   To the honourable the Lord Maior, Aldermen and Sheriffs of the City of Yorke.

My Lord and Gent[lemen].

Since my comeing into this Citty I have receaved divers complaints for the want and neglect of your administracon of publique Justice among the people especially by your failing to keepe those courts of Justice wherewith you stand intrusted by your charters and which is one of the principall priviliges of the Citty. I shall not need to put you in mind that by your neglect herein you indainger the forfiture of that liberty or that as Burgisses and Cittizens you stand bound by oath to preserve your priviliges, yet you must suffer this admonicion that you forthwith discharge the duty which lyes upon you and performe your trust over the people that there may be noe failing of Justice in this kind the Parliament of England intends the preservacon of our Lawes as the best and onely meanes to keepe English subiects in order and the due execucion of them I must carefully looke to where I have powre to comaund. So rests

Your Lordship and the rest very effectionate freind

Fer[dinando] Fairfax.

Yorke 13th August 1644.

(37) 30th September 1644.

Alderman Hoile [Hoyle] declared unto these presents that the Parliament had made an ordinance that he should be Lord Maior for the residue of this yeare, which ordinance being redd all these presents very cherefully and readily submitted unto and were very desirus to performe to the utmost.

fo. 108b (38) 1st October 1644.

[The streets and barsteads of the City were to be repaired and paved].

[The Lord Mayor was to keep in safety the remainder of the City's plate delivered to him. But if any should be taken from him 'forceablely in these times of Warre' he should not be charged to make them good].

fo. 109b (39) 4th October 1644.

[Three parishes, St. Crux, St. Margaret's and St. Deny's were to maintain three sentries, at Walmgate Bar, the Red Tower and the Bean Hills, with the same allowance for fires as they had previously, and the Provost Marshall was to maintain the fires in the Merchants Hall].

fo. 110 (40) 19th October 1644.

And now it is ordred that the wardens of Monckwarde doe viewe St. Maurice Church and by advising with the parishioners take co[u]rse for preservacion of the stalls, books and other things belonging the sayd Church it being in parte broken downe and the houses in the sayd parish burnt downe.

fo. 111 (41) 8th November 1644.

[Thirty beds to be provided for wounded and sick soldiers at St. Anthony's Hall].

fo. 112b (42) 21st November 1644.

[The soldiers imprisoned in the City to be restrained from begging].

fo. 115b (43) 11th December 1644.

[The Guildhall could not be used, it being full of arms, cloth and other things].

fo. 118 (44) 11th January 1644/5.

[Ordered that Edward Giles, the City Husband, should provide lime and other necessaries as soon as possible for repairing the City walls. The Aldermen and Twentyfour were to survey them the following Thursday.

Following an ordinance of both Houses of Parliament dated 1st January the following six Aldermen being very much disaffected to the service of the King and Parliament, were to be removed from office and others elected in their stead, — Sir Roger Jaques, Sir Robert Belt and Sir Edmond Cowper, knights, William Scott, Robert Hemsworth and John Myers].

fo. 121b   (45)   22nd January 1644/5.

Ordred that Alderman Henry Thomson Alderman Watson Mr. Sheriff Taler and Mr. Edward Calvert shall repaire with S[i]r Robt. Barwick to my Lord Generall and make him acquainted in what great decay the Citties walls are in and how according to law and the Citties charters they ought to be repaired And desier [desire] his Excellency assistance and helpe for repairing them accordingly.

fo. 122b   (46)   17th January 1644/5.

That it be moved to Common Counsell on Monday next for making an order for building houses upright from the ground on brick.

fo. 123   (47)   31st January 1644/5.

And now Mr. Alderman Leonard Thomson and Alderman Cowton certified this Court that they had veiwed the tower at St. Leonard's Landing and found the same in great decay and the ferry boate gone and that theirfore they thought fitt yf this Court soe pleased that Mathew Malton repairing the Tower and makeing a new ferry boate at his owne charge have a lease of both for 21 yeares at 30s. rent per annum.

Whereupon it is ordred that he have a lease theirof accordingly to begin at Lady Day next.

fo. 125   (48)   10th February 1644/5.

Ordered that Edmund Giles the Cittyes husband take order that there be seates made in the Centry [Sentry] houses where there is need.

And that he likewise take order there be a watch house of fur deales maid for the Centry at Walmegate barr.

fo. 126   (49)   21st February 1644/5.

Ordered that Edmond Giles have 48 li to repaire the decayes in the Corner of the Cittyes Walls on the ould Baile and the other decay thereto adioyning and make the same answarable in hight to the rest of the Wall according to the late veiw taken of it, and to make a Watch house of Brick or Stone five yards in length and 2 yards and a halfe broad within and he to find all materialls belonging the same and to remove the earth that is there laid at his owne chardge. [An additional 40s. was granted for the work on 20th March 1644/5. (fo. 129)].

fo. 126b   (50)   25th February 1644/5.

[Ordered that Castle gate Postern be opened and that three Aldermen and such workmen as they should appoint should see the same done. They were to view the way and dam at Castle Mills and consider the making of a draw-bridge over the 'clews'[8] there with a sufficient passage for horse and foot at the postern, over the mills and along the usual highway].

Ordered that his Excellency be moved that Skeldergate posterne may be opened for conveniency of vessels cuming up the river soe soone as the same may conveniently be done.

fo. 127   (51)   25th February 1644/5.

And now also his Excellencyes order for drawing up the pallisadoes at the Crane was re[a]d viz:–
It is ordered that the pallisadoes over the river of Owse be forthwith taken away for more conveniency of pasage for the vescels and the same shall be dune by imposing such a sume on every vessell or boate that shall traid or such other wayes as the Lord Maior and Aldermen shall thinck fitt.

fo. 128b   (52)   14th March 1644/5.

And now my Lord Maior and Mr. Alderman Watson are desired by theise presents to goe to my Lord Generall and the Comisiners to move them that parte of the Citties assess-ments may be allowed for the repaire of the Walls and to putt them in mind that three hundereth pound was collected by a former assessment at the motion of my Lord Generall and Sir Jo[hn] Meldram [Meldrum] for that purpose.

fo. 129   (53)   20th March 1644/5.

Ordered that a watch house be biulded of brick at Walmegate barr and the Cittyes husband to see the same done presently.

Ordered that Boothome barr be forthwith vewed by Alderman Horner and Mr. Dossy and they to see what is needfull to be done for preventing/stopping upp[9] the passage there and to get the same affected accordingly.

fo. 129b   Ordered that Alderman Coulton and the rest that are to vew the Toft Greene vew also Skeldergate Posterne and taking some workmen with them consider how a convenient watch house may be maid there for watching the River and what the charg thereof may be.

fo. 131   (54)   28th March 1645.

Ordered and agreed by Edward Giles that he shall and will build a platt forme for a peece of Ordnance and a gaurd house on Toftegrene which shall be in length five yards and in bredth three yards and he to have for doeing the same 60 *li* out of which he is to pay 40s. to Tho. Haggas and Michell Hindley for repaireing the Walls neere the Corner of the Tower att Toft Greene.

And now Alderman Horner and Alderman Coulton are desired to vew the ditch about the Read Tower neere Walmgate barr and to take care that the same be maid soe deepe that nether horse nor man cann come or goe that way forth of or into the Citty.

Ordered that Edward Giles take care for the river Fosse at Castle milnes to stopp the clowes and preserve the water at such a reasonable marke as he shall see cause for preservation of the Citty and to be done with all speed.

Ordered that Abraham Smith doe presently repaire the walls at Fishergate posterne and in all other places soe that noe persons may clyme over the same ether into or out of the Citty.

Ordered that Edward Giles and Abraham Smith doe take care for the present repairing of the draught house at the fare end of the stath and they to have satisfaction for the same.

fo. 132b   (55)   21st April 1645.

Ordered that the Inhabitants of Ruffurth, Knapton and Hessey shall demolish the worke in Houlgate and the brest-worke in Bishoppfeilds on Fryday next and Alderman Leo. Thomson & Alderman Coulton to see the same dune.

Ordered that there be a Comon day worke on Wednesday next at Castle Millnes and every housholder of St. Sampson's and St. Savour's parishes to send an able person with spades or shovels to worke there all that day and 12 men likewise to be hired to worke there with spades and Alderman Horner and Alderman Coulton are desired to take care to get the workmen and to see the worke done and who makes defa[u]lt in sending a fitt person provided for the purpose aforesaid to pay 12d a peece and the same to be levied by distresse.

fo. 133b   (56)   5th May 1645.

Ordred that upon the petic[i]on of Alce Bugg touching a horse taken from her from the parish of Trinities for the publique service it is thought fitt by the Court that the Constables of the said parish shall procure an assessment of 3 *li* the price of the said horse to be maid and they with speed

169

to gather the same and pay it to the said Alce Bugg according to my Lord Fairfax order signified in that behalfe by Col. Needome and others.

Ordred that a Comon day worke be appointed for the demolishing of the worke att the Brickillnes in or neare Holegate Feilds & the same to be done by an able person from every housholder in the townes of Moore Munckton & this to be done on Fryday next & the Cheife Constables to be there and Alderman Leo. Thomson and Mr. Sheriffe Tayler are desired to see the same done and in defalt of appearance and doing the worke to pay 12d to be levied by distresse.

Ordred that a Comon day worke be by the Inhabitants of Acaster Selbie to demolish the worke in Midlethorpe Inggs[10] & this to be done on Fryday next and Alderman Leo. Thomson & Sheriffe Taylor are desired to see the same done and in defalt of appearance by any in doing thereof the same to pay 12d to be levied by distresse.

fo. 134   (57)   14th May 1645.

[Upon the petition of Eliz. Varey and Mariall Smith, the City's tenants in Holgate, it was granted by the Court that they should have abatement of three half year's rent arrears and have the coming year's rent provided they built a convenient house[11]].

fo. 135b   (58)   20th May 1645.

And now it is certified to the Court by Alderman Horner and Alderman Coulton that Edmond Giles hath well performed the plattforme for a peece of Ordnance & a Guard house on Toft Greene for which he was to have 60 *li*, 50 *li* whereof is paid & he hath maid a buttris more convinant for which the Court thinkes fitt to give 3*li* 10s. more to him in all 13*li* 10s.

fo. 138   (59)   10th July 1645.

Ordred that a chalder[12] or two of lyme shalbe taken upp and prepared for mending the walls aboute the ould bale and Edward Giles, the Cities husband to take care the same be donne as alsoe that he and the officer of the ward take from Phillipp Wallers the iron that came of Walmgate Barr and take order it be brought away and laid upp in safetie for the citties use.

fo. 143   (60)   28th July 1645.

And now itt is ordred that Edmund Giles the Cities husband shall furthwith provide a locke and key for Castlegate postran [postern] and make the gate fitt for opening and

170

lockinge and use meanes to way upp and lett downe the portcullis to th'end that the postran may be opened and shutt when further order shalbe given for the same.

fo. 147b   (61)   11th August 1645.

[George Hunter, tenant of a frontstead and garth in Micklegate and formerly of the house there which was pulled down in the Marquis of Newcastle's time, petitioned to buy the inheritance thereof. He was to be granted it for £10 in respect of his great loss and sufferings].

fo. 148b   (62)   18th August 1645.
                [Commons assented thereto].

fo. 148b   (63)   18th August 1645.

[Petition of Anne Watson, widow, tenant of a tenement without Micklegate Bar which was pulled down, except for a chimney, in the Marquis of Newcastle's time. A stable on the frontstead was granted to her for a dwelling rent free] in regard of her great age and the poore estate she is now in.

fo. 158   (64)   11th October 1645.

[A weaver who formerly lived at Monk Bridge end and contributed to the weavers of the City, and now lived within the City because his house was burned and pulled down by the Marquis of Newcastle's party, was to be admitted to the freedom].

fo. 158b   (65)   11th October 1645.

And now it is ordred and Stephen Watson and Robert Horner Aldermen are desired to sett on workemen presently, to take upp the stones which are throwne into the mine at Walmegate barr and cawse the same to be preserved and laid upp for the Citties use and order that the mine be fild upp with earthe and that the barr stead and cawsey theirabouts where nede is be paved.

fo. 163b   (66)   3rd December 1645.

Ordred that William Smalwood the officer of Boothom Ward shall looke unto and see when the ammunicion and other materiall of warr are all removed from the Comon Hall and give notice theirof to Robarte Horner, Symon Cowton, Aldermen, and Thomas Harbarte, gent. who or two of them are theirupon desired to vew and consider of the reparing of the Inner Roome which is falne downe and what materialls of wood and other things are nedefull for reparing the same as alsoe the windowes and what ells is nedefull to be repared aboute the hall and they are desired and authorished by the Courte to repare the same with spede can be and sett on

171

workemen for that purpose and the chardge theirof to be borne by this Corporacion.

fo. 171b (67) 12th February 1645/6.

[Three Aldermen, or two of them, were to view the 'Gyme' (?gin) without Castlegate postern and Edward Giles to stop the same as they directed].

fo. 180b (68) 2nd April 1646.

[Ordered that an assessment of £317 should be laid on the City; £117 to be paid for the money already disbursed for the repair of the City Walls, and the other £200 to pay for the repair of the] gavell end of the ould Chappell or Bursse on Owsebridge.

And whereas there are also great decayes and breaches in Walmegate Barr, the coveringe of Bowtham barr, the Comon Hall, the Castle Milne damme, and other parts of the Cittie wall, the repaireinge whereof will require a greater some then at present can well be rased in this Cittie, therefore it is ordered that the same bee respited for three munthes and then the Lord Maior and Aldermen to lay such assessment on this Cittie for that purpose as they shall thinke nessecary, and in the meane tyme the Burgesses to bee desired to try if the Parliament will al[l]ow anythinge towards the said repayres.

[Three persons (two of them Aldermen) were appointed overseers of the work to be done on Ouse Bridge. A further eight persons were to assist them to advise what necessary repairs should be made to the bursse and bridge].

fo. 181 (69) 15th April 1646.

[The parishioners of St. Cuthbert's petitioned that a land assessment might be made for the repair of the church. It was ordered that it be viewed by the City Husband and two others].

fo. 184 (70) 3rd June 1646.

[The Castle Mill dam was being repaired by the City to prevent any further danger from the breach there, although the work ought to be done by the owners of the Castle Mills, now pulled down].

fos. 187–187b (71) 1st June 1646.

[Henry Penrose, plaintiff, exhibited a bill of complaint to stay the suit brought against him by John Kay, defendant. As a result of a letter written by the late Edmund Kay, son of the said John, from Heslington to York in 'the Leaguer time,' by which some of the Marquis of Newcastle's party learned of their whereabouts, both he and Henry Penrose being 'well affected to the Parliament's cause' were imprisoned in the Merchant's Hall, the latter for six months at least and Edmund Kay until his death. The plaintiff had suffered great loss by the plundering of his goods and by imprisonment. He had paid part of his debt to Edmund Kay, who had acknowledged before his death that the debt was now £13, of which he forgave half as he was the cause of the plaintiff's imprisonment. The remainder was to be paid when he was able. Although the defendant sued for the whole debt, the plaintiff was ordered to pay him £6. 10s. and 20s. costs].

fo. 199   (72)   18th November 1646.

[Some abatement of arrears of rent was to be made to Sir George Palmes as he had no profit from his lands in the leaguer time].

fo. 204.   (73)   8th March 1646/7.

Ordered that Edmond Gyles shall have such timber out of the Sequestracion house in Mint Garth as is necessarie for the repayre of the Citties gates.

fo. 204b   (74)   8th April 1647.

[Edmund Giles was to see that the east end of Holgate Bridge was speedily repaired, and to provide two fothers of lead for the repair of Bootham Bar].

fo. 212   (75)   21st November 1647.

[The Common Council asked that in proportioning the cost of quartering of soldiers, allowance should be made for] the povertye of the Cittye by want of traide and by burneinge of the suburbs.

fo. 226   (76)   26th April 1649.

Whereas the horsefaire hath constantly beene kept without Walmegate barr untill that by these late warres the houses there were destroyed and that streete made unfitt for that purpose, now for as much as the sayd streete is clensed and fitted and diverse convenient houses there erected; it is therefore thought fitt and soe ordered that the said horsefaire and markett be kept without Walmegate barr.

fo. 226b   (77)   3rd May 1649.

Timber   It is ordered that Laurence Williamson & Robert
at Mount   Hardy for the Comittee and Bryan Thackwray &
            Edward Bawderston for the Contractors for
Castle Milnes view the Timber lately imployed at the Greate
Mounte and value the same at there discretion and both this
Comittee and the said Contractors are content that the said

173

Contractors shall have the same at such raites as the said Viewers shall agree on

Fran[cis] Whelewright.

fo. 74   (78)   18th July 1655.

Ordered that the stone at Lathropp [Layerthorpe] Posterne be taken out of Fosse and secured by Edmond Giles & Alderman Horner, and Alderman Tophan is desired to take care that this worke be done and an arch made if they thincke fitt.

fo. 74b   (79)   18th July 1655.

[The estate of Christopher Warde (or Waide) deceased was henceforth to pay the 20s. per annum rent bequeathed by him to the Churchwardens and Overseers of Trinity parish in Micklegate for the use of the poor. All arrears prior to Christmas last were to be forgiven as the greatest part of his house was burned and pulled down in 'the Leaguer time,' a bulwark made in the garth and the fence destroyed. It had yielded no profit until the defendant rebuilt it at great expense].

fo. 103   (80)   2nd October 1657.

[The bells of St. Lawrence's Church were to be weighed and secured] in regard the steeple is in dainger to fall.

fo. 104   (81)   26th November 1657.

[Three bells were removed from St. Lawrence's Church,[13] the largest and smallest of which were broken, the tongues removed and most of the ironwork stolen. They were weighed in the Chapter House. Their weights are given].

B. *City of York Chamberlains' Rolls*, C. 23 (1640–1645). MS. in York Public Library.

The following extracts, covering the years 1642–1645, are all those which have any reference — however remote — to the siege, its preparation, conduct and aftermath. Spelling is as in the original.

1642[14]   *Expenses Necessary*

fo. 27   (1)[15] To Oswald Buckle for 7 *li* of lead.   1s.

(2)   For lyme, sand, brick and workemanshipp for makeing upp a doore at Muncke bridge moate   12s. 11d.

(3)   For lime, bricke, sand, stone and workemanshipp at Munckbar and walles there   10s. 10d.

Thomas, 3rd Baron Fairfax.   The medal was awarded at Naseby.

PLATE XXVI

Major-General David Leslie, 1st Baron Newark. Artist George Jamesone.

fo. 27b	(4)	Paid to divers Souldiers for sundrie daies worke at St. James Church Hill 28s. 6d.
	(5)	For brick, lime, sand and stone at Walmegate barr 7s. 6d.
	(6)	For six deales 7s. 1d.
	(7)	For brick, lime, sand and workemanshipp att Munckbarr and makeinge upp a dore 15s. 6d.
	(8)	To 30 souldiers for one dayes worke at St. James Church Hill at 6d. *per diem* 15s.
	(9)	To one for carryinge and recarryinge picks to St. James Church Hill and for his worke there 2s. 6d.
	(10)	For carryinge Centrie [sentry] houses to divers plac[e]s 20d.
fo. 28	(11)	To James Ettie for worke and Timber aboute the barrs 39s. 7d.
	(12)	To him more by order of [the] Lord Maior 48s. 8d.
fo. 28b	(13)	To Symon Richardson for mendinge the Citties walls £2. 5s. 8d.
	(14)	To Richard Maison for a hundreth waite of sluggs 16s.
fo. 29	(15)	To John Besst for carryinge earth per Lord Maiors note 11s.
	(16)	To John Cammell for Iron worke done at Beane Hills[16] 13s. 4d.
	(17)	To John Bovell for worke done at Micklegate barr 3s.
fo. 29b	(18)	To Thomas Higson & Symon Smith for watchinge the magazine at Common Hall from the 10th of Februarie [1641/2] till the 20th Julie [1642] at 8d. *per diem* and 8d. *per noctem* £23. 8s. 4d.
	(19)	To them for the like from the 27th of August 1642 till December the 31st 1642 at the rate afforesaide £9. 10s.
	(20)	To Mr. John Williamson the Citties husband for worke done aboute Cas[t]le Milnes the Citties Walls and other plac[e]s as appeareth per note £12. 13s. 4d.
	(21)	January 7 [1642/3] For watchinge at the Common Hall two weekes more 20s.
	(22)	To Thomas Sawer for 200 weight of [?] Carbine bullets *et al.* 22s. 6d.
fo. 30	(23)	To Sir Roger Jaques for expences when he and Mr. Hewley went with a letter to Sir Hugh Cholmley 5s. 6d.
	(24)	To Sir Tho[mas] Glemhams man for a passe for Alderman Thomson *et al.* to Pomfrett [Pontefract] 12d.
1643		
fo. 29	(25)	To Thomas Hixon & Simon Smyth for 3 weeks watch at the Magazine 29s. 9d.
	(26)	More for watching the Magazine 5s. 8d.

	(27)	For mending the grate at Bootham barr 15s. 3d.
fo. 29b	(28)	For work done at Monck bar 5s. 4d.
	(29)	To Capt. Mason for his charges when he went post to Pomfrett [Pontefract] 10s. 8d.
	(30)	For stocking and [?] winding peice 7s. 6d.
	(31)	For 5 [?] hanglocks 7s. 4d.
fo. 30	(32)	To Alderman Thomson *et al.* at their going to Pomfrett [Pontefract] 23s. 6d.
	(33)	More to Capt. Mason for going post to Pomfrett [Pontefract] 10s.
	(34)	To Edmund Gyles for glasing [glazing] at St. Anthonies 48s. 6d.
fo. 30b	(35)	For 27 metts (*sic*) of coales for St. Thomas and St. Anthony's and cariage 30s.
	(36)	For cariage of 2700 turves to both hospitalls 2s. 3d.
	(37)	For a band for Common Hall gate and setting up 4s. 2d.
	(38)	To Mr. Whittacres parson of St. Saviours for St. Anthony Hospitall 3s. 4d.

1644

fo. 49	(39)	To the Secratary to Lord Generall for a warrant not to billett soldiers 2s. 6d.
	(40)	For a warrant from his Excellency for safe guarding Tanghall[17] 2s. 6d.
	(41)	For a lock for the Barr 4s. 0d.
fo. 50	(42)	To Thomas [?] Haggis for setting grate at Bowtham bar 4s. 0d.
	(43)	For the grate sett there 3s. 0d.
	(44)	For carying the Iron Barr at Walmegate Barr to the Chamber 16d.
	(45)	To Wrights and Tylers for worke done at Walmgate barr £6. 14s. 8d.
	(46)	To Jo. Watson for coales and for cariage of them & cariage of turves to the hospitalls 32s. 10d.
	(47)	To Roger Garnett for worke done at Walmgate bar 12s. 4d.
	(48)	To [blank] for locks for the barrs 19s. 10d.
	(49)	For reparing and making fitt St. Anthonies Hall for maimed soldiers £27. 8d.
fo. 51	(50)	To Edward Whalley for locks at St. Anthonies 3s. 0d.
	(51)	For redeeming Ed. Trumpeters badge per order of Court 10s.
	(52)	To Lord Generalls secretary for letters to the Aldermen to come in 5s. 0d.
	(53)	To Mr. Whittacres for St. Anthonies Hospitall 3s. 4d.

1645

fo. 29   (54) To Mathew Batchler for worke done att Walmgate barr 16d.
           (55) To Abraham Smith towards repaire of the walls[18]
                                                           £9. 17s. 8d.
fo. 29b   (56) To Edward Giles being his last payment for making a platt
                 forme and a guard howse and for other work donne att Tofte
                 Grene   £13. 10s. [19]
           (57) To Abraham Smith more towards the repare of the walls
                                                           £9. 17s. 4d.[19]

1644   *Foreign Payments*

fo. 58   (58) To Mr. Robert Scott and Francis [?] Wainde for a butt of
                 sack and one tunn of French wyne presented to his Excellency
                 the Lord Fairfax   £47.
                        Rewards to his Majesties Pursivants

fo. 59   (59) For a proclam[ation] for punishing strag[g]ling soldiers[20]
                                                           3s. 4d.

C. Constables' Accounts

Constables' Accounts for the York parishes for the period
of the Civil War are potentially rich sources of information
concerning the siege. Unfortunately those for only one parish —
Holy Trinity, Goodramgate — seem to have survived. The
original MS. is in York Public Library. Abstracts from it were
published by George Benson over fifty years ago.[21] His work has
many inaccuracies as well as lengthy omissions. Below is printed
for the first time all the entries in this book for the period covered
by the siege. The assessments are dated 22 April, 28 May and
23 September respectively, while the disbursements cover the
period January 1644 to May 1645.

In the list of assessments, spellings of surnames are as they
appear in the first list, later alternatives being added in brackets.
Christian names are given in their modern spelling. Marginal
notes relating to the amounts actually paid also appear in brackets.
Generally, the names appear in the same order in each list; any
exceptions are noted in square brackets. Spelling is the same as
in the original while all abbreviations are extended according to
modern usage. Capital letters are also given according to modern
usage. The folios are unnumbered in the original.

Holy Trinity, Goodramgate, Constables' Account Book, 1636–1734.

[Trenetyes] Goodrungatt

An asessment maid the 22 of April, 1644; toward the dissbursments: John Cundill and Christopher Foster, Cunstable[s] of the said parish.

[also]

An asessment maide for the Cunstables disbursments, James Wilson and Thomas Fawcitt, the 28th of May, 1644.

[also]

One other assessment maide the 23th of September for the disbursments of James Wilson and Thomas Fawcitt beinge Cunstables this yeare, 1644.

Pettergaitt	22nd April	28th May	23rd September
Christopher Foster	0–3–6	0–6–0	(paid 5s) 0–6–8
Henry Leeds	0–4–0 (paid 7s)	0–9–0	(paid 8s) 0–9–0
Thomas Fawsitt (Fawcit, Fawcitt)	0–3–0	0–4–6	0–4–6
William Williamson	0–2–0	0–4–0	0–3–6
Mathew Cartwright	0–1–0 (unpaid)	0–1–6	0–2–0
Mr. William Kictchinman (Kitchinman)	0–4–3	0–8–6	0–8–0
William Dalkine (Dalkin)	0–4–0	0–7–0	(paid 6s) 0–8–0
An: Willkinson (Wilkinson, Wilkinson)	0–1–6	0–3–0	0–3–0
Mr. George Robinson (Robbinson)	0–4–6	0–8–6	0–9–0
Henry Peareson (Pearson)	0–3–6	0–6–0	0–6–0
Mr. John Housman (Howesman) for part of his dwelling(e) house and (new) house and stable(s) and gardin(ge)	0–4–9	0–6–0	(paid 5s) 0–8–0
Colronell Dakers[22]	———	0–8–0	
Mr. William Robbinson	———		(paid 8s 6d) 0–10–0

Goodrumgatt (Goodrumgaite, Gooddrumgaite)

	22nd April	28th May	23rd September
Edward Mainman (Maineman, Mayneman)	0–1–0	0–1–0	0–1–0
Mr. Thimby (Thimblebye)	0–4–0	0–8–0	—
James Clarke	0–1–0	0–1–6	0–1–6
Corronell [Colonel] Nedom for Mr. Thomas Wilson howse			(unpaid) 0–9–0
William Fourbanke (Firbanke)	0–1–0	0–1–0	0–1–0
William Barnes	0–2–3	0–4–0	(paid 4s 6d) 0–5–0
Christopher Harrison (Harrisson)	0–1–0	0–1–6	
An: Tiplin [appears after William Pimloe in list for 23rd September]	(unpaid)	(unpaid)	
Philip Cosseltyne	0–1–3	0–2–0	0–4–6
John Salkeld (Salkilde)	0–3–3	0–6–0	0–1–6
Roger Keempe (Kempe)	0–1–9	0–3–0	0–6–0
Robert Salkeld (Salkilde)	0–1–0	0–1–0	0–3–0
An: Salkilde	0–1–0	0–3–0	0–1–0
Jane Laysonby (Lasinbe, Lasinbye)	0–1–9	0–3–6	0–2–0
William Robinsonn (Robbinson, Robinson)	0–1–3	0–2–6	0–3–8
Richard Thomson	0–2–0	0–3–6	0–2–0
Thomas Stevenson (Steavenson)			0–2–6
An: Steavenson			
Thomas Eggelfeld (Egleffeld)	0–1–0	0–1–6	0–2–6
William Sire (Syer)	0–1–0	0–2–0	0–1–6
Edward Dickinson (Dickonson)	0–1–0	0–1–6	0–1–6
Ailes [?Alice] Smith			

	22nd April	28th May	23rd September
James Burnestaill	—	—	0-1-6
William Pimlay (Pimloe)	0-4-3	0-7-8	0-9-0
Thomas Were (Weare)	0-2-6	0-4-6	—
John Greene (Grene)	0-2-6	0-4-0	0-4-0
John Huchisson (Hutchinson)—[near end of list for 23rd September]		(unpaid)	0-1-0
An: Smith	0-0-9	0-1-0	0-1-0
Edward Rods	0-0-4	0-0-6	0-1-6
William Corney	—	—	0-1-0
Robert Dry	—	—	0-9-0
Mr. Brian Richisson (Richardson)	0-4-9	0-9-0	0-6-0
Sir Timothy Fetherston	0-4-9	0-8-6	0-3-6
John Cundill (Cundall, Cundell)	0-2-6	0-5-0	0-6-0
Thomas Grainger	0-1-9	0-3-0	0-6-6
Christopher Grainger	0-0-6	0-1-6	(paid 6d) 0-1-0
James Willson (Wilson)	0-3-3	0-6-0	0-6-0
George Crowder	0-3-3	0-6-0	0-3-6
William Tireman (Tyerman)	0-1-6	0-3-0	0-1-0
Robert Jacksonn (Jackson)	0-1-0	0-1-4	0-2-0
Mr. Francis Blacke (Blaicke)	0-1-6	0-2-0	0-2-6
Margaret Danbrought (Danbrough)	0-1-0	0-2-6	
Philip Swinbanke	0-1-6	0-3-0	0-2-6
Mary Swinbanke	—	—	0-8-0
Mr. Lee for hir [? Mary Swinbanke's] howse	—	—	

	22nd April	28th May	23rd September
Jane Oxspring (Oxspringe) [appears after James Wilson in list for 28th May]	0–1–0	0–1–0	—
Churchyard. (Curchyard)			
Elizabeth Dickson	—	—	0–0–8
Henry Hall	0–0–6	0–0–8	0–0–8
Hugh Jaques	0–0–9	0–1–0	—
George Clarkeson	0–0–6	0–1–0	0–1–0 (unpaid)
Henry Nelson	0–0–6 (unpaid)	0–1–0	0–0–8 (unpaid)
Elizabeth Wilkinson	—	—	0–0–8
William Johnson	—	—	0–0–8
Stables			
Mr. Fouthergill (Fothergill)	0–1–0 (unpaid)	—	—
Robert Terry	—	—	0–2–0
Henry Acckinson (Atkinson)	0–1–0	0–2–0	0–2–0
Mr. Henry Tireman (Tyerman)	0–1–0	0–2–0	0–2–0
Mr. James Deane (Deaine)	0–1–0	0–2–0	0–2–0
Mr. Thomas Pratt (Prat)	0–1–0	0–2–0	0–2–0
John Blackborne	0–1–0	0–2–0	—
Capton Wattson (Watson)	0–1–0 (unpaid)	0–2–0	0–2–0
John Calvarte	—	—	0–2–0
	[Total not stated]	10–1–8	10–15–8

The debursments of Christopher Foster, Cunstable for the time being 1644.

In primis, spent at sessment making with neigbors	o–1–o
Item, Paid to 4 shoulgers the 12th of January	1–o–o
Item, paid to 4 shoulgers the 25 of January	2–4–o
Item, paid to 4 shoulger the 2 February	1–o–o
Item, paid for paier of bandileares, the 2 of February	o–2–o
Item, paid to 4 shoulgers the 12 of February	o–18–8
Spent at mustering, 12 of February	o–1–o
Item, for mending John Greene[23] muskitt	o–o–4?
Item, paid to 4 shoulger the 20 of February	o–16–o
Item, paid to 4 shoulgers for mustreing, 20 February	o–2–8
Item, paid to George Masson for fire and candill for bare [? Monk Bar]	o–7–6
Item, paid An: Willkinson for 2 skaborts [?scabbards]	o–3–o
Item, paid to 4 shoulgers the 30 February	o–18–8
Item, paid for mending Edward Mainman's [23]miskitt [musket]	o–o–8
Item, paid to 4 shoulgers the 9 of March	o–18–8
Item, paid to Mr. Mires for lame soulger mony	o–5–5
Item, paid to 14 shoulgers for garding Minster	o–1–o
Item, paid to 4 shoulgers the 4 of Aprill	1–4–o
Item, paid to 4 shoulgers the 21 of Aprill	1–o–o
[24]Item, paid to Clarke to writting downe corne	o–1–o
Item, paid for girdill of Edward [blank]	o–1–8
Item, spent at 2 sessments makeing	o–2–o
Item, paid to Peter Huchisson for warrant	o–o–4
Item, paid to George Masson for fire and candill	o–7–6
Item, for strooe [?straw] to shoulgers, 22 of Aprill	o–2–6
Item, spent at sessment makeing, 24 Aprill	o–1–o[25]
Item, paid for strooe [?straw] for trope of draggounes	o–2–o
Item, paid for bread and drinke for them, 24 Aprill	o–o–8
Item, paid for horse that went post to Selby	?o–2–2
[24]Item, Paid for caring corne to maggittzin by porters	o–1–8
Item, paid to 4 shoulgers the 27 of Aprill	2–19–4
Item, paid for strooe [?straw] for shoulgers the 1 of May	o–1–6

	[26]14–o–4
	(sic)15–1–6

[Next page]

Item, paid to 4 shoulgers the [?] of May	o–16–o
[24]Item, paid for caring of corne to magazin from Geogre Crower [?Crowder]	o–o–2
Item, paid for rammerwand for muskitt	o–o–3
Item, paid for strooe [?straw] the first of May	o–o–10

Item, paid for warrant for Sir Thomas Glaham [Glemham]   0–2–6
Item, paid for lame shoulgers that went from Cunstable to
                                    Cunstable all my time   0–1–6

                                                                  ―――――――
                                                                  1–1–3
                                                                  ―――――――

                                                                  (*sic*)16–2–9

We whose name are here underwritten have audited the
accountes of John Conndill and Christopher Foster and we
fynd that the parish is indebted to them, having 24s allowed
out of ther assessment, the some of 22d. the 28 of May 1644

          George Robeson (mark)
          William Kitchingman
          Henry Pearson
          Henry Leeds (mark)

Trenetyes in   Disbursments by James Wilson and Thomas Fawcitt.
Gooddrumgaite   Cunstables for St. Trennetyes parish in Gooddrumgate for
                      the yeare 1644 as followeth.

Imprimis paid to Richard Davye and spent about the agrement with him
and George Mason for the fyndinge of the sentree fyer and chandles for
Munke Warde wherein a raitement was assessed uppon everey parish what
they should pay and for fyer and chandles which we had to pay for   0–4–0

[27]Item, paid to Captan Fressell,[28] Comannder and overseare of the mill for
groundinge of corne aboute procuringe of St. John del Picke [Pike] parish
to contrebute and pay the full halffe pay for one horse everey day which was
wholy charged uppon our parish at the raite of 16d a day to the bakers that
grounded at George Blaids mill for Genarall Kinge his regement,   0–6–0

[27]Paid aboute gittinge of an order by the helpe of William Dalkinge to the
Quartr Maister to the Marques of Newcasle for the grantinge and gittinge
of an order or presedent in writinge to shewe to the Quartr Maister of Generall
Kings regement for the clearinge of our parish for the horse gryndinge any
more at George Blaides mill.   0–2–6

[27]Paid to Capton Fressell for a newe order from him that the bakers and the
milners should fynd horses themselves for corne gryndinge at George Blaids
mill and the five parishes of Munke Ward to be dischardged, which order the
Captan delivered to George Blaids for the discharge thereof, which coste us
for our parish parte paid uppon the sessinge of the bill.   0–1–0

[27]Paid for the halffe pay with St. John del Picke [Pike] for one horse gryndinge at George Blaids mill for our parish shaire untill the tyme of our agrement which was 14 dayes after 16d a day is   0–9–4

                                    183

Paid to the traine band the 6th of June   0–6–9

Paid to William Syer the same day   0–0–6

Paid the 8th of June to our traine soulgers   1–6–8

Paid more to William Syer   0–3–4

Paid to George Maison for an arreare which the ould Cunstables lefte unpaid
for fyer and chandles for the sentres   0–6–0

Paid to Richard Davye the 12th of June for sentres fyer and chandles for one
month for our parish shaire beinge ended this 12th of June instant   0–7–6

Paid the 12th of June to John Grene, Edward Maynman and John Craw and
William Syer, so all is paid unto them untill this 13th of June, 1644[29]   0–5–4

Paid at William Pimlow howse at Mr. Clarke firste cominge to our parish
by consent of Mr. Richardson and Mr. Robbinson and William Pimloe and
otheres   0–2–0

Paid to Edward Maynman, John Crawe, Robert Jackson for 3 wecks pay ever
one of them this 13th of June[29]   1–1–0

Paid more the 14th of June beinge Fryday, to John Grene, Robert Jackson,
Edward Maynman, and John Craw, being traine soulgers, and lefte in arreare
by the ould Cunstables, John Cundell and Robert Wilkinson, and allowed
upon by and with the audetinge of there accounts   3–4–0

Paid to John Grene and William Syer for 3 wecks pay betwext them both
after 2s 4d a wecke according to my Lord Maior order with warrant for
that purposse   0–7–0

Paid to William Syer for a muskett, insteaid of a musket that Robert Jackson
brocke when he hurte his faice,[30] which Mr. Richardson intreated me to
b[u]y for the parish instead thereof   0–4–0

Paid the 19 of June to William Syer   0–1–0

Paid the 4 traine soulgers the 22th of June for one wecks pay everey one of
them after 2s 4d a wecke is   0–9–4

              ——————

          (in margin)   (*sic*) 9–9–0

Paid more to the 4 traine soulgers the 29th of June for one whole wecks pay
ever one of them beinge ended the 27th of June   0–9–4

Paid more to the 4 traine soulgers for one whole weckes paye beinge ended
the 4 of July, 1644   0–9–4

Paid more the 12 of July to the 4 traine soulgers for one wholl weckes pay
beinge ended the 12 of Julye   0–9–4

[31]Paid to two men for buryinge of dead horsses and for aile [ale] to them
beffore they went to bury them   0–1–6

[31]Paid to two men to helpe to clence [cleanse] the barsteed   0–1–4

[32]Paid the 20 of July to the 4 traine soulgers for carryinge of the parish armes
and delyveringe of them up to the maggazin and for halffe a wecks pay dew
to them   0—5—4

Paid the 20 of July to Richard Davy for the sentres fyer and chandles from
the 14th of June untill the 14 of July   0—7—6

Paid at the firste assessment makinge with concent of the sessors   0—3—0

Paid for sentree fyeres and chandles from the 14th of July untill the 14th of
September   0—15—0

Paid to the 4 traine soulgers beinge warned to appeare beffore Captan Crooke
at Trenetyes in Micklegaite   0—1—4
                                                                                            _____

                                        [in margin]   (sic) 12—12—0

Paid for fyer and chandles for St. Antonyes Hall   0—4—6

Paid to William Dalkin for his horse for postinge and for horsemeait to the
postemaister   0—6—0

Paid by the consent of the parishoners for a coppe [copy] of the agrement
betwext my Lord Faireffax and Sir Thomas Glemham uppon the yeldinge
up of this Cittye   0—1—0

Paid to the oversears of St. Anthonyes Hall and the lame soulgers which we
carryed thether uppon barrowes   0—2—0

Paid to a ma[i]med soulger which we did carry to the Manner Howse by the
appoyntment of my Lord Maior   0—1—0

Paid for the sentres fyers and chandles from the 14th of September untill the
14th of October   0—7—6

Paid for centree fyers and chandles from the 14th of October untill the 14th
of November   0—7—6

Paid more for centry fyers and chandles from the 14th of November untill the
14th of Desember   0—7—6

Paid for centres fyers and chandles from the 14th of Desember untill the 14th
of January   0—7—6

Paid more for centres fyers and chandles from the 14th of January untill the
14th of February   0—7—6

Paid more the sentrees fyers and chandles from the 14th of Fabruary untill
the 14th of March   0—7—6

Paid to the 4 traine soulgers and we Cunstables at the receavinge of the newe
armes and at the vewe day beffore   0—3—4

Paid for two poste horsses charged uppon our parish by a warrant   0—12—0

Disbursed for our parish with the new Quarter Maister Gennerall at William
Foster's[33] at the quartringe of newe soulgers   0—0—6

Paid for sentres fyres and chandles from the 14 of March untill the 14th of Aprill 0–7–6

Disbursed about the second sesment makinge [with consente of the sessers][34]

0–2–0

Paid to the 4 traine soulgers everey one of them for 2 watches and ones traninge ever one of them 0–10–0

Paid for sentres fyeres and chandles from the 14th of Aprill untill the 14th of May 0–7–6

Paid more to the 4 traine soulgers for six watches and two dayes traninge 1–8–0

Paid more to the 4 trane soulgers for five watches and one day traninge 1–2–0

For writing of all our accounts over which is more then usially haith bene beffore tyme which is usuallye allowed in the laste accounte 0–2–0

Disbursed uppon the audetinge of this accounte 0–2–0

Som is(*sic*) 20–10–7

The ?26 of May 1645

We whose names are here underwritten have audited the accounte of James Willson and Thomas Faucitt and we fynd the parish is indebted to them the some of 2–12–4.

    [Signed]   William Kitchingman.
                    Brian Richardson (his marke),
                    Henry Pearson (his marke),
                    Roger Kempe (his marke).

Receaved at the hands of William Dakin and George Crowder the newe Cunstables the somme of 2–12–4 which the parish was indebted to James Wilson and Thomas Fawcit as by the audeters accounte appeareth, I say receaved this 19th of June, 1645

    By me   James Wilson,
                   Thomas Fawcett.

APPENDIX III

CASTLE MILLS AND BRIDGE

THE FOLLOWING DOCUMENT in the Borthwick Institute of Historical Research in York[35] has an important entry relating to the
Castle Mills and the nearby bridge in the period of the siege and
immediately before it. It dates to 24 December 1649 or soon
afterwards. The income of the Sir Thomas Heskith Hospital in
Heslington came from rents and tolls on the Castle Mills, hence
the presence of this document in the Yarburgh muniments
which, until a few years ago, were housed in Heslington Hall.

fo. 8

Memorandum that upon the fourth day of October 1642
castle gate postern was shutt and banked upp strongly with
earth and the portcullis lett downe for the safety of the citty
of yorke against Hoothams [Hothams] and others which had
an intent to beseige it.

And after that the bridge at castle milles was broken downe
and taken away.

Upon the xxiij th day of December then next after was the
great flude at the said castle milles with all the drawing doores
and stoups driven away by force of the water floodd which
then prevaled.

Upon the sixt seaventh eight ninth and tenth daies of January
then next after the said flude or floodgate was made up againe
with six piles of woodd having iron piles in the lower endes
driven into the ground and spruce fir deeles of whole length
nailled to the same for stopping the streame of water which
was done by order from the lord Savile at the costes and
charges of the said citty he being then governour of the same.
In February then next after divers people were sett on worke
by the then governor of the said citty and his officers to digg a
trench through the mill damme neare unto Saint Georges

187

posterne purposely to bring the streame of the river of Fosse
to runn into the moat dike towards Fishergate by meanes of
which said trench and a flood of water coming presently after
did make such a breach through the Calsey [Causeway] and
way towards Fishergate that by violence thereof a great ash
tre[e] root was eradicated and driven away above ten yards
from the place where it stood besides much earth driven away
from the corner of Mrs. Weddelles close there adioyning.

Upon the one and twentyth two and twentyth thre and
twentyth fower and twentyth daies of March then next after
the said breaches were begunn to be made up againe by
setting fower and twenty piles of woodd thre yards long in one
of the breach[es] and as much in another of them with
boords nayle[d] thereto to stopp the waterflood and earth
likewise to make the same firme and strong the banke be-
longin[g] to the said mill damm and the other banke be-
longi[ng] to Fishergate Calsey [Causeway] at the citties
costes and charges.

fo. 8v

But prevailed litle to any purpose in regard the breaches
which the waterflood had made were very depe and brode
war[n?]e and could not spedily be made firme and sound.

Shortly after one [blank] Emmerson enters upon the Castle
milles and out of two of them contrives one mill for grinding
gunpowder and when the same was effected and broughte to
passe upon a certaine day the same being sett on work for
grinding gunpowder and now left in the mill butt all fast
locked upp it chanced in the grinding to sett itselfe on fier
and by the blast of the gunpowder destroyed itselfe and the
other milles also.

Afterwards and in the sommer season at the citties cost and
charges and by common daie worke[36] the damm belonging to
the said castle milles was made up againe very strong and
firme and also the calsey way [causeway] into Fishergate.

There was no rent paid for the said castle milles from the
fift day of December 1642 untill the 24 day of December
1649 by reason the said milles were demolished and lay waist
at the most of that tyme.

Many petitions and su[i]tes were made by Richard Kendraw
Maister of Sir Thomas Heskethes Hospital at Heslington on
the behalfe of himself and the rest of the poore people at that
hospitall unto noble menn and others for help to gett the said
castle milles builded up againe and for the releafe in the
meane tyme but no prevaling saving only that Colonell John
Bellassess [Bellasis] of his noble mind and charitable dis-

188

position did give unto the the said Richard Kendraw tenn poundes in money to be distributed among the poore people of the said hospitall which was then done accordingly.

APPENDIX IV

EXAMPLES OF ANTI-ROYALIST PROPAGANDA

(i)

The Marquis of Newcastle who never laid any Religion to heart, nor hath anything of a Souldier in him, but is wholly steered by Generall King, Sir Thomas Glenham [Glemham], Sir William Widrington, Colonell Goring whilst he was there, &c. men who have not an Acre of land in our County; Lastly that the most of the Captaines and Souldiers are Tygers and Beares for cruelty, Bores [boars] for wast and devastations, Swine for Drunkenesse, Goats and Stallions for Lust &c. in so much as Captaine Legg, when John Owsman the Post-Master of Yorke did come and tamely enough charge him for violating the Lawes of Hospitality so farre as having, the Command of his whole house he had got his daughter with Child, the Captaine took it very ill that he should complaine, and said he had done more then [than] so, he had laine with all in his house, save himselfe, and his Oastler. (*New-come Guest*).

(ii)

Let us all look up to God, without whom all this arme of flesh is no better then [than] an Egyptian Reed. The arrivall of more Irish Rebells is daily expected. O that the Protestants would now unite themselves as one man, for the cutting off of the Anti-christian crew of Papists and Rebels, to the advancement of the glory of God, the establishment of the true reformed Protestant Religion, the honour of the King, the Priviledges of Parliament, the Liberties of the Subject, the Laws of the Land; that peace may be upon us and the whole Israel of God. (*Hulls Managing*).

(iii)

Rupert's Spirit. But if his Highnesse, be such a Bug-beare, such a Goblin-Prince to fright folke, how chanced it that his Highnesse did not transmit some of his Spirit at Yorke? Why did his Highnesse runne away, and leave so many thousands blushing in their own Crimson? But the truth is, his Highnesse Spirit is not a fighting, but a Plundering Spirit; and that he can transmit to his cavalry at all seasons.

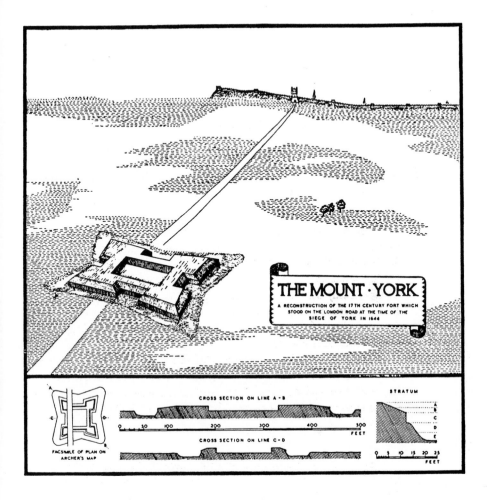

PLATE XXVII

Reconstruction of the 1644 Sconce on the Mount, York.

PLATE XXVIII

Oliver Cromwell.   Artist Sir Peter Lely.

Pitti Gallery, Florence.

(*Mercurius Britannicus* no. 75, dated Monday 17th March — Monday 24th March 1645).

(iv)

It is certified that the Catholik Marquesse of Newcastle is gone from Amsterdam to Flanders, and from thence intends for France. It is no great matter whither, unlesse he will doe us the courtesie to come and help Rupert to another beating: never did any Stage-player act his part worse than he hath done, to be hist [hissed] off the Stage by both Parties.

(*Mercurius Britannicus* no. 76, dated Monday 24th March — Monday 31st March 1645).

APPENDIX V

ELIZABETH COLE AND THE FERRYBOAT 1640

IN THE *Calendar of State Papers* (*Domestic*)[37] are abstracts of three documents bearing on this subject — the Petition of John Cole and his wife Elizabeth, the account or 'perticular' of the conduct of Sir Paul Neale in 1640, and the Certificate of Francis Farbank, a gaoler, and five other York inhabitants confirming the imprisonment of Elizabeth and her father. The 'perticular' gives the affair in the greatest detail and the full version (as opposed to the printed abstract) follows :—[38]

To the Kings most Excellent Majestie.[39]

A Perticular of the disaffection and disservice of Sir Pawle Neale Knight to your late Royall Father of ever blessed memory, Together with the petitioners' particular losses and damages susteyned by the said Sir Pawle Neale and meerly for their Loyalty and faithfull performances of their Trusts in his said Majesties Service.

In the yeare Anno Domini 1640 the Petitioner being imployed and intrusted by Alderman Watkinson of Hull, and one of his Majesties Servants to carry severall goods of his said Majestie by water betwixt Hull and Yorke against St. Georges day in the same yeare, the said Sir Paule Neale did not only obstruct and hinder the petitioners passage with the said goods to Yorke but with many blasphemous oathes and imprecacions threaten that he would not only sink the petitioners keele (or boat) and his Majesties said goods but would alsoe kill the petitioner and her father then in the boat who was above 80 yeares of age. And accordingly with a boat hooke the said Sir Paule, with all the malice and strength he had, strucke at the petitioners aged father, which blow the petitioner by Gods providence happily rewarded from of [off] her father, yet it fell soe heavy that it splitt the bing of the petitioner's boat, and if it had hitt him as hee intended, the said Sir Pawle had then (certainly) killed the petitioners aged father. But when the petitioner and her father did see the desparatenesse of Sir Pawle they putt of [off] the boat from the shoare with all the strength they had to save their lives and told him the goods were his Majesties and alsoe shewed him the warrant or comission they had from his said Majestie and asked him why he was soe unreasonable against his Majesty to hinder [illegible] that be but servants. Hee answered the petitioner and her father that he cared not (a Phillop) for his Majestie and in a slighting manner and in contempt of his Majestie and of his aforesaid warrant did hold up his hand and philloped with his fingers, and said that his said Majesty had noe right to the River of Ouze for it belonged to his father and him though the contrary be well knowne to most men thereabouts.

The petitioner and her father haveing a ferry boat wherewith they did constantly gett 10s a day the said Sir Pawle in malice to the petitioner and her aged parent and to deprive them of that livelyhood did cause the said ferry boat not only to be suncke for three yeares but alsoe to pay the rent of the ferry whereby the petitioner was damnifyed above £1000 as wilbe made appeare.

That the said Sir Pawle to consumate the designed ruine of the petitioner, her children and her aged parents, without any just cause very maliciously did cause the petitioner and her aged father to be imprisoned for the space of 37 dayes and threatining to starve them (like a toad upon a pricke) in which time he sent his servant to see them severall times saying to him are they not yet starved, and that he would starve them before they should come forth which wicked designe of his [illegible] tooke effect. But that Joseph like God inclined the hart of the jalor to shew the petitioner and her aged father some favour, which false imprisonment (besides [Sir] Pawles wicked conspiracy against the Petitioner and her father) at five pounds an houre according to the Statute for the time aforesaid is £4440. The petitioner [be]ing by her birth and name of the ancient family of the Vaversours in Yorkeshire as is well knone to divers persons of good quality of that County.

That the petitioner in Anno 1642 did petition your Majesties late royall father to be relieved in the premisses by the said Sir Pawle, as by the said petition and reference thereon appeares. And your Majestie being then Prince and at Yorke was gratiously pleased to take notice thereof and of your petitioners aforesaid sufferings, and sent for the said Sir Paule, and in Sir Arthur Ingram his garden asked the said Sir Paule how he could finde of his hart to imprison such a fine old man and this good woman, who answered your then Highnesse "It was not I but my father.' And the petitioner then affirming before your Majestie and him, that the abuse was his and not his fathers your Majestie said 'Sir Paule, pay them all their losses and damages.' Sir Paule answered your Majestie 'I have not money.' Your Majestie gratiously answered him, 'Sir Paule, you doe not well to lay it on your father that is dead and gone.' And your Majestie said 'Sir Paule I will lend you gold.' Sir Paul then answered Your Majestie, 'I will pay them at Doctor Easdens house to morrow.' Your Majestie said further, 'Sir Paule, Sir Paule, remember what I have done for you and looke you give them full sattisfaccion least you incurr our further displeasure. And if he doe not, good woman, come to me and I wil be thy paymaster.' But the said Sir Paule did not according to his promise pay the petitioner one penny, and being here demanded why he did not pay the petitioner according to his promise, he replyed and said to the petitioner that there was never any promise made but that it was either broken or kept, and is now the only cause of the petitioner further troubling your Majesties redresse herein.

The 'petition' adds the further fact that Elizabeth's father was called Robert Austin and that she was the mother of an unspecified number of children. The 'Certificate' says that she was imprisoned for thirty days, (during which time she had 'a young infant sucking att her breast,') and the father for seven days.

APPENDIX VI

DEPREDATIONS OF THE SCOTS

THE FOLLOWING document[40] gives an insight into the kind of depredations committed by the Scots in North Yorkshire in the two years following the siege of York. These may be taken as representative of the same sort of excesses committed by them during the siege time around the city (see pp. 22-3).

> A remonstrance concerning the misdemeanours of some of the Scots souldiers in the County of Yorke.
>
> Subscribed by divers Gentlemen of the Committee of Sequestrations in that County; and sent up to Thomas Westrop Esquire (publique Agent) to be presented to the House of Commons. December 6. 1646.
>
> This remonstrance is appointed to be printed, and is signed, by Richard Wynne, Edmond Hall, Thomas Bate, Henry Lyle, Thomas Peeres, John Humfray. London, Printed for T.V. 1646.
>
> Sir,
>
> There is but little possibility that the Scots will leave us this winter, for they have charged horses to goe to Newcastle for more armes, and planted themselves by Troopes in severall places of the Country: I will give you some particulars of their deportment.
>
> Five Souldiers quartered with a Widdow of Hutton a fortnight together, and though they had twelve pence a day allowed them for dyet, they paid her onely six shilling for them all, she told them they must provide other quarters, for she was not able to maintaine them at that rate, they answered they would; bought a six penny loafe, caused her give them milke to it, and went into the fields, brought home a fat sheepe where with they supplyed their leane Commons: Thus are quarters paid, Easton [?Eston] men were forced to pay a penny per diem for every shilling that wanted of their Assesse; thus are monies collected.

195

A Souldier at Hemlington broke his Landlord's head, cut his servants lip, threw the meat about the table, broke the Pales [Pails], Kettles and Piggons, because his Landlord would not give him two shillings per day, and bid him complaine if he durst; thus is the Country abused; the Officers have double pay for themselves and unseen souldiers.

The Post boy of Durnton [?Darlington] was robbed by the souldiers of Worshall, and his horse and purse taken from him; no wonder though letters miscarry.

A G[u]isb[o]rough man had two Horses and three pound in money taken from his servant, by one Hamilton, as he was coming from Thrisk [Thirsk] Market, the man and horse was found out by the owner, and complaint made to the Captaine but no restitution; whereupon a Petition was presented to the Lieutenant Generall upon Saturday was seven night at G[u]isb[o]rough, who seemed to be very much offended, and commanded that the party should be brought before him, but he kept close enough till the Lieutenant Generall[41] removed, and that very day the Captaine and three more fell upon the owner (being Constable) and beat him very sore, three swords being drawn upon him at once, and had slaine him at his owne doore, if very good helpe had not been presently made, since which time the Constable is forced to abandon his ownt house; this is sharpe law.

The Country at the same time when the Lietenant Generall was at Grisbrough [Guisborough], was about to present a Petition wherein was represented their great sufferings by the Scottish Army in particular expressions: and their humble suite for the removall of two Regiments before the Petitioners were totally consumed; but the Lieutenant Generall was gone by three of the clock in the morning, wherby the Countries intentions was prevented, yet three men were sent after him to Richmond with the Petition; but of their successe I cannot write because the Messengers are not yet returned that I heare of.

The Justices of Peace of our Wapentakes, and other substantiall Inhabitants have quite left the Country. It would mollifie an Adamantine heart, to heare the bitter complaints and ru[e]full moanes that are ecchoed out in every quarter; this is but cold comfort to hungry soules that have sold their goods, borrowed monies, and mor[t]gaged their lands to satisfie the souldiers: I wish the Commanders of that army would read the fifth Chapter of Nehemiah, and make him their pattern; or that they would make a generall (not a particular use) of the Covenant, they would then finde that delinquents not brought to condigne punishment, but protected and quartered amongst us, that the liberty of the subject is not maintained, but grossely abused. God in mercend [mercy send] them out of this Kingdome, that the Country be not totally consumed, nor like to this poore Wapentake in a ready way to ruine and beggary, divers that have lived in an honest and substantiall way, wanting bread to put in their childrens mouthes when they cry out for hunger; Sir no more for the present, but that I am

Your Worships most humble Servant,
Tho[mas] Bate

Stampton 20. Novemb. 1646

Upon a meeting of us whose names are subscribed we doe not only ratifie what is written but also certifie.

That one Bogden a Wollen Draper of Rippon, was slaine neare Cattericke bridge upon the tenth of November last, by foure Scots, who tooke both his horse and money.

That upon severall complaints of the country, the Leiutenant Generall hath issued some Orders for regulating the souldier, but to no purpose, for both Officer and souldier exact to their liking, some a third more, some halfe, or to speake more properly every man what he please; and when one man is utterly wasted and his estate spent, (as in every township some fall daily) then they inforce the rest of the Inhabitants of that Township to pay the decayed mans proportion, which tends to the generall ruine of all; and if a Landlord complaine to any superiour Officer, for the exaction of the souldier, he is referred to make peace with the souldier, and that is his doome. Wee have intreated Mr. Lyle, to repaire to the Committee at Yorke with the Petition and answer of the Lieutenant Generall, who will report their result to you and so rest,

Your very humble Servants,

Dated at Ayton
21 November 1646
For the Worshipfull Thomas
Westrop, Esquire. London.

Rich. Wynne.
Edmond Hall.
Thomas Bate.
Henry Lyle.
Thomas Peeres.
John Humfray.

APPENDIX VII

EXTRACTS RELATING TO THE SIEGE FROM *THE ARMY OF THE COVENANT*

THE FOLLOWING are the items in the period April–July 1644 relating to the Scottish army and the Siege of York which are included in *The Army of the Covenant*, SHS vol. XVI and XVII (1917).

p. 15⁴²   *Charge.*

Armes and Amunition received by the Generall of Artillery or hes Deputts, out of the Scotts or English Magazines for the Expedition to England, begun January the first, 1644, and ended Jan[ua]ry. the 30th, 1647.

| | *Scotch Charge.* | | | Pairs of |
June 26 1644	Powder	Match	M[usket] Ball.	Pistols with hulsters (*sic*)
From James Menteith by James Fisher at Mid[d]lethorpe			6,500	
pp. 16–17	*English Charge.*			
May 14·1644 From Hull by Andro Meine at Mid[d]lethorpe	6,000	6,000	2,000	
May 27 1644 From Hull by Wm. Duncane of Mid[d]lethorpe	4,000	9,000		
June 26 1644 From the Earle of Manchester by James Fisher	10,000	3,000		
p. 21 From the Earle of Manchester by James Fisher				494½

[*Issues from the Magazine to*] *the Traine of Artillerie.*

1644		Coyles of Wt. towes	Powder	Musket Ball	3 lb. Ball	11 lb. Ball	12 lb. Ball	18 lb. Ball
May 3	Given out for ye ye gunnes w[hi]ch went to Fairfax Leagour		200					
— 26	Given out at Mid[d]lethorpe for charging the frames		100	100		12		
— 29	Sent w[i]t[h] ye gunnes w[hi]ch went to Manchesters q[ua]rters						5	244
—	Given out for ye gunns w[hi]ch were taken from ye hedges		200	100				
July 2	To Ro[ber]t Colquhoune for ye great and smale canon[43]		1100	200	84			
— 10	Sent to Akum [Acomb]		200					20
—	To ye gunnes in ye fort against Yorke		650					16
— 11	Given out at Mid[d]lethorpe for ye culverin and 2 salkers (*sic*)							32
—	Given out for drawing ye canon alongst the bridge of Mid[d]lethorpe[44]	1						
— 12	Sent to Akum [Acomb] by Jam[es] Trotter for ye gunns there.		600					
—	To Ro[ber]t Colquhoune for ye gunns beyond Akum [Acomb][45]		200					
— 13	To ye fort before York							

APPENDIX VIII

ROMANO-BRITISH CEMETERY AND 17th CENTURY GUN EMPLACEMENT ON THE MOUNT, YORK[46]

A LARGE Romano-British cemetery has long been known to extend from outside Micklegate Bar to Mount Vale, bordering on the Eboracum-Calcaria (York-Tadcaster) Roman road, the predecessor of the present Blossom Street-Mount-Mount Vale, Dringhouses road, a sector of the A 64. A few years ago one part of this, in Trentholme Drive, was carefully excavated under modern archaeological disciplines ;[47] another, on the Mount, was uncovered in the 17th century. This article is concerned with the latter.

The following is an extract from the *York Courant* dated 29 June 1742 :—[48]

> York, June 29. Last Month our Magistrates made an order to level Part of a Piece of Ground called the Mount, out of Micklegate Bar ;[49] designing to widen the High-Road, which was before too strait for Carriages, Coaches, &. to pass and repass in that Place. Tradition tells us, that the old Road lay on the South-Side of this Mount; and a Part of the Pavement, or Causway, had been dug up, on that Side, in the Memory of some Men living; the former Authority, also, assures us that this present Road was only cut through when King James I came first out of Scotland to this City; in order as is supposed, to make the Road look more streight and even from the Bar, and pay some Complement to the new King. This place, called the Mount, has been, plainly, raised from the Surface, and might have, antiently, been an exterior Fortification on the Road, as an advanced Guard to the City, being about two great Bowshot from the Gate. The like of which is to be seen, about the same Distance, out of the North-Gate at Lincoln. The Hill at York is not so regular as to pronounce it absolutely a Roman Work, but, be that as it may, it has all the Appearance of a once fortified Place.

Thus much being thought proper to premise, the next is, that the Workmen, in cutting through this Hill, met with a surprizing Quantity of human Bones; and though they did not level more than fifteen yards of it at the most, yet, by the Number of Sculls dug out, the Overseers cannot compute it at less than that twelve or thirteen Hundred Skeletons of dead Bodies were removed. The Bones were all found in two paralel Ramparts, having an Area, or Platform, betwixt them, and were from within two Foot of the Surface to about ten deep, promiscuously laid; and, what is remarkable, not above two or three Skeletons of any Size less than of Manhood were observed amongst them.

In removing the Bones, it was expected that some Curiosities would be found, which might give some Light for a Conjecture to what People, Age or Accident, this great Repository of the Dead might be assigned; and a strict Charge was given to the Overseers to see that the Labourers secreted nothing. But with all their Caution not above one Roman Coin was discovered, which was of the middle Brass of the Emperor Nerva . . . . Nerva came to the Empire A.v.c. 850, or the 96th Year of Christ. The Romans were then Masters here, but whether this Coin has lain near so long in the Ground, as from that Time, is very uncertain. In removing a Brick Wall that stood as a Fence to the Ground, in the Foundation was found a Roman Sepulchral Inscription of Millstone Gritt, but so miserably broken, that no Art nor Contrivance could put the Pieces together to make it legible. There could only be read on one Piece ENTISSIM, and must have been either *Pientissimus*, or *Merentissimus*, two Epithets well known to be common in Monumental Inscriptions. There were found, also, two portable, not pensile Lamps, of red Clay, one of them very elegant, having a Figure of a Man with the Head of a Swine, a Falchion in one Hand and a round Ball in the other, impressed upon it: The Head of a Dart, or some Missive Weapon, about nine inches long, of Iron: A Roman Fibula, or Buckle for their Garments: A Piece of Metal enameled, and another Metalic Affair which cannot be Understood: An Urn of blue Clay, with the burnt Bones in it. Add to these, two Canon Bullets and a Cross-Bar shot, with some Musket Balls.

It will seem very strange that these Bullets should be found along with Things of a much greater Antiquity; but this is easily accounted for. In the Time of the last Siege of York, *Anno* 1644, this Mount was made use of by the Besiegers as a Battery against the City, and these Bullets were shot against them by the Besieged from a Battery of Cannon placed on Micklegate Bar; the Shot being all lodged in that Rampart which faced the Bar. But the vast Number of human Bones already dug out, and the much greater Quantity which are still contained in this small Compass of Ground is not so easily accounted for; there having been not one third Part of the Hill cut away, and the Strata of Bones appearing visibly to go on in the Remainder.

The Conoiseurs in Antiquities are therefore invited to give their Judgments on this remarkable Discovery.[50]

This account was written by Francis Drake, the York historian.[51] The discovery excited great interest amongst the antiquarians of the mid-18th century.[52] One of these was William Stukeley.[53] Stukeley visited York twice — in 1725 and again in 1740 — on both occasions, it will be noted, before the discovery took place. In 1725 he recorded[54] that he passed the Mount and recognised the battery under discussion, viz :-

> We still kept on the Roman Road all the way hither [from Tadcaster to York]. A great sconce a little way off York called the Mount, consisting of four bastions raised in the civil wars. It is a most delicious country, over-flowing with plenty.

In his *Courant* article Drake was undoubtedly correct in his opinion that the road widening in 1742 had revealed archaeological evidence of two quite separate and distinct historical epochs. The ramparts, 'two Canon Bullets and a Cross-Bar shot (*sic*) with some Musket Balls' doubtless related to the siege of York in 1644, while the skeletons and other finds were almost certainly Roman.[55] Conclusive proof of the 17th Century origin of these 'ramparts' is supplied by an original and unpublished map of York[56] now in the York Public Library. It measures 4ft. 6 in. by 3ft. 6in.; it is in a modern frame. The title reads :-

> By His Ma[jes]ties, Spetiall Commands. Plan of the Greate, Antient & famous Citty of York. Delineated by Capt. James Archer one of His Ma[jes]ties. Ingeniers.

Though bearing no date it can be dated closely. James Archer was commissioned on 20 December 1671, was in Flanders on war service in 1673 and died about 1690.[57] It might be argued that a work of this importance would be undertaken towards the end rather than at the beginning of his career as a commissioned officer.

A likely date would seem to be during the years 1682–88, when Sir John Reresby was Governor of York. Reresby's strong monarchial sympathies antagonised the citizens, and relations between him and the City were strained throughout his governor-ship. His fear of armed insurrection in the City during these years was very real, and is indicated on page after page in his *Memoirs*. The climax was reached with the suspension of the City's charter and the refusal — in January 1684 — of the Corporation to answer a *quo warranto* inquiry ordered by the King.[58] It is probably no coincidence that Lord Chief Justice

George Jeffreys (in the following year to be President of the notorious 'bloody' western assize) was one of the two Judges of Assize to the City that year.[59] It is therefore postulated that — at the latest — the map was drawn up by January 1684. It is however, possible to go further and suggest that the following extract from Reresby's *Memoirs*[60] may supply the actual day and month as well as the year, 1682, when the City was surveyed and presumably the plan was drawn :–

> Oct. 17 1682. Being at Doncaster . . . . I recieved a letter from Colonel Leg, Master of the Ordinance, intimating that Sir Christofer Musgrave, Lieutenant of the Ordinance, was ordered to come down to Yorke by the King to take a vewe of the condition of that garrison, which occasioned my speedy journey to that place. I gott thether early the next day, and waiting upon the lieutenant, he tooke the dimension and scituation of the Tower and Castle by the helpe of a survayer brought with him to that purpas, took an account of the stoors and ammunition in Cliffords Tower, and tould me the King intended we should be better supplyed, and that his Majesty would be at the charge to repair the defects of the Tower (especially the parapet which was too weake), and to bring the river about it.

The 'survayer brought with him' may well have been Captain James Archer. The statements that (i) the surveyor 'tooke the dimension and scituation of the Tower and Castle' and (ii) 'His Majesty would be at the charge to repair the defects of the Tower . . . and to bring the river about it,' are of particular interest in connection with Archer's map. The latter shows both the plan of Clifford's Tower and its attendant defences — merely as part of the over-all plan of York — and also a separate drawing, called on the map *Profil of Cliford Tower with the Castle Walls*, which is an elevation of the tower and mound and shows water in the ditch surrounding it. As described by Reresby the visit of the lieutenant and the surveyor appears to have been short and hurried. As will be indicated later, Archer's map shows considerable evidence of haste and of hurried and, in certain instances, of faulty workmanship.

The execution of the plan would suggest a military author even if the Captain's name did not appear on it. Emphasis is laid on the City's defences — especially the walls, gates, and vantage places such as churches and large public and private buildings (e.g. the Minster, Clifford's Tower, etc.) — together with some detail as to the depth and flow of the Ouse under Ouse Bridge (then the only bridge spanning the river) during the summer and winter seasons, viz :—

> The owse Bridge Consists in 7 Arches the midle most Arche is wyde 27 yards. From ye Highest Stone of the said Bridge yts [that is] to say of ye Midle Arche to ye Bottom of the River is 17 yards. The River some tymes flows of a suden that scars [*Sic* = ? scarce] a litle boat will passe under it. In sumer tyme it [is] very challow at the Bridge some tymes 1½ & 2 fo[ot of] water. Below and above the Bridge in seaverall [places] there is 5. 6. 7. 8. 9. and 10 fo[ot] of water in sumer tyme. The figures[61] will shew the places. In winter tyme there is water plentifully. Bottoms of 3 & 4 score [tons] comes to ye Kay on High Spring tydes. Art & monny might bring Bottoms of a Hundred Tons to the Towne.
>
> In winter tyme the Fosse is full of water & in sumer tyme little or none at all.

There is a table on the plan listing the distances between one important landmark and another — its value for artillery purposes being obvious, viz :—

Dimention of the Circomferrens
Longitude & Latitude of ye citty.

	Yaards[62]	Feete
From Skeldergate Posterne to Micklegate Barr	800	...
Thens to North Posterne	745	...
thens Crosse ye Owse	44	...
thens to Bowthame Barr	446	...
thens to Munck Barr	643	...
thens to Lathorp Posterrene	328	...
thens to ye Red Tower	342	...
thens to Walmegate Barr	294	...
thens to Fishergate Posterne	342	...
thens to Cast[l]egate Posterne	179	...
thens to Cliford Tower Post	344	...
thens to ye Owse	46	...
thens Crosse ye Owse to Skeldergate posterne	57	...
Circomferrens	4608	...
Circoṁs. of ye mannor [i.e. The King's Manor]	931	...
from Micklegate Barr to Munck Barr	1320	...
from Bowthame Barr to Walmegate Barr	1200	...

That Archer, in drawing up his plan, was conversant with the principal outworks of the 1644 siege is shown by the following two entries under what he calls *Table Alphabethik to know all the*

Edifises & Remarkable Places in ye Citty, i.e., the key to the letters
and numbers he uses on the plan to identify the different places :–

D   The Towrell that was blowed up by ye Enemy

29   A Mont where ye Enemy had a battry

The first of these refers to St. Mary's Tower under which General
Crawford sprang a mine on Trinity Sunday, 16 June 1644. In
the case of the second, the reference number (No. 29) cannot be
found on the plan as it is now framed. The site of Lamel Hill —
to which this certainly refers — is about half an inch outside the
present visible part of the map in the right hand corner ; if the
frame were removed doubtless the number would be visible there.

To Archer the most important item on the plan would
appear to have been a 4-gun emplacement, some 200 yards
square, and surrounded by a dry ditch 40–50 ft. wide,[63] which is
depicted on the highest part of The Mount. Under No. 28 in the
Table Alphabethik it is described as 'A Little fort without ye
town.'[64]

Archer's plan has every appearance of having been drawn
hastily and haphazardly. Distances on his plan which can be
checked against present-day measurements — e.g. those between
the salient points along the line of the walls as listed in the table
reproduced above — can be shown to be quite untrustworthy.
Large buildings are shown clearly and boldly, but without detail,
and their exact sizes are open to doubt, while smaller ones such
as private dwelling houses are indicated in so conventional a
manner as to throw doubt on their exact size, shape and position.
Most of his roads appear to be drawn too straight and too wide,
(the Micklegate Bar-Mount road is a good example while many
of his road junctions are unquestionably incorrect — e.g., that
of the Boroughbridge Road (now Holgate Road) with the
London Road (now Blossom Street). In this particular instance
it is instructive to compare the road junction as shown on Archer's
plan — Plate X — with the same one as shown on Horsley's —
Plate XXXI — which dates only about 12 years later. One last
criticism, the north compass point as shown by Archer is incorrect, it is 45° too far to the west. It is easy to see how such an
error arose. Archer placed the 'barb' by which he denoted his
north point on the wrong pointer of his 'compass ;' this is an

understandable mistake, but one which clearly underlines the hasty nature of the work. These are merely a few of the more obvious criticisms which can be levelled against the work. To sum up, the plan has every appearance of being a stylised composition, intended to give little more than a rough indication of the buildings, defences and chief vantage points — as seen through the eyes of a military engineer — in and near the City. Archer seems to have been particularly interested in vantage points which could be used in the siting of artillery; hence, perhaps, his plotting of the many windmills (of which more later) around and outside the city walls.

In view of these strictures it will be realised that it is by no means an easy or straightforward matter to transpose — after re-scaling[65] the Mount battery as sited on Archer's map on to a modern Ordnance Survey map. This, however, has been attempted in plate XXIX.[66] In siting it thus, the following factors have been taken into account.

As shown on Archer's plan the distance from the mid-point of Micklegate Bar to the centre of the sconce is $555\frac{1}{2}$ yards. As indicated earlier this is — on *a priori* grounds — suspect. Two further considerations rule out entirely the possibility of its being in fact this distance from Micklegate Bar. (i) Placed thus it would not be on the highest part of The Mount — some feet higher, be it noted, in 1644 than it is now — but on the city side of the northern slope. As will be indicated later, there is reason to suppose that, when built, it was intended to command both the southern approaches to The Mount as well as The Mount-Micklegate Bar area. (ii) Placed thus it would lie over the site of the present Nunroyd House. The earliest parts of the existing house on this site date to the early 18th century, though there are structural remains which might indicate an earlier 17th century building on the same site. In the deeds belonging to the house there are hints that the site was acquired from the Corporation *c.* 1660 by the then Lord Mayor, Christopher Topham[67] so that he might build on it a house worthy of a man in his position. It is not clear whether in fact there was any building there during his lifetime. The fact, however, that he acquired the site at all at this date is sufficient to suggest that the battery — then in a ruinous,

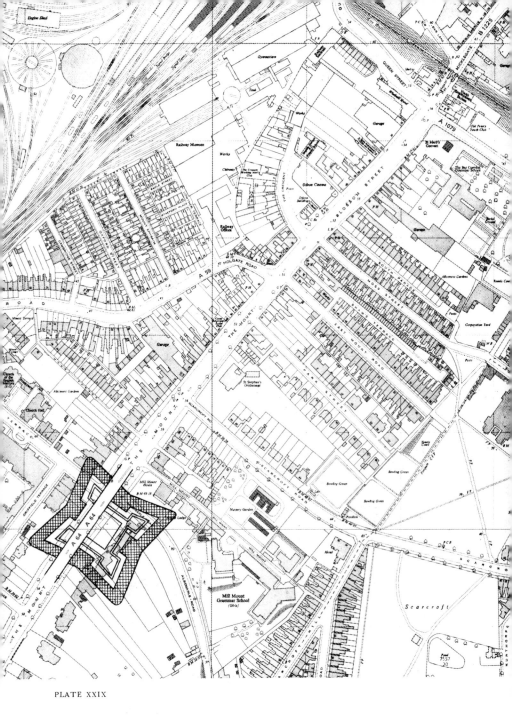

PLATE XXIX

Plan of the Mount Battery super-imposed on a Modern Ordnance Survey Map.

Reproduced from the Ordnance Survey Map with the Sanction of the Controller of H. M. Stationery Office. Crown Copyright Reserved.

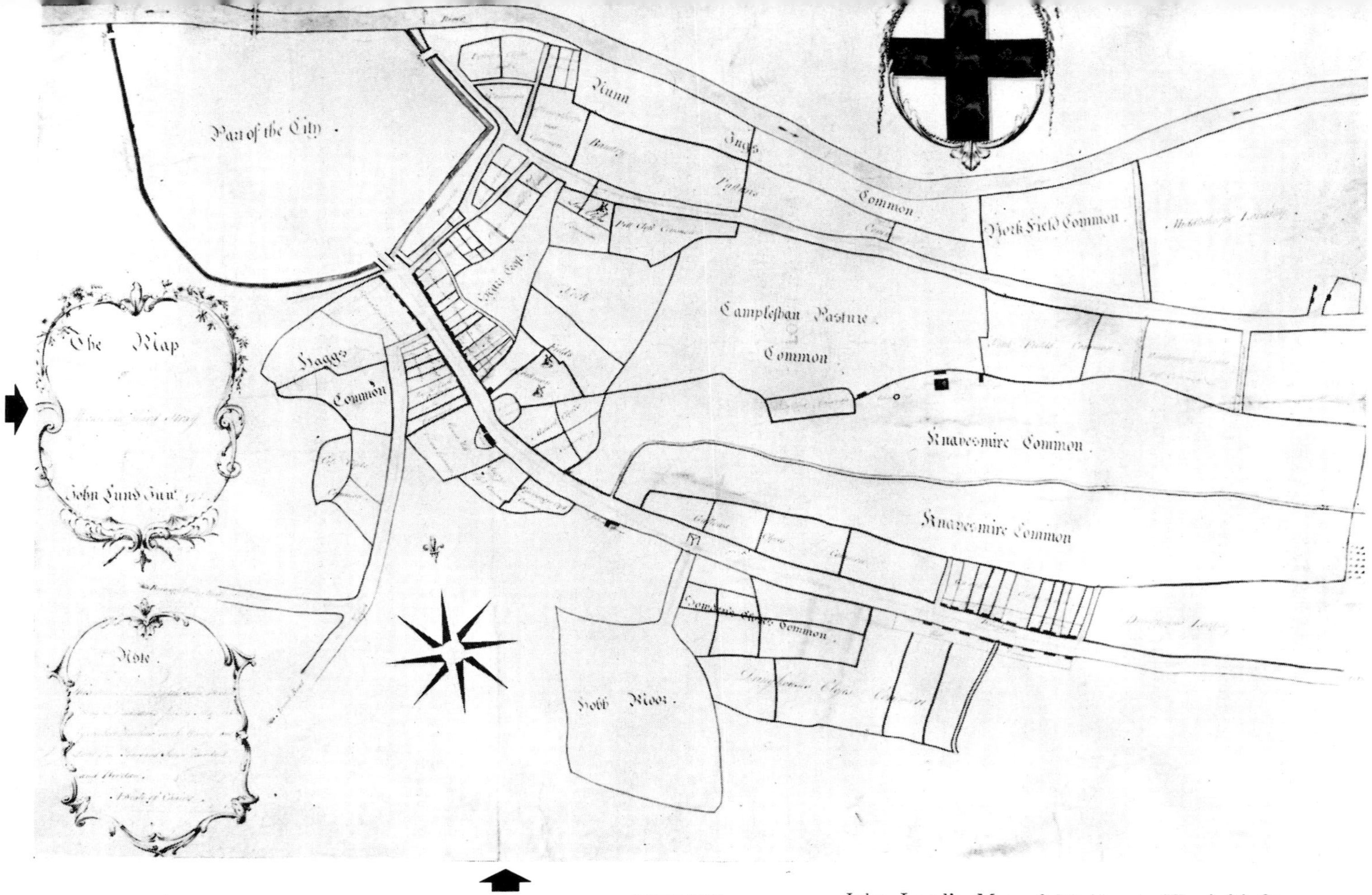

PLATE XXX

John Lund's *Map of Micklegate Ward & Stray* 1772

but nevertheless, from a prospective builder's point of view, 'formidable' state — did not straddle the immediate vicinity of this house.[68]

The clue to the precise siting of Archer's battery seems to be supplied by two windmills. He shows one on the north (his north-west) 'horn' of the sconce and another 750 ft. almost due east of this. The earliest Ordnance Survey map of York, dating to 1850,[69] shows what is called a '*tumulus*' in the north-east corner of the grounds of the Mount House (pulled down about 1865), known as the Driffield estate after the family which owned it. It is shown roughly circular with a diameter of 50 ft. Its centre is approximately 200 ft. south of the middle of the Mount Parade roadway (Dalton Terrace did not exist then, being built some 17 years later) and some 40 ft. west of the west edge of the road (now The Mount). On a modern Ordnance Survey map (on which it is not marked) the centre of the '*tumulus*' would be a few yards west of the Dalton Terrace-Mount road junction and close to the pavement on the city side of Dalton Terrace. It is suggested that this '*tumulus*' was, in fact, no more than the steading of a windmill.[70] On this same Ordnance Survey map there is shown 780 ft. due east of this '*tumulus*', a windmill called 'Mount Mills' (it does not appear on the present Ordnance map), lying at the eastern end of the Mill Mount Road which led to it. This 1850 '*tumulus*' and windmill coincide so closely[71] with the two windmills as shown on Archer's map that they have been taken as the decisive points in fixing the site of the sconce, as shown on plate XXIX. As drawn, the sconce bestrides the road at its highest point, with the south-west 'horn' over the front garden of what is now called Hennebique House. The 1937 Ordnance Survey map shows a steep slope on the south side of this garden — until a few years ago clearly visible on the site — which may represent the last vestiges of this 'horn.' The whole of the front garden of this house was removed in 1952–3 to a depth of 7–10 ft. In section it revealed 4–5 ft. of dark disturbed 'made-up' soil and below this the undisturbed brown clayey subsoil. A stone coffin and pottery of Roman origin were found 3–4 ft. below the surface of the top layer, which suggests that at least 2 ft. of the top dark soil was there in Roman times.

Another map dated 1772 confirms this siting :[72] it has this explanatory note — 'This map was drawn with some alterations and additions from a map taken by Robert Kershaw in the year of Our Lord One Thousand Seven Hundred and Nineteen.' At the highest part of The Mount it shows a roughly square enclosure with rounded corners some 18,000 sq. yds. in size. It is labelled 'The Mount Common.' Two windmills to the east of it can be linked with similar structures on the 1850 Ordnance Survey map so that the area concerned can be located exactly. It was part of the sconce. It is evident from Archer's map and from other sources quoted above that only about two-thirds of the original sconce was on the east side of the road. This 1772 map indicates that the rest — on the other side (the west) — had been absorbed back into the neighbouring enclosures certainly before that date. The indications are that in the eighteenth century that part of the sconce to the east of the road was still visible and the ground thereabouts was so disturbed and uneven that it had never been taken into the neighbouring fields. Instead it remained as an isolated 'common.'

As shown on Archer's map the sconce was built straddling the road. It was built by the military. Three entries in the City 'Chamberlains' Rolls'[73] show that in 1642–3 46 shillings at least were paid to 'divers souldiers for sundrie daies work at St. James Church Hill.' St. James' Church (or, more correctly, St. James' Chapel), a mediaeval foundation dating from the 12th century, was sited roughly where Nunroyd House now is. After the dissolution of the chantries it fell into ruins : one authority[74] says that part of it was still standing in 1651. The highest part of The Mount took its name from this building being variously called St. James' Hill[75] or, as above, St. James' Church Hill. The date of these three entries as given in the 'Chamberlains' Rolls' is 1642, no details of the day and month being added. This is the Old Style reckoning and so could be any time before 25th March 1643.

The sconce was, in fact, built by the Royalists as one of three outposts to the City's defences on the south.[76] The others were eventually captured by the Parliamentarians and used against the city. After being in Parliamentarian hands for a very short time this particular sconce was re-captured, being held by the Royalists until the final capitulation.[77]

It is clear that the sconce was not maintained after the Civil Wars. A minute[78] in the York City 'House Books' dated 3 May 1649 almost certainly relates to it and suggests that there was timber revetting supporting the 'ramparts' and that this was removed immediately the wars ended.

William Lodge's *Aspect of York* (plate XXXII), dated *c.* 1678,[79] shows the ruinous condition of the emplacement at that time, the road running through it and a windmill on the north-west corner. Archer's plan, dating — if the arguments advanced on pages 202–3 are correct — to some four years later, shows the windmill on the north-west corner. Benedict Horsley's map (Plate XXXI) — surveyed 1694, dated 1697[80] — shows the whole of the emplacement, but it is difficult to reconcile the details of it with those of Lodge's *Aspect* or — what is more important — with those of Archer's plan. For instance, the road is shown running through the ramparts apparently much too far to the east. Horsley shows three windmills on his earthworks — two to the west of the road and one to the east. One of the former is presumably to be identified with that of Lodge and Archer on the north-west corner, but its position as shown is puzzling.

Less than a hundred years after the battery was abandoned even a local historian as reputable as Francis Drake was hazy as to its precise purpose and date. Writing in 1736,[81] he said :—

At a good bow-shot from it [Micklegate Bar] is a place called the Mount; which is said to have been thrown up in our late civil wars; but to me it seems of much greater antiquity; and I take it to have been an outwork, or Roman fortress, erected for the greater security of this land side of the city, as I may so call it. Whoever will take a view of the antient Lindum, Lincoln, drawn out by that diligent and intelligent antiquary Dr. Stukeley, will find such an outwork as this but larger to have been made, *extra muros* of that famous city.

In design the sconce is typical of those used during the Civil Wars.[82] Thrown up into the 'ramparts' of this emplacement when it was constructed *c.* 1644, would be the skeletal remains and grave furniture of the Romano-British cemetery which extended around it on all sides,[83] though it is impossible to believe that the skeletal remains found in 1742 represented anything like the 'twelve or thirteen Hundred Skeletons' of the *Courant* account.

The height of the original 'rampart' is unrecorded but a figure of 8–10 ft. — arrived at after the following considerations — is postulated. The heights of similar sconces found elsewhere in the country lie between these limits. In the *Courant* account above Drake says that — 'the Bones . . . were from within two Feet of the Surface to about ten deep.' This is taken to mean that the top two feet of the rampart as cut through in 1742 produced few or no bones (Plate XXVII, stratum B). On the assumption that the soil from the lowest part of the ditch around the emplacement would most certainly be thrown on to the highest part of the ramparts during the course of its construction, the paucity of bones there is understandable. As will be shown later, it is probable that the lowest part of the surrounding ditches penetrated into the undisturbed subsoil below the original Roman cemetery to a depth of between 2 and 3 feet (Plate XXVII, stratum E), i.e., the ditches were 7–8 feet deep. On the analogy of the Trentholme Drive excavations in 1951–2 into the nearby Romano-British cemetery — only 200 yards to the south of the area covered by the battery — the interments here are unlikely to have been deeper than 4–5 feet under the Roman ground level. Again, on the analogy of the Trentholme Drive excavations, it is assumed that the ground level in 1644 was practically the same as when the Romano-British cemetery was abandoned some 1400–1500 years earlier. Assuming that Drake's 8 feet layer containing bones (his 'ten feet deep' minus the 'Two feet of the surface') represents (a) 4 feet of undisturbed cemetery containing complete skeletal remains (Plate XXVII, stratum D) under the Roman ground level[84] and (b) 4 feet of disturbed bones above this level (Plate XXVII, stratum C), a rough cross section of the ditch and rampart can be attempted. As shown on pages 173–4, it is almost certain that the ramparts were supported by a wood revetment. When this was removed in ?1649 the whole of the earthen ramparts must have splayed outwards in all directions. Taking this into account, it is not unreasonable to add another 2–3 feet to the top of the rampart (Plate XXVII, stratum A). This would imply that in 1644 the ramparts were at least 8 feet high. That the centre of the emplacement was 'hollow' is clear from Archer's drawing (Plates X and XXVII), Horsley's drawing (Plate XXXI), Drake's *Courant* account (viz., '... two parallel ramparts, having an area betwixt them.'); Stukeley's account (viz., '... four Bastions) and from analogies elsewhere in the country. Normally the ammunition for the guns was stored there.

It is interesting to note that, assuming the cross section of the ditch and rampart to have been as drawn on Plate XXVII and bearing in mind that the four 'horns' or corner platforms (on which the actual guns were mounted) were of approximately twice the cubic capacity of a corresponding length of 'ordinary' rampart, the cubic content of the ditch (assuming a 7 feet depth) is approximately the same as that of ramparts and 'horns.'

There is no record of what happened to the skulls and other finds of this 1742 levelling — the two lamps, the coin, small metal objects and the fragments of an inscribed ?gravestone (all certainly Roman), and the two 'Canon Bullets,' 'Cross-bar shot' (*sic*) and musket balls which certainly dated to the 1644 siege.

APPENDIX I

[1] For full title of the tract see p. 10 note[2].

APPENDIX II

[2] These numbers do not appear in the original MS. They are merely inserted here for ease of reference.

[3] 'The district known as the Ainsty adjoins the city of York and is contained between the rivers Ouse, Wharfe, and Nidd, with a western boundary across the land from the Nidd by the Ainsty Cross to the Wharfe, east of Wetherby.' (Benson, *Later Medieval York* 1919, p. 73). The City of York had considerable jurisdiction over this area particularly as regards matters of defence.

[4] Similar entries occur 3 February 1637/8 (fo. 1b); 3 February 1638/9 (fo. 19) and 3 February 1639/40 (fo. 37).

[5] Details of this area are to be found in Benson, pp. 32–3.

[6] Probably Mr Gervas Nevil, Providore-General of the Royalist Army (Newcastle p. 165).

7 From 29 April to 8 July 1644 the *House Book* B. 36 is blank. The entry dated 8 July does not concern the siege: then follow the two entries dated 12 and 25 July (Nos. 32 and 33). The next one (No. 34) is dated 2 August and, from then onwards, regular entries are resumed.

8 'Clows' — sluice or floodgate. OED.

9 Interlineated.

10 Middlethorpe Ings is the name of that stretch of the river Ouse near Middlethorpe Manor. Near this house the Scots had their ammunition depot (see Appendix VII). It is to be assumed that it was protected by earth-works and it is probably the demolition of these to which this 'Housebook' entry refers.

11 The presumption is that their house was destroyed during the siege.

12 'cauldron'. OED.

13 The bells were placed in the church of St. John's, Ousebridge.

14 Only rarely is a precise date given in the original MS. Where this is so the date is quoted.

15 These numbers do not appear in the original MS. They are merely inserted here for ease of reference.

16 Bean Hill was just outside the City Walls in the Fishergate area, *cf.* Raine, pp. 298–9.

17 This entry is crossed through.

18 Crossed through. Marginal note — 'this is upon the walls accountes.'

19 Crossed through.

20 Marginal note — 'Allowed.'

21 *Associated Architectural and Archaeological Societies' Report and Papers* xxix Pt. 1 (1907), pp. 659–672. Benson, p. 659, says — 'Amongst York Parish Books, Constables' Books are rare — though there may possibly be others, this is the only one I know of.'

22 Presumably Sir Richard Dacre, Colonel of horse during the Siege and at Marston Moor.

23 Probably soldiers of the Trained Band.

24 These entries doubtless relate to the conservation and rationing of food which we know was ordered by the Marquis of Newcastle as soon as he entered the city on 22 April 1644. The 'magazine' was presumably used as the collecting centre, 'the stoir hous' of p. 15.

25 This item is crossed out.

26 This figure is crossed out.

27 This, and other entries relating to the grinding of corn at George Blaid's horse-driven mill, probably conceals a problem of major embarrassment to the Royalist authorities responsible for feeding the besieged. In a report dated 8 June a Parliamentarian scout wrote (HMC Luke, p. 664 No. 157) — 'Divers which came out of the city say that they have bread and drink enough in York, but cannot get their corn ground fast enough, having only 4 windmills, which sometimes stand still for want of wind.'

28 This was probably Colonel (later Lord) John Frecheville who was Governor of York in the reign of Charles II. For his biography see A. C. Wood, *John, Lord Frecheville of Staveley*. DAJ liii (1932). See also J. T. Brighton, *The Heraldic window in the Frecheville Chapel of Staveley Church*. DAJ lxxx (1960).
29 The men listed are soldiers of the Trained Band.
30 Perhaps his musket blew up in his face?
31 These two entries may relate to the 'cleaning up' of the city necessitated by the chaos and confusion following the Royalist defeat on Marston Moor: and the precipitate retreat back to the city and the hurried departure of the remnants of Prince Rupert's army soon after dawn on the following day (3 July). Monk Bar, which was in the parish of Holy Trinity, Goodramgate was the exit by which the Prince left the city on that occasion.
32 The city surrendered on 16 July so that this and all subsequent entries relate to the time when the Parliamentarians were in control.
33 Mine host of Ye Olde Starre Inne, Stonegate (see p. 115).
34 The entry in the brackets is crossed through.

APPENDIX III

35 *Yarburgh Muniments: Sir Thomas Hesketh's Hospital Register.*
36 The date of this was almost certainly 25 February 1644/5, see YCHB, Appendix IIA, p. 168 no. 50.

APPENDIX V

37 1661–2, p. 501.
38 By permission of the Keeper, Public Record Office.
39 King Charles II.

APPENDIX VI

40 B.M., T.T. E 365 (9).
41 David Leslie. His headquarters were at St. Nicholas, a country house on the outskirts of Richmond in Yorkshire.

APPENDIX VII

42 All these page numbers relate to vol. XVI.
43 These were presumably used at Marston Moor.
44 This would be the bridge of boats across the Ouse linking Middlethorpe (Scots) and Fulford (Fairfax).
45 All these columns are blank in the original.

APPENDIX VIII

46 This article was first published in YAYAS Report for 1952–3, pp. 18–34. It is reproduced here by permission of the Council of the Yorkshire Architectural and York Archaeological Society.

Subsequent research has resulted in some additions, omissions and amendments to the original text. Those portions relating more particularly to the Roman discoveries have been omitted.

47 L. P. Wenham, *The Romano-British Cemetery at Trentholme Drive, York,* HMSO 1968.

48 In all documents, etc. quoted in this appendix, the spelling is given as in the original.

49 Two entries in the City of York 'House Books,' vol. 43 (1739–56), MS. pp. 72 and 75 relate to this matter. (i) On 28 April 1742 'Mr. Alderman Clarke, Mr. Alderman Eskricke and Mr. Matthews of the Four and Twenty are appointed a Committee to superintend and direct the levelling of the Mount and finishing it is such manner as they shall think proper for making it a safe and convenient road. And that the Expence thereof not exceeding twenty Guyneas shall be paid out of the Comon Chamber.' (ii) On 14 July 1742 this committee reported 'That they have put the order in that behalfe [i.e. the levelling of The Mount, etc.] in Execution and made a very convenient and hansome road to this City but the Expence of compleating this work has amounted to the sum of Fifty two pounds nine shillings and seven pence which exceeds the sum ordered at the last House for that purpose. This House haveing taken the premises into consideration Do order That the excess being Thirty one pounds nine shillings and seven pence be paid out of the Comon Chamber of this City but that this be no president for the future for exceeding any limited sum.' Cf. Davies, *Walks through the City of York* 1880, p. 105.

50 A much abbreviated summary of this account appeared in the *Gentleman's Magazine* xii (June 1742), pp. 330–1. It states that the bones were found 'within two Foot of the Surface *to about* 20 *deep.*' (my italics): the *Courant* statement that these were 10 feet 'deep' is more likely to be correct. G. Benson, *York* iii (1925), p. 170, perpetuated the '20 foot' error, quoting the *Gentleman's Magazine* as his authority. Cf. also Benson, *op cit.* ii (1919), p. 162.

51 B. 1696; d. 1771. Author of *Eboracum, or the History and Antiquities of the City of York.* Wm. Bowyer, 1736. For his biography see DNB and YAJ. iii (1875), pp. 33–54.

52 Dealt with in detail in the original article.

53 B. 1687; d. 1765. A member of the Society of Antiquaries and the outstanding antiquarian of the 18th century. DNB.

54 *Itinerarium Curiosum*, Centuria II ed. 1776, p. 75.

55 This opinion as to the Roman origin of the skeletal remains is based on the accumulative evidence of the past 220 years.

56 It is referred to in YAJ. xxxvi (1946), p. 376. Little is known of the previous history of the map. It was purchased in York by the late Mr J. B. Morrell for the City Corporation a few years before the outbreak of the Second World War.

57 Information supplied from the records of the Institution of Royal Engineers, Chatham.

58 Drake, pp. 209–10 and *Memoirs of Sir John Reresby* ed. A. Browning 1936.
p. 334 *et passim*.

59 *Memoirs of Sir John Reresby*, pp. 341–3.

60 pp. 279–80.

61 The reference is to the numbers written at intervals on that shaded part of
Archer's plan which represents the River Ouse. They indicate the depth in feet
at those particular places.

62 It should be noted that the distances between the various places around the
walls as given by Archer in this list bear little or no similarity to a table of
measurements between the same points in Drake, p. 261, which was drawn up
in 1664–5.

63 In the strict military sense this is not a ditch as it served no defensive purpose.
It represents no more than the hollows left all round the emplacement after the
soil from which the ramparts were raised had been dug out.

64 There are many other outposts, batteries and fortifications connected with the
1644 siege of York to which Archer's map makes no reference. The best known
of these was that, already mentioned, on Lamel Hill. (see pp. 147–9). By a
curious coincidence it, like the fortification under discussion, had also been
superimposed on a cemetery.

Dr. Thurnam, who excavated Lamel Hill most thoroughly in 1849 (cf.
Arch. Journal, vi (1849), pp. 27–39 and 123–136 (for shorter version see
YPSR, i (1847–54), pp. 98–105) concluded that the topmost 10–12ft. of
disturbed human bones — had been thrown up to support the Parliamentarian
battery in 1644. Underneath this, to a depth of some 4 ft. below the pre-1644
ground level, Thurnam found undisturbed skeletons indicating a cemetery of
considerable extent; he uncovered 20–30 complete skeletons 'and detached
bones of at least as many more.' After weighing up carefully the evidence for a
Romano-British as against an Anglo-Saxon date for this cemetery, he decided on
the latter, concluding that it was Christian and was 'to be attributed to . . .
the seventh or eighth century.'

65 Here again we cannot be certain of the accuracy of Archer's measurements of
the actual battery. If the point made later about the front garden of Hennebique House is correct, the battery should almost certainly be slightly larger
than he shows it.

66 Reproduced from the Ordnance Survey map with the sanction of the Controller
of H.M. Stationery Office, reduced to quarter scale from the 25 inch map of
Yorkshire (York), New Series, Sheet clxxiv 10 (ed. 1966).

67 B. 1632; died in January 1670/1. Skaife, *Civic Officials . . . .of York* (MS. in
Public Library, York) p. 774.

68 I am indebted to Dr. Eric Gee for this information about Nunroyd House.

69 York Sheet, 14, 5 ft. — 1 mile. Surveyed 1850. Published 1852. Copy in the
Public Library, York.

70 There is a long-established tradition in York that a number of British (pre-
Roman) *tumuli* exist in the Mount area. For example Benson, *York,* ii (1919),

p. 7 stated — 'The Brigantes of York . . . . They buried the bodies on the glacial ridge which commanded the trackway from the south. The chieftains were buried under *tumuli*, two of which near the Mount are shown on the Ordnance Map. Other *tumuli* have been levelled, but human remains have been found all along the ridge.' In fact, no well-attested pre-Roman finds have been recorded from this area. The 'human remains' are unquestionably Roman. It is far more likely that these '*tumuli*' were the steadings of windmills to which the elevated aspect of the area lent itself, and for which there is evidence of many on early maps of York, e.g. Archer's and Horsley's — to quote but two.

71 The discrepancy between Archer's 750 ft. and the Ordnance Survey's 780 ft. is easily accounted for — (i) the possibility of error in Archer's measurement and (ii) the 'conventional signs' used on the one map for the windmill and on the other for the '*tumulus*' are so large as to be quite disproportionate.

72 'The Map of Micklegate Ward Stray by John Lund Junr.' 1772. Original in York Public Library.

73 Quoted in full in Appendix IIB, p. 175 nos. 4, 8 and 9.

74 Gent, p. 190.

75 Raine, pp. 306-7.

76 See pp. 143-7.

77 See pp. 96-7.

78 See Appendix IIA p. 173 no. 77.

79 So dated on the slide in the Evelyn Collection in the Public Library, York, from the negative of which Plate XXXII is taken. The original engraving is in the Evelyn Collection in the Art Gallery, York: it was reproduced as frontispiece in Benson, *York*, ii (1919) where it is undated.

80 Original engraving in the Public Library, York. Drake's 'Plan of the City of York' (*Eboracum*, p. 244), though not ascribed to Horsley, is clearly a reproduction of his map.

81 p. 60. It will be noted that this work was published six years before the 1742 discovery. G. T. Clark, 'On the Defences of York,' YAJ iv (1877), p. 17., stated categorically that this earthwork and that on Lamel Hill 'served as batteries during the Parliamentary siege of York.'

82 Numerous examples might be quoted. Cf. RCHM Newark, fig. 3 (The Queen's Sconce) and Plate 10 (The King's Sconce).

83 The evidence of recorded finds in the immediate vicinity of the earthwork is conclusive for the existence there of the Romano-British cemetery even without that of the 1742 discovery.

84 This argument implies that the road widening in 1742 cut into the undisturbed Roman cemetery well *below* the 1644 ground level; the assumption is based on these considerations:— (i) The present day cutting through which the road passes at the Mount. It is significant that this cutting begins at about the northernmost part of where the sconce was originally sited. At Hennebique House which is comparatively near the highest part of the cutting it is interesting to note that the removal of the soil in the front garden there in 1952 revealed a

Roman coffin the top of the lid of which was found 3 feet *above* the level of the existing road surface. (ii) Trenches in the modern roadway near the Mount dug in connection with road repairing, &c., precisely where the battery must originally have been built — have all shown the brown clayey soil, which in the Hennebique House garden formed the undisturbed subsoil 3–4 feet under the black disturbed topsoil, *immediately below the present surface*, indicating that here the topsoil has been entirely removed. Cf. Hargrove, *History . . . . of York* iii (1818), p. 511 — 'The high road to ancient Calcaria, now Tadcaster, runs over the Mount, and though repeatedly cut into to relieve the ascent, it has every time exhibited numerous relics of mortality.'

Bibliography

BIBLIOGRAPHY

(The abbreviated title preceding each entry is that by which the work is designated in the text).

A. *Contemporary tracts or newspapers.*

Articles of Surrender.

The articles of the Surrender of the City of Yorke to the Earle of Leven ....
on Tuesday July 16, 1644. Together with an explanation of some part of the
Articles. London. Printed for Mathew Walbancke, July 23. 1644.
B.M., T.T. no. E 3(5). Wing A 3876.

Exact and certaine Newes

Exact and certaine Newes from the Siege at Yorke .... July 3. London.
Printed for Mathew Walbanke. 1644
B.M., T.T. no. E 53(12). Wing E 3592.

Exact Relation

An Exact Relation of the Siege before Yorke: Of the taking of the Suburbs, and
of the Approaches made within 40. yards of the Walls: Of the taking of the
King's Mannor house there .... As it is sent in severall Letters, dated at the
Leaguer before York, the 6. and 7. of June. London. Printed for R. White.
June 12. 1644.
B.M., T.T. no. E 50(30). Wing E 3697.

Extract of Letters

Number 7. Extract of Letters, Dated at Edenburgh the 14, 16, and 17. of
April. 1644 .... As Likewise a Letter from the Scottish Armie neare York,
wherein severall passages from the 16. of March to the 20. of April, formerly not
Printed, are fully and truely exprest. London. Printed by Robert Bostock and
Samuel Gellibrand, dwelling in Paules Church-yard. 1644.
B.M., T.T. no. E 44(10). No Wing number.

Full Relation

A Full Relation of the late Victory obtained .... By the Forces under the
command of Generall Lesley .... Against His Majesties Forces under the
command of Prince Rupert .... Fought on Marstam (sic)-Moor, within five
miles of York, on the Second of July, 1644 .... By Captain [William] Stewart
.... London. Printed by J. F. for L. Blaiklock, July 11 1644
B.M., T.T. no. E 54(19). Wing S 5530.

Hulls Managing

Hulls Managing of the Kingdoms Cause .... To which is added .... the
posture of the English and Scots Armies before York, with the manner of the
siege; .... London, Printed for Richard Best at Grayes-Inne gate. June 18.
1644.
B.M., T.T. no. E 51(11). Wing H 3362.

Intelligence no. 2.

Number 2 *The Continuation of True Intelligence. From the Right Honourable, the Earl of Manchester's army. Since the taking of Lincolne; May 6th. untill the first day of this instant June,* 1644. By Sim[eon] Ash and William Goode, Chaplains to the said Earl. London, Printed for Thomas Underhill, at the Bible in Woodstreet. 1644.

B.M., T.T. Formerly no. E 50(33), now Wing C 59 g 20(33).

Intelligence no 4.

Number 4 *A Continuation of True Intelligence from the English and Scottish Forces . . . . now beleaguering York, from the eighth of this instant June to the 17th thereof . . . .* By Sim[eon] Ash and William Goode . . . . London. Printed for Thomas Underhill . . . . 1644.

B.M., T.T. no. E 51. No Wing number.

Intelligence no 5.

Number 5 *A Continuation of True Intelligence, From the English and Scottish Forces . . . . now beleaguering York, from the 16th of June, to Wednesday the 10th of July* 1644 . . . . by Sim[eon] Ash . . . . London, Printed for Thomas Underhill . . . . 1644.

B.M., T.T. no. E 2(1). No Wing number.

Intelligence no. 6.

Number 6 *A Continuation of true intelligence from the Armies in the North, from the* 10. *day to the* 27 *of this instant July* 1644. *Wherein is given a full and particular Accompt of the Surrender of York* . . . . By Sim[eon] Ash . . . . London. Printed for Thomas Underhill 1644

B.M., T.T. no. E 4(6). No Wing number.

Manifest Truths

Manifest Truths, or an inversion of Truths Manifest, Containing a Narration of the Proceedings of the Scottish Army . . . . [by Edward Bowles] London. Printed by M.S. for Henry Overton in Popes-head-Alley, and Giles Calvert, at the Spread Eagle at West end of Pauls, 1646.

B.M., T.T. no. E 343(1).

More Exact Relation

A more Exact Relation of the late Battell Neer York; Fought by the English and Scotch Forces, against Prince Rupert and the Marquess of Newcastle . . . . [Two letters, signed respectively 'Lion Watson' and 'R. Grifen'] London. Printed by M. Simmons for H. Overton, 1644.

B.M., T.T. no. E 2(14). Wing W 1082.

New-come Guest

A New-Come Guest to the Towne. That is, the Descriminant Oath which the Earle of Newcastle imposeth upon the Countie and Citie of Yorke . . . Written by a Yorke-shire Gentleman, for the good (especially) of his Countrie-men . . . .

London, Printed for Matthew Walbancke, at Graies-Inne Gate. June the 5th. 1644.
B.M., T.T. no. E 50(14). Wing N. 600.

Particular List

A Particular List of Divers Of the Commanders and Officers taken Prisoners at Marston Moore neer York (otherwise called Hesham Moore) .... [By T.M.] London, Printed for Ralph Rounthwait, 1644.
B.M., T.T. no. E 54(8). Wing M 84.

Particular Relation no. 1.

Number 1. *A Particular Relation of the severall removes, services, and successes of the* .... *Earle of Manchesters Army* .... *April* 20 *to* .... *May the 6th* 1644 .... *sent by Mr. William Goode* .... *& Mr. Simeon Ashe* .... London. For Thomas Underhill, 1644.
B.M., T.T. no. E 47(8). Wing G 1098 = P605.

Particular Relation no. 3.

Number 3. *A Particular Relation* .... *of the most Remarkable Occurrences From the United Forces in the North* .... *From Saturday the* 1. *untill Munday the* 10th. *of this instant June.* Sent from the Leagure before Yorke, By Sim[eon] Ash, [and] Will[iam] Goode .... London, Printed for Thomas Underhill at the Bible in Wood-street. M.DC.XLIIII.
B.M., T.T. no. E 51(3). No Wing number.

Sermon

A Sermon preached in the Metropoliticall Church of York, upon the 19. *Day of May, being the fourth Sunday after Easter last, by William Ranson, Vicar of Barton upon Humber, before His Excellencie The Marques of Newcastle, Lord Generall, &c. And Published by his speciall Command.* Printed at York by Stephen Bulkley, 1644.
Not a T.T. Copy in B.M. with pressmark G 3842(2) Wing R. 249.

B. *Contemporary, or near-contemporary sources, published.*

Analecta

Sir Thomas Widdrington. *Analecta Eboracensia. Some Remaynes of the Ancient City of York* (ed. Caesar Caine), London 1897.

Baillie

David Laing (ed.), *The Letters and Journals of Robert Baillie. A.M. Principal of the University of Glasgow* 1637–1662, vol. ii. Edinburgh 1841.

Bernard

Edward Bernard (ed), *Catalogi librorum manuscriptorum Angliae et Hiberniae* .... Oxford. 1697. vol. i. (The relevant entry is by White Kennett, a noted antiquary and later Bishop of Peterborough).

PLATE XXXI

Part of Benedict Horsley's
Map of York, 1697,
showing the remains of the
Mount Sconce in the left
foreground.

PLATE XXXII

William Lodge's *Aspect of York*, dated *circa* 1678, showing the ruinous state of the Mount Sconce in the foreground.

Carmen

Paganus Piscator [= Payne Fisher], *Marston-Moor: sive de obsidione praelioque Eboracensi carmen.* London. Thomas Newcomb. 1650.

Cholmley

Sir Hugh Cholmley, 'Memorials touching the Battle of York.' EHR. vol. v, no. xvii (1890), pp. 347–352.

Correspondence

H. W. Meikle (ed), *Correspondence of the Scots Commissioners in London 1644–1646.* (The Roxburghe Club). Edinburgh 1917.

CPAM.

Calendar of the Proceedings of the Committee for the Advance of Money (Domestic) 1642–1656. HMSO 1888.

CPCC.

Calendar of the Proceedings of the Committee for Compounding . . . . 1643–1660. HMSO 1889.

(N.B. Some of the entries in this work are printed in greater detail in YRCP listed below)

CSP., Add.

Calendar of State Papers (Domestic) Addenda 1625–1649. HMSO 1897.

CSP., Dom.

Calendar of State Papers (Domestic) 1644. HMSO 1888.

CSP., Dom. 1661–2

Calendar of State Papers (Domestic) 1661–2. HMSO 1861.

CSP., Ven.

Calendar of State Papers (Venetian), vol. xxvii (1643–1647). HMSO 1926.

CTC.

Calendar of Treasury Books 1660–1667. HMSO 1904.

Douglas

'The Diary of Mr. Robert Douglas when with the Scottish Army in England 1644.' (Printed in *Historical Fragments, relative to Scottish Affairs from 1635 to 1664*), Edinburgh, 1833.

Drake

Francis Drake, *Eboracum: or the History of the Antiquities of the City of York . . . .* London, 1736.

Dudhope

'Letter by James Scrymgeour, and Viscount Dudhope[1] from "Ye Leaguer at York ye 28 of May, 1644".' YAJ vol. xxii (1903), pp. 301–2.

Fairfax

'Letter by Ferdinando, Lord Fairfax to the Committee of Both Kingdoms. Dated 20 April 1644.' HMC Report and Appendix 1881.

Gent.

Thomas Gent, *The Antient and Modern History of the famous City of York
.... The whole diligently collected by T[homas] G[ent]* 1730.

Hildyard.

*A List or Catalogue of all the Mayors .... of Yorke. From the time of King
Edward the First until .... 1664 .... York Published by a true Lover of
Antiquity ....* Printed by Stephen Bulkley 1664.

(N.B. This work is incorporated into James Torre, *The Antiquities of York
City .... Collected from the papers of Christopher Hildyard ....* York.
Printed by G. Waite for F. Hildyard .... 1719.)

HMC Luke.

HMC. The Letter Books 1644–45 of Sir Samuel Luke. HMSO 1963.

Journal.

'The Journal of Prince Rupert's Marches 5 September 1642 to 4 July 1646,'
ed. C. H. Firth. EHR., vol. xiii, no. xlix (Jan. 1898), pp. 729–741.

Ludlow.

Memoirs of Edmund Ludlow .... London, printed for T. Becket and P. A. de
Hondt and T. Cadell, in the Strand; and T. Evans, in King Street, Covent
Garden, 1721.

Memorials.

Robert Bell (ed.) *Memorials of the Civil War comprising the correspondence of
the Fairfax family ....* Forming the concluding volumes of the *Fairfax
Correspondence* London 1849.

Miscellanea.

A. Raine, 'Proceedings of the Commonwealth Committee for York and the
Ainsty.' YAS Record Series, cxviii (1953), *Miscellanea* vol. vi, pp. 1–30.

Monckton Papers.

E. Peacock (ed.) 'The Monckton Papers,' Philobiblon Society, *Miscellany*,
p, xv.

Mace.

Thomas Mace, *Musick's Monument; or, a Remembrancer of the Best Practical
Musick, Both Divine and Civil ....* London, 1676.

Ogden.

'Mr. Ogden's Narrative', dated Richmond, July 6 1644. TRHS., NS, vol. xii
(1898), pp. 71–2 (being Appendix II, to C. H. Firth's 'Marston Moor').

Parliaments of Scotland

The Acts of the Parliaments of Scotland vol. VI 1643–1651. 1819.

Rushworth.

J. Rushworth, *Historical Collections*, vol. ii, pt. 3. London, 1692.

Short Memorial.

Thomas, third Lord Fairfax, 'A Short Memorial of the Northern actions;
during the war there, from the year 1642 till the year 1644.' In Arber's *An*

224

English Garner. Stuart Tracts 1603–1693 with an introduction by C. H.
Firth. Westminster, 1903.

SHS vol. XVI or XVII

'Papers relating to the Army of the Solemn League and Covenant, 1642–1647,'
vols. i and ii. (*Publications of the Scottish History Society*, 2nd series, vols.
XVI and XVII).

Slingsby.

D. Parsons (ed), *The Diary of Sir Henry Slingsby of Scriven*, Bart . . . .
London. 1836²

(N.B. This supersedes an earlier, less detailed, version :- *Original Memoirs,*
written during the Great Civil War; being the life of Sir Henry Slingsby, and
Memoirs of Capt. Hodgson with notes &c. Edinburgh, 1806).

Somervell.

'J. Somervell to James Scott of Bonyntoun. Giving an account of the proceedings of the Scots army'. Dated 1 May 1644. HMC vol. x, pt. 1, Appendix.
1885.

Stockdale.

'Mr. Stockdale's Narrative', dated 8 July 1644. (Harleian MS 166,87)
Printed in TRHS., NS vol. xii (1898), pp. 73–76 being Appendix III to
C. H. Firth's 'Marston Moor.'

Thurloe.

Thomas Birch (ed.), *A Collection of the State Papers of John Thurloe, Esq.* . . . .
containing authentic memorials of the English affairs from the year 1638 *to the*
Restoration of King Charles II. London, 1742.

Warwick.

Sir Philip Warwick, *Memoirs of the Reign of King Charles the First.* Edinburgh,
1813.

YRCP.

J. W. Clay (ed.), *The Yorkshire Royalist Composition Papers or the Proceedings*
of the Committee for Compounding with delinquents during the Commonwealth,
3 vols. (YAS Record Series. vol. xv. 1893).

C. *Biographies.*

Markham.

C. R. Markham, *A life of the Great Lord Fairfax*, London, 1870.

Newcastle

C. H. Firth (ed.), Margaret, Duchess of Newcastle, *The Life of William*
Cavendish, Duke of Newcastle. London, 1886.

Ridsdill Smith

Geoffrey Ridsdill Smith, *Without Touch of Dishonour. The Life and Death of*
Sir Henry Slingsby 1602–1658. Roundwood Press, 1968.

Terry

Charles S. Terry, *The Life and Campaigns of Alexander Leslie, First Earl of Leven*. London, 1899.

Warburton

Eliot Warburton, *Memoirs of Prince Rupert and the Cavaliers*. London, 1849.

D. *Parish Registers.*

(a) *The Minster*

R. H. Scaife, 'The Register of Burials in York Minster, accompanied by Monumental Inscriptions, and illustrated with biographical notices.' YAJ vol. i (1870), pp. 226–330.

(b) *All Saints', Pavement*

The Parish Register of All Saints' Church, Pavement in the City of York vol. i. 1554–1690 ed. T. M. Fisher, YPRS, vol. c 1935.

(c) *St. Crux*

The Parish Register of St. Crux, York ed. R. B. Cook and Mrs F. Harrison. YPRS vol. lxx (1922).

(d) *Holy Trinity, Goodramgate*

The Parish Registers of Holy Trinity Church, Goodramgate, York. ed. R. B. Cook. YPRS vol. xli 1911.

(e) *Holy Trinity, King's Court (or Christ Church).*

The Parish Register of Holy Trinity, King's Court (otherwise Christ Church), York 1716–1812 ed. W. J. Kaye. YPRS vol. lxxxv 1928.

(f) *Holy Trinity, Micklegate.*

The Parish Registers of Holy Trinity, Micklegate in the City of York 1586–1777, ed. W. H. F. Bateman. Delittle, York 1894.

(g) *St. Laurence*

The Parish Register of St. Laurence, York 1606–1812, ed. E. C. Hudson. YPRS vol. xcvii 1935.

(h) *St. Martin, Coney Street.*

The Parish Registers of St. Martin, Coney Street, York. 1557–1812, ed. R. B. Cook, YPRS vol. xxxvi 1909.

(i) *St. Martin-cum-Gregory.*

The Parish Register of St. Martin-cum-Gregory in the City of York 1539–1734. ed. E. Bulmer, Delittle, York 1897.

(j) *St. Mary Bishophill, Junior.*

The Parish Register of St. Mary, Bishophill, Junior, York. 1602–1812, ed. F. Collins. YPRS vol. lii 1915.

(k) *St. Michael-le-Belfrey.*

The Registers of St. Michael le Belfrey, York. Pt. I 1565–1653, ed. F. Collins. YPRS vol I 1899.

(1) *St. Olave*

The Parish Register of St. Olave, York Pt. I 1538–1644. ed. Mrs F. Harrison and W. J. Kaye, YPRS vol. lxxiii 1923.

E. *Other published works.*

Benson

George Benson, *An Account of the City and County of York from the Reformation to the year* 1925 (being volume 3 of his History of York). Cooper and Swann, York 1925.

Cooper

T. P. Cooper, *York: the story of its walls, bars and castles* . . . . London 1904.

Defoe

D. Defoe, *A Tour through England and Wales* 1724–6. vol. II of Everyman Edition 1959.

Raine

A. Raine. *Mediaeval York. A topographical survey based on original sources.* London 1955.

RCHM Newark

Royal Commission on Historical Monuments (England) *Newark on Trent. The Civil War Siegeworks.* HMSO 1964.

Wedgwood

C. V. Wedgwood, *The King's War* 1641–1647. London 1958.

F. *Unpublished Material*

Constables Acc. Book

'Holy Trinity Goodramgate. Constables Account Book 1636–1734.' MS in York Public Library.

Giles

William Giles, 'York and the Civil War: extracts from the records of the proceedings of the York Committee of the Association of the Six Northern Counties with Notts and the City of York & town of Hull.' MS in York Public Library.

Keep

H. Keep 'Monumenta Eboracensia.' MS history of York in the library of Trinity College, Cambridge. Date *c.* 1680.

YCCA

'City of York Chamberlains Accounts.' MS in York Public Library C 23 (1640–1645).

YCHB
'City of York House Books.' MS in York Public Library. B 36. (1637–1650) and B 37 (1650–1663).
G. *Fiction*.

Beatrice Marshall, *The Siege of York. A story of the days of Thomas, Lord Fairfax.* Sealey and Co., London 1902.

Florence Bone, *A Rose of York.* Religious Tract Society, London. (n.d.)

[1] He died of wounds received at Marston Moor (SHS. vol. XVI, p. xxvi).
[2] The MS of this Diary was long considered lost. A few years ago it was discovered in the Manuscript Department of the University of Nottingham (cf. Ridsdill Smith, p. 33).

Index

T HE IMPORTANCE OF The Siege of York in the history of the English Civil Wars cannot be exaggerated. It was the direct cause of the Battle of Marston Moor, the greatest battle fought on English soil and the one which lost the north for King Charles I.

Peter Wenham's book is the fruit of many years of research. Admirable use is made of untapped contemporary tracts and of unpublished as well as published material from the York City Archives. The York parochial muniments, printed and unprinted, were also combed for relevant entries. All these, together with a host of other sources, including many newly-discovered documents, continue to throw a flood of light on an enthralling episode in the history of York.

In this book Peter Wenham, although his sympathies obviously lie with the besieged, is very fair-minded in his approach. He does full justice, for example, to the Fairfaxes. The author's intimate knowledge of the locality about which he is writing is a first-class asset; in him the reader can rely upon an impeccable authority for the topography of the siege; his guidance is especially useful for those wholly or only slightly familiar with York and its environs.

This is a scholarly, well documented, and exhaustive monograph on a subject of intense interest to students of the Civil War.

PETER WENHAM MA, M.LITT, M.ED, FSA was born in Richmond, North Yorkshire. He graduated from the University of Durham and from 1963 to 1974 was Head of the Department of History at St John's College in York. For many years he was Editor of the Yorkshire Archaeological Journal, and was widely known as one of Yorkshire's leading archaeologists and historians.

Retiring to Richmond, he became Honorary Curator of The Richmondshire Museum, until his death in 1990. Successful sales of this book will support the Peter Wenham Memorial Trust which was established to continue his researches.

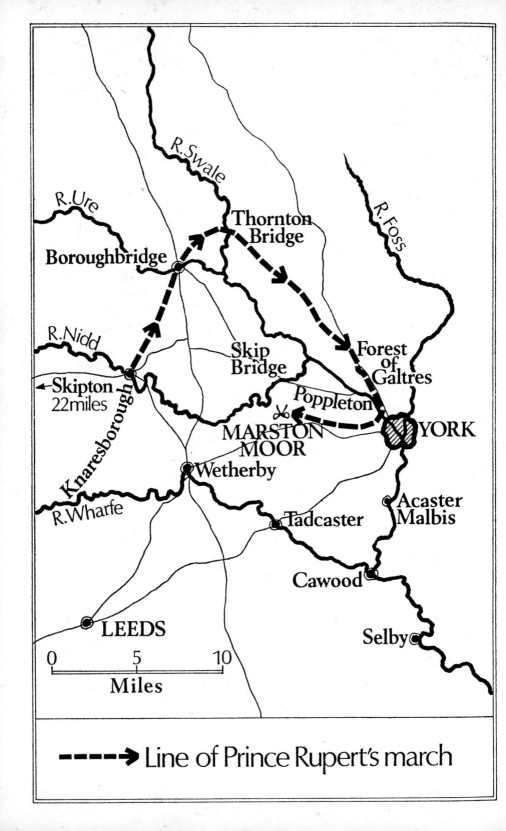

R.Swale

R.Ure

R.Foss

Thornton
Bridge

Boroughbridge

R.Nidd

Skip
Bridge

Forest
of
Galtres

Skipton
22miles

Poppleton

Knaresborough

MARSTON
MOOR

YORK

Wetherby

R.Wharfe

Tadcaster

Acaster
Malbis

Cawood

LEEDS

Selby

0   5   10
Miles

------➤ Line of Prince Rupert's march